19/95

The Bold Vegetarian Chef

adventures

in flavor with

soy, beans,

vegetables,

and grains

the BOLD Vegetarian Chef

Ken Charney

JOHN WILEY & SONS, INC.

This book is dedicated to Cheryl.

For sticking through the good, the bad and the ugly.

For keeping me up to standard.

For your love.

Published by John Wiley & Sons, Inc. New York.
Published simultaneously in Canada.

This publication is designed to provide accurate and authoritative information in regard to the subject matter covered. It is sold with the understanding that the publisher is not engaged in rendering professional services. If professional advice or other expert assistance is required, the services of a competent professional person should be sought.

Wiley also publishes its books in a variety of electronic formats. Some content that appears in print may not be available in electronic books. For more information about Wiley products, visit our web site at www.wiley.com.

Library of Congress Cataloging-in-Publication Data

ISBN: 0471-21278-4

Printed in the United States of America.

Book design by Richard Oriolo

10 9 8 7 6 5 4 3 2 1

Contents

Acknowledgments

Thank you Gary Isenstadt, formerly of the Natural Gourmet Cookery School, for being one of the first to truly inspire me and believe in me. It's been a long time, but I still remember.

Thank you Louis from the defunct Luma in New York City, for letting me burn my fingers (as you laughed) and allowing me to see the difference between school and the real world.

Thank you Jonathan, for being my friend through all these years and working with me and putting up with me and listening to (and helping me) in all my failures and accomplishments in the early years.

Thank you Maryellen, for believing in me when I wanted to change careers and seeing some light at the end of the tunnel.

Thank you chef, writer, and traveler Rick Bayless, for inspiring several dishes in the book. I found your knowledge and insight on Mexican cuisine stirring.

To all those who believed in me over the years and who took the time to listen. Much obliged.

To my parents, who support me unequivocally and believe in me; I couldn't have done it without you.

To my editor, Susan Wyler. This book would not exist without her. Her superb editing and dedication made the book what it is.

And finally, a heartfelt thanks to Dad. For being in the right place at the right time . . . and for your inspiration in all your creative accomplishments.

INTRODUCTION:
Vegetarian Delights

So you want to be a bold vegetarian chef and master the art of vegetarian

cuisine? Open your mind, warm your hands, and seek a path of culinary

excitement. A lively world of senses and inspired songs of fare await you.

Why vegetarian? Why this book? I love animals. I stopped eating meat in the

late 1980s when I read *Animal Liberation*, by Peter Singer. It was a turning point for me, and the main reason I passed up a traditional cooking school for one that specialized in natural and vegetarian foods. The emotion I felt when reading that book is still with me.

In today's society I have found that being a vegetarian has become synonymous with eating healthy, but this is not always the case. Much is based on people's perceptions.

There are many folks who eat fish and chicken twice a week but still consider themselves vegetarian. I define a vegetarian as someone who doesn't eat any animal or seafood. A strict vegetarian doesn't eat meat, chicken, fish, or any animal by-products. While I put myself in the former camp, I am comfortable eating dairy, eggs, and cheese, especially if their origin is strictly monitored. By this I mean if the products are made from animals that have been treated properly (raised free range) and fed organically.

While this book is defined by vegetarianism, it is my wish that we move away from labels. For example, I prefer the ancient Asian terms for the soybean: "meat from the earth" or "meat without bones." Food is nutrition, whether in the form of milk or cutlet or roast or butter—all words that can be used interchangeably for meat or for vegetarian products.

The art and craft of bold vegetarian cuisine encompasses several areas with which you should be familiar. It means exciting flavors and a variety of international ingredients. It means different textures and tastes and the ability to target as many senses as possible. Yet, as with a painter's canvas, there are times for broad, masterful strokes and times for simplicity and clean lines.

The beauty of simplicity is apparent in the luscious flavors of polenta with fontina cheese and roasted garlic, while the three-mushroom chipotle chile ragout that accompanies it offers a more complex range of flavors. Each dish has its place and purpose, and each is exquisite in its own way. Sometimes the white of the canvas is part of your art. Sometimes silence is part of your song. The same goes for good food.

The obvious is occasionally forgotten: Don't be satisfied until a dish is right. Create handsome, beautiful works of art, but know when to say "Enough—we're done." Learn the techniques, tips, and tools that make this sort of cooking second nature. Understand when to add a third or fourth ingredient and when to leave it out. Remember that homemade stock, for example, makes the difference between a good and an extraordinary taste. Take pride in your food, knowing that the little things go a long way in satisfying and exciting your friends and family or whomever you cook for.

You are likely reading this book because you truly enjoy cooking or are eagerly interested in learning more about it. You enjoy shopping for local foods because they have traveled less distance and because they are of your soil and earth—your home. At the same time, you recognize that our world is becoming smaller and that interesting, exotic produce and grocery items from around the world are far easier to access then ever before. What's more, many traditional natural food markets—like the one I work for, the largest chain of co-ops in the country—and epicurean shops now carry a wide variety of fresh ingredients that make creating gourmet dishes a whole lot easier.

Almost every week I see prepared basic ingredients in the grocery store that used to take a lot of time to make myself—for example, roasted garlic, fresh roasted peppers, preserved lemons, quality stocks, ready-made sauces, and so on. You shop for organic foods because they sustain the earth and contain no added toxins. You shop for fresh foods because that is what makes culinary sense. If the chanterelle mushrooms listed in the ingredients are soggy and somewhat long in the tooth, then shiitakes or creminis will work fine. I often have to remind myself of this. It's a real effort to pull myself away from a particular ingredient, because I want to make the dish just so, but the substitution is usually the right thing to do. This is the essence of the art of vegetarian cuisine.

If you like to shop for fresh, organic ingredients, if you like to garnish your plates with beautiful extras that embellish your food, then this book is for you. If you like learning about foods you've never tried before, then this book is for you. If you like taking extra steps to give good food an extraordinary air, then this book is for you. But don't panic: I'll hold your hand and pass along all the tricks I've learned both in my personal kitchen experiences and as a professional vegetarian chef. Once you're comfortable with the recipes here, I hope you'll experiment on your own. Be bold. Be assertive. Touch on all the taste senses: salty, sour, sweet, bitter, savory. I'm not big on a lot of fancy ingredients and techniques, though I don't mind a few—but I've found it is worth taking an extra step or adding that extra ingredient to give a dish real character and depth.

This is a book filled with recipes, but it is really about ideas, techniques, and templates; it's about being creative and alive in the kitchen. It represents, at times, a merger of the worlds of natural foods and traditional cooking. I find both can be restrictive standing alone; the two combined are more than the sum of their parts.

I like to think that a good cookbook makes good bedtime reading. Why not? Look over the particulars, get an idea of what ingredients you'll need, what kind of preparations to think about and what kitchen tools you'll need—hopefully you will be inspired. At this point, you'll feel prepared when you're ready to start cooking. In other words, start the process *before* you start the process. I assure you that this will create a much more enjoyable cooking experience.

The best teachers are those who do not profess to know much, but rather are willing and eager to learn more. I like to think I've discovered, created, and adapted some great flavor and food combinations. I gladly offer these to you not only as recipes, but also as tips and templates for you to use in creating your own masterpieces. You learn from me some of the secrets of bold vegetarian cooking, and I learn from you humility and patience.

Tips, tools, techniques, and ingredients for a bold vegetarian kitchen

WHAT WE HAVE HERE are those little extras that will make your dishes and presentations special. Some are explained in more detail in recipes or other chapters. This is by no means an exhaustive list. What I've tried to do is include a number of ideas that will help make your meals memorable. They will show you care about food and cooking and all things culinary. None are especially complicated, yet many lend an air of sophistication and flair. Some may be unfamiliar to you; others will be old hat. They are in no particular order other than alphabetical.

Beans: When you're planning to use dried beans in a recipe, start soaking them either before you go to bed at night or before you go to off to work in the morning. This saves a lot of time and hassle, so they will be ready to go when you're ready to go. After a soak of 6 to 8 hours, beans usually cook fast enough so that by the time you've finished your prep work, they're done or close to it. What most cookbooks don't tell you is that it's not too late, even if you have only 4 to 6 hours to soak beans. The bottom line: every hour of soaking will speed up the cooking process. (See page 166 for details.)

Blender: A blender is generally used for liquids or things that liquefy easily, like tomatoes, tomatillos, and chunky soups. A blender simply will not puree or properly blend tofu or reduce hard bread to crumbs. There's no doubt that in small batches you could manage to accomplish the task, but it would likely prove exasperating and only add to your time and cleanup in the kitchen. Get a food processor!

Bulk spices: I discourage you from buying spices in jars. While some quality companies produce gourmet or even organic jarred spices, I think your chances for freshness are considerably higher with bulk. If you can find a small, reliable shop in your area or a spice company catalog to order from, please do so. It will be well worth the effort. Look for a shop with high turnover and relatively small inventory.

Try this test if you're skeptical. Take a jar of any dried spice and smell it. Maybe it's not bad, you think. Leave it out on the kitchen counter with the lid off and see if your kitchen smells fragrant after an hour or two. Do the same with *freshly* bought spices from the bulk section of your natural foods market, spice shop, or spice catalog. See if you notice the difference. Some spices hold their potency longer than others, so I can't say absolutely how long your spices will keep their freshness. It may range from a few weeks to two or three months.

Volatile oils, flavors, and fragrance dissipate quickly from many spices. Certain spices, like black pepper, cumin, and nutmeg, to name just a few, taste infinitely sharper when kept whole, then ground, crushed, or grated as you need them.

Caramelizing onions: This is a classic technique I use quite often. I find many people actually don't understand what it means. Caramelizing does not mean that you add sugar, but that you bring out the natural sugar present in the onion. Sauté an onion in oil as you would any other, but keep cooking it over a slightly lower heat, stirring every few minutes. The onion will gradually become browner and softer and beautifully sweet.

Cast-iron skillet: This is an indispensable kitchen tool—a must have. A fair number of recipes in this book use the cast-iron skillet. If you did not inherit one from your mother or grandmother, buy one today, or even two or three of different sizes. They're slow to heat but hold heat longer and more evenly than most other pans. They move from stovetop to oven, not to mention campfires, easily. They deglaze, they blacken chiles and tofu or tempeh, they brown onions like nobody's business, and they stand up to very high temperatures. Take good care of your skillet by following directions on seasoning and cleaning, and it will last forever. Whenever I use mine I always dry it thoroughly with a paper towel and coat it lightly with oil.

Cheesecloth and kitchen twine:
These items are used for a number of reasons, as you will see in several recipes. Make sure to have some on hand.

Chiles:
These spicy dried peppers of the capsicum family are not just about heat—they're also about flavor. There are many, many dozens of chiles in the world. You will have to try at least a few of them yourself to get a feel for what they are all about. Tasting chiles might be compared to tasting wine. There's more than one flavor in a single chile, sometimes several, which add a certain complexity and richness to dishes. And depending upon the season, the amount of rain, where they were grown, and the fickleness of that particular chile, you will find the same type tasting different or having varying degrees of heat than the one you sampled before. And if that wasn't enough, chiles often have local names that vary or are mislabeled in the store, meaning you will have to become the expert on what's what.

Dried chiles are supposed to be dry but not brittle. They should be soft, supple and fragrant, without holes or tears. Usually they are toasted before using, being careful not to let them burn. Look for a slight color change and a fragrant aroma.

Coffee or spice grinder:
Essential for creating spice mixes or powders. If you use your grinder for coffee, you'll have to buy another one exclusively for spices. To clean, don't rinse in water, but wipe out with a pastry brush.

Crispy shallots, leeks, and sage:
These are brilliant garnishes and toppings that add crisp and crunch as well as visual appeal to soups, mashed potatoes, and pasta.

For *shallots,* remove the skin and cut off any hard root bits. Slice into very thin, waferlike pieces. Heat canola or safflower oil to medium-high heat. The oil is hot enough when it changes its consistency and begins to shimmer and smoke ever so slightly. This is something you will learn to recognize with practice. Fry shallots in small batches until golden brown. With a slotted spoon, *quickly* scoop onto a paper towel. Sprinkle with salt.

Cut *leeks* in half lengthwise, then slice only the white or very tender green parts into very thin half-moons. Clean by dropping into a large bowl of water and thoroughly rinsing out any dirt or debris. Strain and spin or pat until dry. To fry, follow the same procedure as for shallots.

For *sage*, pick the largest leaves off of the stems. Fry in small batches, following the same procedure as for shallots. Remember, though, that sage leaves cook faster than shallots or leeks. As soon as they stop bubbling, remove them quickly from the oil with tongs or a slotted spoon and gently lay them on a paper towel. No need to salt.

Dairy, cheese, and eggs:
Use organic dairy products and organically produced free-range eggs whenever possible. Cows and hens raised organically by and large are treated more humanely than others, and your ingredients will remain as clean as possible.

Food processor:
If you'll be working with tofu or anything else that you want thoroughly smooth and creamy, this is a very important tool. The standard-bearer is the Cuisinart brand. They've been around a long time and should last for many years without problems.

Knives and knife skills:
Good knives are a critical component of your kitchen. A whole set is not necessarily needed. To start, a good chef's knife, 7 to 10 inches long, a heavy-duty cleaver (optional), a couple of paring knives, an offset serrated knife, and a fillet knife will serve virtually all your purposes. A whole chapter could be written on knives—but, in summary, look for well-known, established brands like Henckels, Wüsthof, and others that make hand-hammered carbon steel blades. Shop around for the right fit in your hand. Buy a knife skills video or attend a class on proper knife technique. The better your knife skills, the faster and easier your prep work will be. There's a good chance that if you learn just a few good knife techniques, you will actually look forward to doing your prep work. You will look forward to going into the kitchen and getting to work. Can you believe it?

Mandoline:
A hand-operated slicing device with adjustable blades for thin and thick slicing, julienne, and other cuts; a mandoline is great for French fries and salads. If you want to spend a little money, get a good stainless-steel model. Otherwise you can find decent plastic mandolines that do the trick, at least until they wear out or break.

Marinade tips and ideas:
Marinades are easy once you get the hang of them, which luckily should take all of ten minutes. They enhance portobello mushrooms, tofu, tempeh, and certain vegetable dishes immensely. Marinades often double as sauce or can be reduced to a sauce.

Simple marinade guide

WINE/VINEGAR

Aged balsamic vinegar

Cider vinegar

Beer

Brown rice vinegar

Chardonnay, Riesling

Cider vinegar

Fruit vinegars

Madeira

Merlot, Cabernet, Pinot Noir

Mirin

Port

Sherry

Vegetable stock

FRUIT OR VEGETABLE JUICE, ZEST, OR PUREE

Apple juice or cider

Lemon

Lime

Orange

Peach puree

Pineapple

Roasted pepper puree

Tangerine

SAVORY THICKENERS

Barley miso

Bottled mustard

Chickpea miso

Peanut butter

Pesto

Tomato paste

SWEETENERS

Honey

Maple syrup

Molasses

Unrefined cane sugar

MINCED/CHOPPED

Chives

Cilantro

Garlic (raw or roasted)

Ginger

Lemongrass

Rehydrated dried chiles (blended or minced)

Scallions

Shallots

FRESH/DRIED HERBS

Basil

Bay leaf

Dill

Fennel

Marjoram

Oregano

Rosemary

Sage

Sorrel

Tarragon

Thyme

DRIED SPICES

Caraway

Celery seed

Chili powder

Cinnamon

Coriander

Cumin

Curry

Mustard powder

Onion powder

OIL/CONDIMENTS/MISCELLANEOUS

Extra virgin olive oil

Horseradish (bottled)

Hot sauces

Nutritional yeast

Salad dressings

Salt and freshly ground pepper

Soy sauce

Toasted sesame oil

Wasabi (powder or paste)

Vegetarian Worcestershire sauce

You will find dozens of marinades in this book, mostly in the soy and seitan chapters, with others sneaking around here and there. Some are straight-up marinades; others are sauces that can be or have been thinned out. (Remember that too thick a sauce will not penetrate what you are marinating—or, if it does, will take too long to do so.) Still others may be derived from a dressing or vinaigrette.

chef talk

Go easy with soy sauce and miso—a little goes a long way. Ditto with molasses; too much may leave a bitter aftertaste. In a rush without all night to marinate? Try a citrus-based marinade, which I have found tends to penetrate tofu more quickly than do more savory combinations. On occasion, I've made a marinade that is too thick, and it failed to penetrate the tofu. In other words, I made a sauce, not a marinade. THIS may sound obvious, but don't forget to taste as you go along. This is how you learn: by experiencing the building of flavors. Experiment and perfect your own secret recipes. Don't be afraid to scrap a marinade and start over if you're not satisfied. Don't forget to write down ingredients and use the combination again. Or not. FOR tofu or tempeh, marinate several hours or overnight, or use the pan-fry method described on page 120. Marinades are all about saturation of flavor, which can vary a great deal in tofu, as densities by brand and even batch can shift. Generally, vegetables don't pick up the flavor of a marinade. However, pouring a cold marinade over hot grilled, broiled, or roasted vegetables is a striking way to highlight the flavor of the marinade while enhancing the vegetables' natural simplicity.

The combinations for marinades are infinite, as are the flavors and sources for ideas. When inventing your own marinade, you'll want to mix and match sweet, savory, salty, spicy, and sour flavors or combine like flavors and colors. For example, try three or four different citrus flavors, like tangerine, orange, lemon, plus a light-colored miso, plus brown rice vinegar and light-colored unrefined cane sugar. The colors are consistent in lightness, as is the nimble but persuasive combination of flavors. You have tart, savory, and sweet. Add salt, pepper, and an herb . . . and there you go.

A basic list of marinade ideas is shown on previous page.

Measuring: If you are one of those who need to measure out salt and pepper, please read this. Start paying attention to what a tablespoon or a teaspoon looks like so you can get away from measuring. Here's a trick you can try. Take a large plate, your measuring spoons, and any old dried herb. Measure 1 teaspoon onto the plate eight or ten times. Look at what you've done. Visualize the scenario. Place 1 teaspoon of the herb in the palm of your hand. After this exercise, I don't think you will forget how much 1 teaspoon is. Do the same for 1 tablespoon and for 1 cup of water in a larger bowl. Do it over and again until you know what 1 cup looks like. Warning! Do not attempt this technique when you are baking, which is a science and must be exact.

chef talk

Miso: I suggest having two kinds of this invaluable condiment on hand. Don't worry, miso lasts almost indefinitely in the fridge. I highly recommend keeping chickpea miso (Miso Master brand, if you can find it—my favorite all-around miso), which is mild and flavorful, or a yellow or white miso as well as a dark or red miso. Miso flavors, thickens, and lends complexity to a variety of different types of recipes, from dressings, sauces, and soups to marinades and spreads.

Oil: I like to keep three or four oils on hand—olive, canola or safflower, and peanut. In fact, I use two kinds of extra virgin olive oil, one for cooking and a special expensive one for raw use, as in vinaigrettes or on pasta after it's off the heat. I keep a squirt bottle near where I cook with just enough oil to last a couple of weeks (see Chef Talk).

Depending on how often you use your oils, you may want to keep them in the refrigerator or at least in a cool, dark place. This will keep them from going rancid. Most oils will, however, congeal in the fridge. Thaw by running the bottle under warm water.

Oven-dried tomatoes: If you've never made your own, try these. The flavors are concentrated, and the texture is superb. Slice plum tomatoes lengthwise in half. Place face down on a parchment-lined, heavy-duty baking pan and bake at 175°F (80°C) for 6 to 8 hours or overnight if possible. Sun-dried tomatoes can be substituted for oven-dried but will not carry the day as your own freshly done tomatoes will. These are outstanding in eggs, pasta, or any place you might use sun-dried tomatoes.

Parchment paper: Saves on messy cleanups when you are baking or roasting vegetables and other foods that can stick. When I use parchment I always get at least one funny look that says, "I didn't know you could put *that* in the oven!" You can also wrap foods in parchment to cook them; this is called cooking *en papillote*. Note: The paper usually burns during high-heat baking or broiling.

Pasta (preparing ahead): This is a very useful technique because it takes a lot of hassle out of preparing a large dinner. The pasta and the large pot it needs are finished and done with. Cook pasta al dente, as usual. Immediately strain and run the pasta under cold water. Use your hands to gently toss it so every piece gets exposed to the water. Continue until the water has cooled the pasta completely and stopped the cooking process. Strain thoroughly and sprinkle the pasta with olive oil, again using your hands to make sure every piece is well coated. Cover and refrigerate until ready to incorporate into your dish.

Pastry bag: Used only every so often but a lifesaver when you need it, a pastry bag will save time and trouble when you're trying to get fillings into tight spots. Pastry bags come in many sizes and varieties, including disposable. Decide which is best for you.

Plastic gloves: Have a box of the thin, disposable kind on hand. You'll find them in medical or restaurant supply stores. Made of various synthetics, such as polyvinyl, gloves are great for handling chiles and when mixing, shaping, and coating burgers or any other food mixture that needs hands-on attention.

Produce: If you haven't yet, start talking to your produce managers. Get to know them. They can offer a wealth of information. Here's just one example of what I mean. You're making homemade tomato sauce, and there are three kinds of tomatoes at the market: plum, organic, and vine-ripened. Which is the freshest, meatiest, sweetest red tomato? Ask your produce manager to cut all three open and find out. Is one juicier? One meatier? One more acidic? If you're buying two pounds of tomatoes, you can be sure that a smart manager will help you out. Unfortunately, the large chain stores may not be accommodating and may have less invested in good customer service, though this is not always the case. Don't hesitate to ask questions. A good manager will always let you taste. If not, take your business elsewhere.

Roasted garlic: Here are three methods for roasting garlic.

Method #1: If you want to include roasted garlic in something that will get blended or mashed or pureed or even delicately laid out as an addition to a sauce or side dish, use this method, which guarantees a very soft and browned clove. Instead of roasting the whole head of garlic, cook the cloves *after* you have separated them from the head and removed the papery outer skin. This way there is no squishing out hot garlic all over the place, pieces of skin stuck to everything, getting all over your fingers and making a big old mess. Try this:

Preheat the oven to 300° to 325°F (135° to 160°C). Break apart one head (or more) of garlic into individual cloves. Skin the cloves and cut off the hard bits on the ends. (It's okay if the cloves get crushed while you peel the skin off them.) Coat the garlic cloves lightly with olive oil and cook them in a covered baking dish for 30 to 40 minutes, or until lightly browned and very soft. You may toss them once or so while they are cooking.

Method #2: Probably the easiest way to mellow garlic is to roast it with the skin on. Heat a cast-iron skillet over a medium heat. Place the unpeeled garlic in the pan. Cook for about 15 minutes, turning over the garlic with tongs occasionally but allowing it to get slightly blackened in spots. Let cool and peel.

Method #3: Roasting whole garlic yields a beautiful presentation and a terrific spread for bread. Refrigerating the roasted head enables you to pick out the cloves with a paring knife easily and without a mess.

Preheat the oven to 325°F (160°C). Lay a head of garlic on its side, keeping the root end intact. With a sharp knife, slice off the top eighth or quarter (depending on how fat or big the garlic is) of one or more heads of garlic to expose the tops of the cloves. Lightly coat the cloves with olive oil and cook on a baking sheet for about 1¼ hours. Halfway through the cooking process, coat again with a little olive oil, and then again when the cloves are lightly browned and very soft. For a spectacular antipasto, serve with fresh bread, olives, roasted peppers, cheese, and Rosemary Olive Oil (page 21).

Stocking up:

Your dry goods pantry and refrigerator are where it all starts. Okay, so it all starts with a great attitude, but that's another book. Some of the items listed here are described in this section and some in other chapters, and some are self-explanatory. Because many of the recipes in this book call for at least one of these ingredients, read over this list and think about what you have and what you can buy to add to it. This may be the strongest place to start in creating a bold vegetarian kitchen.

You will find the following ingredients in virtually any natural foods stores, gourmet grocery stores, as well as in many local corner markets:

A variety of dried chiles

Sun-dried tomatoes

Red, chickpea, and white miso

A variety of dried and canned beans

Jasmine, brown, and mixed-blend rice

Vinegars: balsamic, cider, white wine, red wine, aged sherry

Dried mushrooms

Tamari or other "clean" soy sauce

High-quality extra virgin olive oil

Tomato paste in a tube

Canned tomatoes

Vegetable stock

Hot sauce

Chili paste

Tamarind paste

Sea salt

Mirin

Chinese black bean paste

Toasted sesame seed oil

Unrefined cane sugar

Vegetarian Worcestershire sauce

Stockpots, sauce and sauté pans, and skillets:
To avoid scorching, burning, and sticking, purchase sturdy professional-quality pans with even heat-conducting properties and heavy bottoms. Shop in restaurant supply stores or wait for sales. Take care of your pots and pans—treat them right—and they will last for many, many years.

Sugar:
I use unrefined cane sugar exclusively. It's cleaner, much less processed, and slower to go through your system than refined white or brown sugar. You will see "unrefined cane sugar" listed as an ingredient in many recipes throughout this book. Sucanat is the brand I usually use, though natural foods grocery stores generally carry several. These sugars come in dark and light varieties, which is important in some desserts and wherever color is key to the finished product.

Suribachi:
For pulverizing nuts, garlic, or large spices by hand, this grooved ceramic Japanese mortar with a wooden pestle produces outstanding results. It also works well for pastes, pesto, spice mixes, and salsas.

Tomato peeling:
Roasting is the easiest and most satisfying way to peel tomatoes, as it brings out the tomato essence without losing any of the tomato flavor or nutrients in water. Juices that are released can be saved and used. Halve

chef talk
Use the skins and any unused seeds from tomatoes to make vinaigrette. Simply press through a fine mesh strainer and mix with oil and vinegar.

tomatoes lengthwise and set on a baking sheet lined with parchment paper skin side up. Roast in a 400°F (200°C) oven for 25 minutes.

Broiling: Preheat broiler; set rack about 5 to 6 inches from the heat. Slice tomatoes in half lengthwise and set the slices face down on a baking sheet. Broil until the tomatoes are lightly charred and the skins are wrinkled and peeling, about 5 to 7 minutes. Alternatively, broil the tomatoes whole on both sides, 4 to 5 minutes per side. Turn over with tongs.

Boiling: Score a shallow *X* with a sharp paring knife along the bottom of a tomato, drop into boiling water for 30 to 60 seconds or so. Retrieve the tomato with a slotted spoon and run under cold water or drop in ice water. The skin will peel right off.

Tongs: Have a couple of pair, one long and one short. Tongs are useful for working with chiles.

Two spatulas: Yes, two. The best way to handle burgers or other items you might be frying in oil is to use one spatula to press straight up and down against the burger at a 90-degree angle and the other to flip it over. This enables you to flip without much splatter. The same technique works well when you want to coat the raw burgers with bread crumbs or cornmeal before cooking. The burgers will keep their shape, and your hands stay clean.

Vegetable stock: Homemade stock (see page 45) is always the preferred choice, especially in soups and polenta, but several brands are now available in aseptic containers that are useful when only a small amount is needed. Some brands are clearly better than others, so you'll have to try for yourself. Beyond stocks, a number of ready-made soups, such as butternut squash, corn, and tomato, make excellent bases for sauce.

Vinegar: Besides your standard red, balsamic, and white wine vinegars, I suggest having on hand some expensive balsamic or sherry vinegar. The difference between inexpensive and aged vinegar (days versus years) is like the difference between a $7.99 bottle of wine and a $20 or $40 bottle. Both have their place, of course, but for exquisite vinaigrettes or on top of grilled vegetables, aged vinegar is the way to go.

STARTING

OFF RIGHT:

Appetizers
and Snacks

"Starting Off Right" is about piquing your interest and whetting your appetite. It's

about keeping your mouth busy during those uncomfortable moments at a party.

It's deciding that two or three starters make a light meal. What's important to

remember is that those small first tastes make a very big impression. Let's talk

specifics.

For nibbles, I like a good spread or pâté on fresh bread. I've got several that disappear pretty fast at gatherings. The Petite Black Lentil Pâté is not unlike chopped liver, but much better. It is vegetarian, of course, but has a certain depth and character that goes beautifully on crisp, fresh baguettes with goat cheese and olive oil. Besides lentils, it gets its flavors from the combination of walnuts, green beans, and caramelized onions. Another spread, Caramelized Onion Sweet Potato Butter, accomplishes a lot, but ever so simply; its creaminess is not much different than that of butter. Simple ingredients, but a rich taste.

This chapter also contains several fiery chile and fruit salsas to choose from, including Seared Pineapple and Fire Salsa and Mango Avocado Salsa. I think we take salsas for granted, as they have become so popular as condiments (maybe too popular, if you ask me). Some store-bought salsas are, however—as you may have experienced yourself—of reasonably good quality, but none compare to the combination of fresh fruit or tomatoes and chiles mixed with lime and cilantro made just an hour or so before you eat. If you don't have a lot of experience making your own salsa, I think you will appreciate this part of the chapter. And nothing could be simpler.

Also look for more elaborate starters like the Vietnamese Spring Rolls, with four dips to choose from. They are well worth the effort and can be fun to make with friends.

Caramelized onion-sweet potato butter

Perfect for the holidays but great anytime, this spread is used very much like dairy butter and is **best served** at room temperature. Once you've tried the recipe as is, feel free to adjust the amount of oil, maple syrup, and tahini to your own taste. No matter what changes you make, remember two key instructions: the onion should be nicely caramelized, and the spread must be **pureed** until very creamy.

1 large sweet potato or Jewel yam (about 1 pound [500g]

1 large yellow onion, coarsely chopped

3 tablespoons olive oil

1 to 2 tablespoons maple syrup

1 tablespoon tahini

¼ teaspoon salt, or more to taste

Freshly ground pepper

1. Preheat the oven to 325°F [160°C]. **Bake** the sweet potato until soft, 40 to 50 minutes. Let cool, scoop out the sweet potato, and discard the skin.

2. Meanwhile, in a medium skillet, **cook** the onion in 1½ tablespoons olive oil over medium heat until soft and golden brown, 10 to 15 minutes.

3. In a food processor, **combine** the browned onion, 1 tablespoon maple syrup, the remaining olive oil, and the tahini. Puree until smooth.

4. Add the sweet potato, salt, and pepper to taste and **blend** again until very smooth and creamy. Taste and add up to 1 more tablespoon maple syrup if you feel it is needed. Let stand for about 1 hour before serving.

MAKES ABOUT 2 CUPS [500ML]

Petite black lentil pâté

Though you can substitute green or brown lentils, look for the black variety, as they hold their shape well and offer a more distinct color. I strongly encourage you to make this ahead because the flavors build immensely over time. When ready, serve on crackers or fresh bread with goat cheese and mustard or horseradish, or maybe a little extra virgin olive oil.

1½ cups vegetable stock or water [375ml]

3 garlic cloves, minced

1 bay leaf

½ cup petite black lentils or French lentils [100g]

½ onion, finely chopped

2 tablespoons extra virgin olive oil

1 large portobello mushroom, chopped

½ cup broken or chopped walnuts [50g]

10 fresh green beans, cleaned of strings, coarsely chopped

2 teaspoons dried basil

2 teaspoons dried oregano

1 teaspoon salt

½ teaspoon freshly ground black pepper

⅛ teaspoon crushed hot red pepper

1 tablespoon minced fresh rosemary

3 tablespoons fresh lemon juice

1. In a medium saucepan, combine the vegetable stock, garlic, and bay leaf. Bring to a boil. Add the lentils and reduce the heat to a simmer. Cover and cook for about 25 minutes or until the lentils are soft. Remove and discard the bay leaf.

2. Meanwhile, in a medium skillet, cook the onion in 1 tablespoon olive oil over medium heat until softened and beginning to color, about 5 minutes. Add the mushroom and walnuts and cook until the mushroom has released its juices and they have evaporated, 5 to 7 minutes longer.

3. Add the green beans, basil, oregano, salt, black pepper, and hot pepper. Continue to **cook** until the herbs are fragrant and the green beans have softened slightly, about 2 minutes longer. Add the fresh rosemary and 2 tablespoons lemon juice. Cook until the liquid is absorbed.

4. In a food processor, **blend** the onion-mushroom mixture until well mixed. Scrape down the sides to make sure all the ingredients have been well incorporated. Add the cooked lentils and mix again until very smooth. Add the remaining 1 tablespoon each lemon juice and olive oil. Mix well. Adjust the seasoning, if necessary. Let the flavors marry at least 2 hours before serving. If not eating for more than 1 hour, refrigerate. For best results, serve at room temperature.

SERVES 6 TO 8

note The color of the pâté will likely be grayish and muddy right after blending. But, no fear, this will also change over a couple of hours' time.

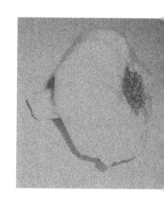

Roasted pepper hummus

Hummus is easy to make and **tastier** than store-bought any day. I particularly enjoy this version in the fall, when the variety of hot peppers is in full stride. I like using a fresh cayenne, roasted in a cast-iron skillet. The roasting helps the chile retain the spiciness but mellows the heat and expands the flavor.

If you prefer no heat in your hummus, **substitute** sun-dried tomatoes or a roasted red bell pepper for the hot pepper, or use roasted garlic instead of raw garlic. Add more tahini if you like a creamier hummus. Serve with diced cucumbers, tomatoes, and warm pitas.

1 fresh cayenne pepper, or more to taste

3 cups cooked and drained chickpeas [500g]

5 garlic cloves

3 tablespoons tahini, preferably roasted

⅓ cup extra virgin olive oil [75ml]

Juice from 2 fresh lemons

Chopped cilantro or parsley, for garnish

1. Make sure your kitchen is well ventilated. **Toast** the cayenne pepper in a dry small cast-iron skillet over medium-high heat, turning every so often, until lightly blackened all over. Remove the stem and coarsely chop the pepper.

2. **Blend** all ingredients except the garnish in a food processor until very smooth. Let stand for an hour or so to let flavors develop. Scrape into a shallow serving dish and drizzle additional oil on top. Garnish with cilantro or parsley.

SERVES 6 TO 8

note Fresh cayenne peppers can be hard to find, depending on the kind of fresh market you have available, or where you live. Substitute another hot pepper, such as jalapeño, or even a rehydrated dried chipotle or canned chipotle in adobo sauce.

Rosemary olive oil

This has got to be one of the **simplest** appetizers ever conceived. I have given just the basic recipe, which, when used with exquisite extra virgin olive oil and fresh rosemary, is all you need. That doesn't mean you can't add a little garlic, a splash of balsamic vinegar, or another herb. Dip fresh, crusty bread in oil. Enjoy with olives, roasted red peppers, cheese, or any of the spreads in this chapter.

1 cup extra virgin olive oil [250ml]　　　4 to 6 sprigs fresh rosemary

Place the olive oil in small glass or ceramic bowl. Add the rosemary to the oil and let **steep** for at least 2 hours and up to overnight.

MAKES ABOUT 1 CUP [250ML]

Guacamole with tomato and cumin

Not much needs to be said about guacamole. It's beauty in taste and **texture** is self evident. Though I add cumin and coriander, plus a generous dose of fresh tomatoes, this recipe is **essentially very simple.**

4 plum tomatoes, seeded and finely diced

2 ripe avocados

3 garlic cloves, minced

1 teaspoon ground cumin seeds*

1 teaspoon ground coriander seeds*

1 teaspoon salt

3 tablespoons finely diced red onion, rinsed under cold water, then drained well

Juice of ½ lime

In a bowl, **mash** all the ingredients until well incorporated but still chunky. Adjust any of the seasonings to your taste.

SERVES 4 TO 6

*If you can mash the ingredients in a suribachi (see page 13), use whole garlic cloves and whole cumin and coriander seeds. Crush in the mortar along with the salt, then add remaining ingredients and mix well.

chef's tip

Rinsing the raw onion removes its bite, which I sometimes find unpleasant in a mild dish such as this.

Tomatillo, roasted fennel, and garlic guacamole

4 tomatillos, husked and rinsed

1 fresh serrano pepper

3 garlic cloves, unpeeled

1 tablespoon canola or safflower oil

3 ounces fresh fennel bulb, sliced (about 1 cup) [90g]

1 teaspoon unrefined cane sugar

2 ripe avocados

1 to 2 teaspoons salt

3 tablespoons red onion, finely diced, rinsed under cold water and drained well

3 tablespoons coarsely chopped cilantro

1. **Preheat** the broiler with the rack set about 4 inches [10cm] from the heat. Spread the tomatillos on a baking pan and broil, turning with tongs once or twice, until they are lightly browned and softened, about 5 to 7 minutes. When done, chop and set aside in a bowl along with any juices.

2. Meanwhile, make sure your kitchen is well ventilated. **Heat** a cast-iron skillet to medium-hot. Dry-roast the serrano pepper, turning every so often with tongs, until it is lightly blackened all over. When done, remove the stem and coarsely chop the pepper; add to the tomatillos. In the same pan, while you are toasting the pepper, roast the unpeeled garlic. Turn over with tongs occasionally but allow to get slightly blackened, about 8 to 10 minutes. Peel, chop, and add to the bowl.

3. Heat the oil in the same pan, add the fennel, and cook until soft and lightly browned, about 10 minutes. **Flatten** the pieces of fennel with a spatula, where you can, to get as many sides onto the heat as possible. Coarsely chop.

4. In a blender or food processor, **combine** the fennel, tomatillos, garlic, pepper, and sugar. Puree until smooth. In a bowl, mash with the avocados until the ingredients are well incorporated but still slightly chunky. Season with salt. Stir in the onion and cilantro. Cover with plastic, setting it right on the guacamole to keep it green. Serve at room temperature.

SERVES 6

Toasted garlic and tomato bruschetta with olives and basil

This recipe has some serious flavor. Bruschetta, a classic favorite, is usually made with raw tomatoes on toasted bread rubbed with garlic topped with fresh basil. I add a little punch to the mix with toasted garlic and olives. If stir-frying, remember to keep the heat fairly low, because extra virgin olive oil has a lower burning point than other more refined oils.

8 pieces thick-crusted Italian or peasant bread, sliced about ½ inch thick [1cm]

2½ tablespoons extra virgin olive oil

4 to 6 garlic cloves, sliced into thin slivers

6 large plum or small to medium vine-ripened tomatoes, finely diced

Salt and freshly ground pepper

1 teaspoon balsamic vinegar

6 to 8 kalamata olives, pitted and sliced

3 tablespoons shredded fresh basil

1. Brush the top of each bread slice with about ½ teaspoon of the olive oil and toast or grill until golden brown on both sides. Set aside on a serving plate.

2. Heat the remaining olive oil in a wok or medium skillet over medium-low heat. Add the garlic slivers and cook until nicely browned, stirring often, about 3 minutes. Add the tomatoes and cook for another minute or so, until they soften. Add a generous amount of salt and pepper and a splash of vinegar. Toss in the olives.

3. Top each piece of toasted bread with the tomato mixture. Garnish with basil and serve at once.

SERVES 4

Horseradish mustard dip

This zesty blend makes an excellent substitute for cream cheese or sour cream spreads. Use on sandwiches or for dipping crudités or crackers. Fresh horseradish is phenomenal in its potency but, sadly, seasonal. When fresh is not available, use a good bottled brand—meaning one prepared with just horseradish and vinegar. Stay away from versions with eggs and cream and preservatives, etc.

3 tablespoons grated fresh or bottled white horseradish

½ pound firm tofu [250g]

2 garlic cloves, crushed through a press

2 tablespoons fresh lemon juice

1 tablespoon apple cider vinegar

1 tablespoon extra virgin olive oil

1 tablespoon stone-ground mustard

1 teaspoon soy sauce

1 teaspoon salt

Freshly ground pepper

1. If using fresh horseradish, mix in a food processor until as finely ground as possible. Add all the remaining ingredients and blend well.

2. If using bottled horseradish, first puree the tofu until smooth and creamy. Scrape down the sides of processor once or twice. Add the remaining ingredients and continue to blend for a minute or two until creamy.

3. For best results, cover and refrigerate before serving. The flavors become remarkably sharp after an hour or two.

MAKES ABOUT 1 CUP [250ML]

chef's tip

To use fresh horseradish, peel what you need and chop into small chunks then grind in a food processor. It will make quite a racket at first but eventually will smooth out. Blend and blend until ground down. Wrap any unused root in plastic and refrigerate.

Sun-dried tomato and roasted garlic spread with mint and maple

This spread goes especially well on crackers and warm baguette slices, but it would be excellent with crudités and can be thinned with extra oil to use as a salad dressing. A cold dollop is perfect on top of Cajun Tempeh (page 146).

1 head of garlic

10 sun-dried tomato halves, soaked in hot water until soft, then coarsely chopped

1 pound firm silken tofu [500g]

Juice of 1 lemon

2½ tablespoons olive oil

2 teaspoons cider vinegar

2 teaspoons maple syrup

1 teaspoon red miso

1 teaspoon nutritional yeast

6 to 10 leaves fresh mint, coarsely chopped

Salt and freshly ground pepper

1. **Preheat** the oven to 325°F [160°C]. Break the head of garlic into individual cloves. Skin them and cut off any hard bits on the ends. Coat the cloves lightly with 1½ teaspoons of the olive oil and cook in a covered baking dish for 30 to 40 minutes, or until golden and soft. You may toss them once or so while they are cooking.

2. Puree the roasted cloves in a food processor. **Add** the sun-dried tomatoes and blend again until well mixed. Add the tofu and blend again. Add the lemon juice, vinegar, maple syrup, miso, yeast, mint, and remaining 2 tablespoons oil. Puree until very smooth, at least 2 minutes, scraping down sides two or three times. Season with salt and pepper to taste.

3. Transfer the spread to a bowl and cover. Let stand 1 to 2 hours or overnight, if you have time, to allow the flavors to develop. **Serve** on crackers or a warm baguette.

SERVES 6 TO 8

White bean and roasted garlic spread

Dried beans, freshly cooked, will give you the most satisfying taste here, but, of course, canned beans can be substituted for convenience. A mixture of herbs contributes the most interesting flavor. Serve warm or at room temperature, preferably with Cumin Pita Chips (page 34).

1 head of garlic

2 tablespoons plus 2 teaspoons extra virgin olive oil

2 cups cooked white beans [330g]

2 teaspoons ground cumin

3 tablespoons fresh lemon juice

3 or 4 dashes of Tabasco sauce

1 tablespoon plus ½ teaspoon minced fresh herbs, such as oregano, thyme, and mint

Vegetable stock or soy milk (optional)

Salt and freshly ground pepper

1. Preheat the oven to 325°F [160°C]. Separate the head of garlic into individual cloves. Skin them and cut off the hard bits on the ends. Toss the cloves with 1 teaspoon of the olive oil to coat lightly and cook in a covered baking dish for 30 to 40 minutes, or until golden and soft. You may toss them once or twice while they are cooking.

2. In a food processor, combine the roasted garlic with the beans, cumin, lemon juice, Tabasco, 1 tablespoon minced herbs, and 2 tablespoons of the olive oil. Puree until smooth. If the spread is too thick, thin with vegetable stock or soy milk, adding 1 tablespoon at a time. Season with salt and pepper to taste.

3. Scrape the spread into a serving bowl (a dark-colored bowl will create the most dramatic presentation) and let stand for 1 hour, if you have time. Just before serving, drizzle with the remaining 1 teaspoon olive oil and garnish with the remaining herbs.

SERVES 6 TO 8

Vietnamese spring rolls

This recipe is typically served instead of egg rolls or fried spring rolls, and it is very refreshing as such. But the opportunity is there if you care to fry half your rolls, for example, and present them alternately with uncooked rolls. Try one and see if you like this method. Lightly coat a medium frying pan with vegetable oil and heat to medium-high. Fry rolls for about 1 minute on each side or until lightly browned. Drain on paper towels and serve warm.

Most important: Clear your space and organize all the ingredients ahead of time. These rolls are works of art. Take your time. Accept your mistakes. Relish the beauty of your successes and use the time to meditate as you prepare this recipe.

Easy tips and techniques:
read this first

The quantities in this recipe will vary to such a degree that you must make this recipe to see how much you will need or use. Trying to follow strict guidelines will only create frustration. Follow the quantity guidelines and you will have no problems, except maybe some leftovers that can be used in a stir-fry or scrambled eggs.

The ingredients list can be taken as a guideline too. Think about adding or substituting blanched snow peas, sun-dried tomatoes, cooked beets, or any other appropriate item you might find appealing.

Rice paper is somewhat fragile. I usually throw away several cracked and broken sheets before I even get started. However, you may be lucky and buy a package where they'll all be perfect. (Be sure to let me know if this happens.)

If my first few experiences are any indication, you will probably tear a few rice paper sheets as you are rolling them. Hence, I will not even guess how many you will need and suggest you just buy a package.

1 small carrot, peeled and cut into thin slivers

2 teaspoons olive oil

4 large fresh shiitake mushrooms, stems removed, caps cut into thin slivers

1 package dried rice noodles (about 16 ounces) [300g]

1 package rice papers measuring 8½ to 9 inches round (usually 20 rice papers per package) [22 to 23cm]

½ red bell pepper, cut into thin slivers

½ yellow bell pepper, cut into thin slivers

½ medium-small cucumber, peeled, seeded, and cut into thin slivers

½ package (6 to 8 ounces) baked tofu, cut into matchsticks [250g]

Salt and freshly ground pepper

1 bunch of fresh basil

1. **Blanch** the carrot slivers in a medium saucepan of boiling water for 30 seconds or so, until just barely tender. Using a small strainer or slotted spoon, remove the carrot pieces and rinse under cold water until cooled. Drain and set aside.

2. Heat the olive oil in a medium nonstick skillet. Add the shiitakes and **sauté** over high heat, tossing, until just tender, 2 to 3 minutes. Drain on paper towels.

3. Add about ⅓ package of rice noodles to a saucepan of boiling water. (You will need about 1 ounce [30g] noodles per roll.) **Remove** from the heat and let stand for 1 minute, or until the noodles are soft. Drain and rinse in cold water until cooled. Drain again and set aside.

4. Fill a large, shallow bowl with cold water. **Soak** 1 sheet of rice paper at a time in the water for 1 to 2 minutes, or until soft. If the edges are still firm, use your fingertips to gently press the edges until they soften. Carefully lift out the rice paper and let drip for a few seconds over the bowl. Place on a clean cutting board. Before you begin to assemble your roll, place another rice paper in the water so it will be ready when you are finished with the current one.

5. Set a small mound of noodles (about 1 ounce [30g]) 2 inches [5cm] from the bottom of the rice paper. Leave a 1- to 1½-inch [3- to 4-cm] margin on the sides. **Top** the noodles with one-tenth of the carrots, mushrooms, peppers, cucumbers, and tofu. After the first roll or two, you will realize how much is too much or too little. Season with salt and pepper to taste.

6. **Fold** the sides up over the filling and carefully begin to roll the rice paper up from

the bottom. After one turn of the paper, add 1 or 2 basil leaves (they will show through the translucent paper) and continue to roll into a tight cylinder.

7. **Roll** the paper all the way over, and the paper will stick to itself—more so as it begins to dry. Your finished product should be about 4 to 5 inches [10 to 12cm] long. Set aside on a large plate and repeat with the remaining rolls. Cover and refrigerate if not eating right away, up to 3 hours. If fried, they're best eaten while still warm.

chef's serving suggestions
Serve with Orange-Sesame Dipping Sauce, Chinese Mustard Dressing, Sweet and Sour Sauce (recipes follow), or the peanut sauce in Charney's Classic Peanut Sauce (page 124). If you have time, make two or more sauces. A choice of dips makes for an excellent presentation.

SERVES 5

Orange–sesame dipping sauce

Here's a citrus-based sauce with a nice **tang** and serious bite. It makes a fine dipping sauce for almost any Asian dumpling and is a perfect as a **marinade** for tofu or tempeh.

3 garlic cloves, minced

1 teaspoon grated fresh ginger

½ cup fresh orange juice [125ml]

1 tablespoon plus 1 teaspoon toasted sesame oil

1 tablespoon plus 1 teaspoon rice vinegar

1 tablespoon honey

1 teaspoon soy sauce

1 teaspoon hot sauce, or to taste

½ teaspoon red miso

1 tablespoon minced cilantro

Salt and freshly ground pepper

Mix all the ingredients very well in a bowl. **Taste** and season additionally if necessary, remembering the flavors will brighten dramatically in the next hour or so. Let stand at room temperature for 1 hour before serving.

MAKES ABOUT ³/₄ CUP [200ML]

Chinese mustard dressing

It's almost too simple to be true, but this sauce is amazing. There are no fancy ingredients—they can all be bought in any Asian or gourmet grocery store—and it's easy to make. The combination of flavors, however, is distinctive. Use as a dipping sauce or over a crunchy salad.

1 tablespoon Chinese mustard powder (hot or regular)

Hot water

½ cup plum sauce [125ml]

3 tablespoons rice vinegar

2 tablespoons toasted sesame oil

1 tablespoon soy sauce

1 teaspoon salt

1 tablespoon unrefined cane sugar

1. In a bowl, blend the mustard powder with just enough hot water to make a paste. Let stand for 10 minutes.

2. Add the remaining ingredients and blend well. For maximum flavor, cover and refrigerate for at least 1 hour before serving.

MAKES ABOUT 1 CUP [250ML]

Sweet and sour cherry-mango sauce

Here's my version of Chinese duck sauce, perfect for dipping spring rolls and other Asian dumplings. I think most people are familiar with the flavor of sweet and sour. This sauce is distinctive with cherries, mango, and raspberry vinegar. Tamarind paste, also known as Indian date, is used in barbecue sauces and Thai noodle dishes and chutneys (probably without your knowing it). It's tangy, slightly sweet, with a somewhat raisiny flavor. Look for it in jars of concentrated paste.

½ cup finely chopped onion [70g]

1 tablespoon vegetable oil

1 cup frozen or pitted fresh cherries, coarsely chopped [150g]

1 mango, peeled, pitted, and coarsely chopped

⅔ cup raspberry vinegar [150ml]

¼ cup unrefined cane sugar [50g]

1 teaspoon tamarind paste

1. In a nonreactive medium saucepan with a heavy bottom, cook the onion in the oil over medium-low heat until very soft but not brown, 5 to 7 minutes.

2. Add the cherries, mango, vinegar, and sugar. Bring to a boil, cover, and reduce the heat to a bare simmer. Cook for 10 minutes. Uncover and cook 10 minutes longer, stirring occasionally so the sauce does not stick to the bottom or sides.

3. Pass the sauce through a food grater or a fine mesh strainer and press until the solids are practically dry. Return to the pan, stir in the tamarind paste, and simmer uncovered for 5 minutes, or until the sauce is reduced enough to coat a spoon heavily.

MAKES ABOUT 1 ¼ CUPS [300ML]

Cumin pita chips

Once you try these, you are likely to become **addicted.** They are easy to make and especially good served warm. Pita chips can be made a few hours ahead. Place in a bowl, cover with a dishtowel or paper towels to keep them crisp, and store at room temperature. Reheat briefly if desired.

Pita bread, about 6 inches in diameter [15ml]

2 teaspoons olive oil per pita

Crushed cumin seeds

Coarse salt and freshly ground pepper

1. Preheat the oven to 350°F [175°C]. Cut each pita into 8 triangular wedges. Cover a baking sheet with parchment paper and lay out pieces of pita in a single layer. Brush the tops of the pitas with olive oil and dust lightly with cumin, salt, and pepper.

2. Bake for 15 minutes, or until lightly browned on top. Turn the chips over. Bake for 5 minutes longer, or until the chips are crisp and lightly browned.

SERVES 2

Mango avocado salsa

I love a good salsa—which is the Mexican word for sauce, by the way. The fresh flavors, from hot to sweet to tangy, all rise together in a crescendo of exciting sensations in your mouth.

This is the salsa that started it all. The combination of colors and vibrant tropical flavors never fails to get rave reviews. The recipe calls for two mangoes, but you may use a third, depending on how juicy and meaty they are; adjust the other ingredients as necessary. Serve over Curried Corn Burgers (page 102), as a relish, or with chips as a dip.

2 mangoes, finely diced

1 small red bell pepper, finely diced

½ red onion, finely diced

1 fresh jalapeño or serrano pepper, minced

Juice of 1 large lime, or more to taste

½ cup [125ml] coarsely chopped cilantro

2 avocados, diced

Splash of peach vinegar*

Salt

In a large glass or ceramic bowl, combine the diced mangoes, red pepper, red onion, and jalapeño pepper. Mix well but with a light hand. Add the lime juice and cilantro and mix again. Fold in the avocados. Add a splash of vinegar and season with salt to taste. Let stand for 10 to 20 minutes before serving.

SERVES 4 TO 6

*This is a specialty item that may have to be ordered from a gourmet food catalog. If not available, use red wine vinegar.

Tomato and kiwi salsa with fresh apricots

For measurement's sake, your plum tomatoes and kiwis should be about the same size. And try to find fresh apricots for this salsa. If, however, they are not in season or have no taste (which is not unusual), substitute 1 mango or a large peach.

NOTE Due to the fragility of kiwis and apricots, this salsa has an especially short life. It's best eaten fresh.

3 kiwis, peeled and finely diced

4 plum tomatoes, seeded and finely diced

2 fresh apricots, finely diced

½ cup thinly sliced shallots [50g]

1 fresh serrano or jalapeño pepper, minced

3 garlic cloves, minced

¼ cup coarsely chopped cilantro [60ml]

3 tablespoons lime juice

½ teaspoon salt

1. In a large glass or ceramic bowl, combine all the ingredients except the lime juice and salt. Mix well but with a light hand.

2. Add the lime juice and salt to taste and mix again. If you have time, cover and refrigerate for 1 hour to let the flavors develop. Toss again and check the seasoning before serving.

SERVES 4 TO 6

Roasted corn and yellow tomato salsa with ancho chiles

Fresh corn is always preferable, and the new super-sweet hybrids have extended the season appreciably, but frozen will work without a hitch.

2 dried ancho chiles, stems and seeds removed

2 teaspoons olive oil

1 cup fresh or frozen corn kernels [120g]

½ pint yellow cherry tomatoes or 1 to 2 small yellow tomatoes, seeded and finely diced [150g]

1 small red onion, finely diced

1 fresh serrano or jalapeño pepper, minced

¼ cup fresh lime juice [60ml]

1 avocado, peeled and cut into small cubes

½ cup coarsely chopped cilantro [125g]

Salt

1. Bring a small saucepan of water to a boil and remove from the heat. **Add** the ancho chiles and cover. Soak for 20 to 30 minutes, or until soft. Coarsely chop the chiles and set aside.

2. While the chiles are soaking, **heat** the oil in a large cast-iron skillet over high heat. Add the corn and cook, tossing or stirring often, until lightly browned, 5 to 7 minutes. (Alternatively, if you don't have a cast-iron skillet, coat the corn lightly with oil and roast on a baking sheet in a 400°F [200°C] oven for 15 to 20 minutes.)

3. In a large ceramic bowl, combine the ancho chiles, corn, tomatoes, red onion, and serrano pepper. **Mix** well but with a light hand. Add the lime juice and mix again. Just before serving, season lightly with salt and fold in the cilantro and avocado.

SERVES 4 TO 6

Navy and black bean salsa with roasted yellow pepper

Needless to say, this salsa is for bean lovers. It's somewhat heartier than the fruit salsas, which makes it a nice side dish with rice and a salad.

2 large yellow bell peppers, roasted, peeled, and diced

1 cup cooked black beans, drained [165g]

1 cup cooked navy beans, drained [165g]

4 scallions, thinly sliced

½ cup coarsely chopped cilantro [125ml]

2 teaspoons minced fresh mint

1 fresh serrano or jalapeño pepper, minced

¼ cup fresh lime juice [60ml]

1 tablespoon cider vinegar

Salt

1. In a large glass or ceramic bowl, **toss** together the roasted peppers, black beans, navy beans, roasted peppers, scallions, cilantro, mint, and serrano pepper.

2. Add the lime juice, vinegar, and salt. **Mix** well. Season with salt to taste. Serve at room temperature.

SERVES 4 TO 6

THE NEXT TWO SALSAS are more authentically Mexican in style, more loose than chunky. Both are intensely flavored. You can use them as bases for sauces. To do so, puree until very smooth. Press through a mesh strainer and fry in a saucepan over high heat with a little oil. Add ½ to 1 cup [125 to 250ml] vegetable stock and simmer for about 15 minutes. Use where you want to plate a beautiful sauce underneath a burger, grilled tofu or vegetable, or swirled into a soup.

Chipotle chile, roasted pepper, and tomatillo salsa

Chipotle chiles, which are dried smoked jalapeños, add a wonderful **smoky flavor** to everything they touch. This richly flavored and exquisite-looking salsa has a beautiful blend of tastes—smoky, sweet, tart, hot, and tangy.

2 dried chipotle chiles, sliced open, seeds, ribs, and stem removed

2 garlic cloves, unpeeled

1 large red bell pepper

4 tomatillos, husked and rinsed

1 tablespoon unrefined cane sugar

2 tablespoons lime juice

¼ teaspoon salt

1. Preheat the broiler with a rack set about 4 inches [10cm] from the heat. **Pour** very hot water over the chiles in a small bowl and cover. Soak until soft, 30 to 40 minutes. Drain, coarsely chop, and set aside.

2. **Arrange** the garlic cloves, bell pepper, and tomatillos on a baking sheet and broil, turning with tongs, until the garlic is soft and spotted brown, 7 to 10 minutes, and the tomatillos and peppers are lightly blackened and softened, about 10 to 15 minutes.

3. Peel the garlic. **Peel** the skin off the pepper and scrape out the seeds.

4. In a blender or food processor, **combine** the chipotle chiles with the roasted red pepper, tomatillos, garlic, sugar, lime juice, and salt. Blend until coarsely chopped. Pour into a bowl and stir in cilantro. Season with additional salt and pepper to taste.

SERVES 4 TO 6

Seared pineapple and fire salsa

Use this salsa on burgers or tacos or in soup. If you have access to a barbecue, grill your pineapple strips. (Brush lightly with oil first.) If that's not convenient, follow the directions below for using a cast-iron skillet. Habañero (meaning "from Havana") peppers are extremely hot but also have a tropical fruit flavor. I find half a plump roasted habañero about the right heat. If you are a serious chilehead, use more— but hold on to your hat!

3 garlic cloves, unpeeled

1 fat, fresh habañero pepper

About ½ fresh pineapple, core removed, cut into 4 long wedges

2 teaspoons olive oil

2 tablespoons orange juice

1 tablespoon lime juice

1 tablespoon unrefined cane sugar

½ teaspoon salt

3 tablespoons finely diced red onion, rinsed under cold water

¼ cup coarsely chopped cilantro [60ml]

1. **Toast** the garlic cloves and habañero pepper in a dry cast-iron skillet over medium heat until the garlic is soft and lightly browned in spots and the pepper is lightly blackened, 10 to 15 minutes. With tongs, turn the garlic and pepper. Lightly press down on the pepper often.

2. When the garlic is cool enough to handle, peel it. **Slice** the habañero in half, remove the stem, and scrape out the seeds and ribs. Coarsely chop half the pepper. Save the other half until you decide whether your salsa is hot enough or whether you need to add more.

3. In the same skillet, **sear** the pineapple in the olive oil over medium-high heat until the fruit is lightly charred on both sides, 1 to 2 minutes per side. Cut the pineapple wedges into chunks; reserve any juices.

4. Put the pineapple chunks and their juices in a blender or food processor. Add the toasted garlic and habañero, orange juice, lime juice, sugar, and salt. **Pulse** until

chopped and well blended; do not puree until smooth. Pour into a bowl and stir in the red onion and cilantro. Season with additional salt to taste. Let stand 30 to 60 minutes before serving, if you have time.

SERVES 3 TO 4

Epilogue on salsa

YOU HAVE TO WORK pretty hard to mess up salsa. In classes I've taught, I don't usually give an exact recipe; rather, I demonstrate one salsa and then give half a dozen ideas so students can make their own. Ultimately, you decide how bold your salsa will be or how many chiles to add. You decide whether there should be more or less cilantro or garlic or a splash of vinegar. The potential modifications are as plentiful as the flavors to choose from.

You've just read about several excellent salsas. However, if you've never made a salsa or aren't sure of the fundamentals, I thought I'd speed things up with a kind of basic, no-fail salsa suggestion guide or template to help you out. If you don't see something you'd like to include, go right ahead and add it. You can modify, multiply, or just be satisfied. Keep in mind my favorite old adage: The most successful people fail their way to the top.

Salsa guide

START WITH
Vegetable, fruit (raw or roasted), or beans. For example: tomatoes, tomatillos, corn, black or white beans, mango, peach, pear, avocado, and so on.

ADD (SINGLY OR IN COMBINATION)
Onion (red, white, yellow), shallots, scallions, chives, leeks, garlic (raw or roasted).

CHOOSE YOUR CHILE: (RAW OR ROAST-ED, SEEDED, RIBBED, OR LEFT INTACT)
Habañero (10), serrano (6–8), jalapeño (5–6), New Mexico (3–4)

What do the numbers mean?
10 = Beyond Hell, 5 = C'mon, you can take it!
1 = Wimp*

ADD
Chopped or whole cilantro plus hints of mint, thyme, or oregano

Lime juice

OPTIONS
Sugar, vinegar, salt

PREPARATIONS
Coarsely chop or pulse in food processor.

REMEMBER
Pay attention to colors and texture and let the flavors walk down the aisle for a while before serving.

*There are no "1s" in this book.

2 SOUPS and STOCKS: Warm Beginnings

Soups are as much about techniques and templates as they are about the actual

recipes. The ingredients may change, but the techniques and templates stay the

same. So how do you make a soup that will draw you in and then hold you,

making each sip (or slurp) an experience that you wish would linger on forever?

Number 1, make homemade stock.

Number 2, practice layering flavors.

Number 3, be versatile, depending on the ingredients available to you.

What is stock?

Stock is simply the essence that remains when you extract all the flavors from vegetables cooking in water. It's what gives soup and other dishes cooked in it richness and what some chefs call integrity. Best of all, there's nothing challenging about creating a stock. You simply bring basic vegetables and herbs to a boil, then simmer them gently for 45 minutes to an hour.

It's hard to go wrong making a vegetable stock. Almost any vegetable scrap will do fine, depending on what you plan to use the stock for. For example, stick with lighter-colored vegetables for a pale soup. Use a stem or two or three of fresh herbs, peppercorns (tie them in up in a cheesecloth bundle, or bouquet garni), corncobs, mushroom stems, scallions, leeks, and garlic. Feel free to experiment with your own combinations. However, avoid strong-smelling vegetables, such as cabbage and asparagus, and beets, which will color the stock dark red. Also, avoid excess use of the outer brown skin or paper from onions, as too much can add bitterness.

Two more tips to remember

There's no need to stir the pot while the stock is simmering; in fact, moving things around may cloud the liquid unnecessarily.

Note the ratio of water to vegetables. Too much water will leave you with a weak stock, without as much flavor as you would like. It's better to have too little water than too much. Look for the liquid to be 2 to 3 inches [5 to 7cm] over your vegetables.

Variations on basic stock

The variations on stock are infinite. Basic Vegetable Stock (page 45) can be slightly altered by sweating the vegetables first in a little oil until they are soft but not brown, then adding the water, wine, and bouquet garni. Parsnips, leeks, fennel, and a few mushrooms can easily be added or substituted. Just remember to keep in mind the color, taste, and final appearance of your finished product, whether it's a stew, soup, sauce, or pot of beans.

Stocks can also be made (for a broth) by roasting or sautéing a variety of mushrooms with a little oil in a stockpot. When the mushrooms have softened considerably and begun to stick slightly to the bottom of the pan, add water and a bouquet garni and bring to a boil. Simmer for 45 minutes to an hour, then strain, pressing to extract as much liquid as possible; discard the mushrooms. Add fresh rosemary stems, or any herb you like, to the hot stock at the end and allow to steep for 15 to 30 minutes before straining.

Additional stock tips

Whenever you cook, save time by freezing your scraps like carrot ends, the hard root end of onions, mushroom stems, sweet, hot, or roasted peppers, and celery leaves in a well-sealed, heavy-duty freezer bag. When you're ready to make a stock, remove the scraps from the freezer and use them in the same manner as fresh.

To store stock, let cool, then pour into cupcake tins. Freeze the tins, then remove the "cupcakes" and seal them in large freezer bags. Use stock instead of water in gravies and sauces and when cooking grains or vegetables; substitute stock for part of the oil in vinaigrettes.

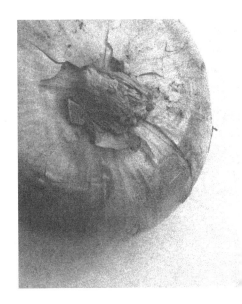

Basic vegetable stock

2 large onions, peeled and quartered

3 carrots, peeled or scrubbed and cut into chunks

2 to 3 celery ribs, cut into chunks

4 to 5 whole garlic cloves, peeled

1 bouquet garni*

Optional vegetables: parsnips, fresh fennel, bell peppers, mushrooms, corncobs

10 cups cold water [2.5L]

½ cup dry white wine [125ml]

2 tablespoons white wine vinegar or champagne vinegar

Salt, freshly ground white pepper, and soy sauce

1. **Add** the onions, carrots, celery, garlic, bouquet garni, and optional vegetables to a large pot. Pour in the cold water and wine and bring to a boil.

2. Reduce the heat to a bare simmer and cook, uncovered, 45 to 60 minutes. If you notice scum floating to the top, skim it off with a large spoon. **Taste** the stock after 45 minutes. If you feel the vegetables have given all they can give, strain and discard them.

3. Return the hot stock to the pot over low heat. **Stir** in the vinegar and simmer for 5 minutes. Season with the salt, white pepper, and a few drops of soy sauce to taste.

MAKES ABOUT 8 CUPS [2L]

*Use cheesecloth and kitchen string to make a fat bundle (2 to 3 inches [5 to 7cm] in diameter) containing fresh parsley and/or parsley stems, peppercorns, fresh thyme, and 1 bay leaf. The flavors of your bouquet garni can be varied to match the type of soup you're creating—meaning you could add cumin seeds, fennel seeds, star anise, or a cinnamon stick, for example, to complement a particular soup.

Roasted vegetable stock

Here's a recipe for a deep, rich, **savory stock,** perfect for soups or sauces. It's essential for French onion soup (page 52). With roasted vegetable stock, it's okay to use beets or even roasted tomatoes or tomato skins, as your stock will be dark-colored anyway.

½ celery root, peeled and coarsely chopped

4 celery ribs, chopped

2 to 3 large carrots, peeled and coarsely chopped

1 head of garlic, divided into cloves, peeled and left whole

3 shallots, chopped

2 large yellow onions, quartered

2 beets, scrubbed and coarsely chopped

1½ tablespoons olive oil

1 teaspoon salt

10 cups cold water [2.5L]

½ cup red wine [125ml]

2 tablespoons red wine vinegar or balsamic vinegar

Salt and freshly ground black pepper

1. **Preheat** the oven to 400°F [200°C]. Place the chopped vegetables in a large bowl. Add the olive oil and salt and toss to coat. Spread out on a large baking sheet or in a shallow baking dish.

2. Roast the vegetables 45 minutes to an hour, **turning** with a wide spatula several times, until they are soft and nicely browned.

3. **Add** the browned vegetables to a large stockpot. Pour in the cold water and wine and bring to a boil. Reduce the heat to a simmer and cook, uncovered, 45 to 60 minutes. If you notice scum floating to the top, skim it off with a spoon.

4. **Taste** the stock after 45 minutes. If you feel the vegetables have given all they can give, strain and discard them.

5. Return the hot stock to the pot and set over low heat. **Stir** in the vinegar and simmer for 5 minutes. Season with additional salt and pepper to taste.

MAKES ABOUT 8 CUPS [2L]

The inner workings of layering a soup

WHILE HOMEMADE SOUPS are actually quite simple and not very time consuming, bold, brilliant recipes require an understanding of how tastes are developed.

Here is a simple illustration of layering flavors for French Lentil Soup with Tarragon and Lemon (page 58). Onions, garlic, celery, and carrots are sautéed with bay leaf, dried tarragon, and oregano. Next they are seasoned with salt and pepper. The lentils and stock are added and brought to a boil.

The onions, garlic, celery (aromatics), and carrots start the soup off with a classic base flavor. The herbs add a distinctive taste, and the lentils bring the combination together with earthy overtones.

Potatoes are added next, and everything is cooked until soft. At this point the flavoring, while somewhat tasty, is rudimentary or undeveloped. How to remedy this? Flavoring accents. First stir in fresh lemon juice and season with salt and pepper.

The lemon juice contributes a real zip. Salt and pepper enhance the flavors that are already there.

Taste your soup again and add a splash of vinegar. At this point your soup is picking up flavor rapidly, but you're not finished yet. Garnish your soup with fresh tarragon or sorrel, which has bright, lemony bite. Finish it with a splash or two of hot sauce, if you like. Stir, taste, and season again with salt and pepper, if necessary.

The garnish adds visual character to the soup, and the hot sauce presents the final staccato note of intensity.

What you have just done is build, layer by layer, a soup that has integrity. For every soup the layers will change, the flavors will differ, and the herbs and spices will vary widely, but you will still build and build until you are satisfied. Then, and only then, will you serve your soup. That said, layering does not by any means have to be complicated. Simple layering works just as well. The bottom line is not to flavor and season all at once, especially not just at the very beginning or the very end of the cooking process.

Garnishing and finishing ideas

- Keep in mind color, texture, size, and design.

- Top your soup with thinly sliced garnishes of watercress, sorrel, spinach, arugula, fennel leaves, cilantro, chives, or mustard greens.

- Bring out the flavor of soup with lemon, vinegar, wine, citrus juice, or hot sauce.

- Swirl in yogurt, sour cream, nut butter, tamarind, miso, tomato paste, or maple syrup.

- Keep in mind all things crunchy, such as fried shallots, leeks, bread, chopped nuts, and tempeh croutons. Often that final touch brings it all home.

Be versatile

Shop for what's freshest, local, and organic, or something you've never used before. Pay attention to colors and textures and different flavor combinations: sweet, sour, salty, bitter, and savory. Often the best ingredients are what you have in your pantry or fridge. For example, tomatoes, beans, or leftover potatoes can be added to soup just as they are, or they can be pureed and added for thickness and flavor. Leftover herbs can steep in your broth or be sautéed with your layer of onions and garlic. A splash of fruit juice can cool and contrast with the heat and taste of a chile or hot sauce. Leftover rice can build a soup into a meal.

That said, I must admit I have some good soups to share with you. I think you will enjoy them enough to make them over and over again.

Beautiful black bean and avocado soup

Cook this soup slowly and drink in its beauty and aroma. The taste is righteous. Silky avocado may sound like a strange addition to a bean soup, yet, in fact, it works perfectly to accent and beautify the soup.

2 tablespoons olive oil

1 medium red onion, chopped

4 garlic cloves, minced

1½ tablespoons whole cumin seeds, crushed

2 to 3 teaspoons chipotle chile powder,* to taste

2 cinnamon sticks

2 tablespoons unrefined cane sugar

2 teaspoons salt

1 cup coarsely chopped cilantro [250ml]

6 medium-size tomatoes, seeded and coarsely chopped

4 cups cooked or canned black beans [650g]

4 cups vegetable stock [1L]

2 ripe but firm avocados, cubed

Juice from 1 fresh lime

Freshly ground pepper

1. In a large soup pot, heat the olive oil over medium heat. Add the red onion and cook, stirring occasionally, until soft, 5 to 7 minutes.

2. Add the garlic, cumin seeds, chipotle chile powder, cinnamon sticks, sugar, salt, and ½ cup of the chopped cilantro. Cook, stirring often, 2 to 3 minutes, until the spices are fragrant.

3. Add the tomatoes and beans and cook an additional 2 to 3 minutes. Pour in the stock and bring to a boil. Reduce the heat and simmer for 15 to 20 minutes.

4. Remove about 1½ cups [375ml] of the beans with some liquid and puree in a blender or food processor. Stir back into the pot.

5. Just before serving, add the avocados, lime juice, and remaining cilantro. Season with additional salt and pepper to taste.

SERVES 6 TO 8

*If the powder is unavailable, use ½ to 1 dried chipotle chile soaked in hot water and minced.

Creamy carrot soup with miso-tamarind swirl

This is a snazzy soup with a wonderful texture. You can make it as thick or as light as you like by adjusting the amount of liquid. The miso-tamarind sauce provides a beautiful contrast in flavor and color, as the orange soup is sweet and the reddish brown sauce has distinctive tang to it.

NOTE Make the Miso-Tamarind Sauce while your soup is cooking.

1 medium-large onion, coarsely chopped

1 cinnamon stick

1½ tablespoons vegetable oil

5 medium-large carrots, peeled and cut into chunks

1 large sweet potato, peeled and cut into chunks

5 cups vegetable stock or water [1.25L]

½ teaspoon grated nutmeg

⅛ teaspoon ground cloves

¾ teaspoon salt

Miso-Tamarind Sauce (recipe follows)

1. In a heavy-bottomed soup pot, cook the onion and cinnamon stick in the vegetable oil over medium heat until the onion is softened but not browned, about 5 minutes. Add the carrots, sweet potato, and vegetable stock. Bring to boil, reduce the heat to a simmer, cover, and cook until the carrots and sweet potatoes are soft, 15 to 20 minutes.

2. Remove from the heat and discard the cinnamon stick. In small batches, ladle roughly equal amounts of vegetables and stock into a blender or food processor. Puree until very smooth.

3. As each batch is pureed, pour it into a large bowl. When finished, return the pureed soup to the pot. Stir in the nutmeg, cloves, and salt.

4. To serve, reheat if necessary. Ladle the hot soup into bowls. Decorate each serving with a swirl of Miso-Tamarind Sauce.

SERVES 6

Miso-tamarind sauce

2 teaspoons maple syrup

1 teaspoon red miso or barley miso

1 teaspoon tamarind concentrate

3 garlic cloves, crushed through a press

1 tablespoon finely minced fresh ginger

½ cup vegetable stock or water [125ml]

1 teaspoon tomato paste

1. **Combine** the maple syrup, miso, tamarind, garlic, ginger, and 1 tablespoon of the stock in a small saucepan. Stir until smooth. Blend in the remaining stock.

2. Warm the sauce over medium-low heat. When it begins to bubble lightly, stir and continue to cook for 1 minute. **Stir** in the tomato paste. Simmer for 2 or 3 minutes until the sauce thickens. Remove from the heat and set aside to cool.

3. When cooled, **pour** the sauce into a squeeze bottle. If you don't have a squeeze bottle, pour the sauce from a measuring cup or drizzle it from a spoon. Design your own swirls over each individual cup of soup.

MAKES ABOUT ²∕₃ CUP [150ML]

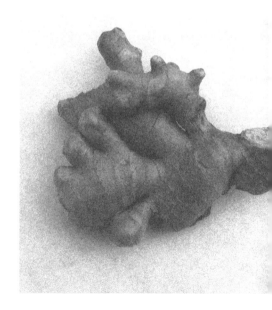

French onion soup with caraway and Gruyère cheese

This soup is not only as good as the classic that's made with beef stock, it's better. Sweet, savory, complex—the buttery flavors melt in your mouth. Roasted Vegetable Stock (page 46) is important to this recipe; it adds a rich color and taste and is well worth the effort. If you have a mandoline, use it to slice your onions paper thin.

3 pounds sweet yellow onions (such as Vidalia), very thinly sliced

2 tablespoons olive oil

Salt and freshly ground pepper

1 tablespoon caraway seeds

½ cup port wine [125ml]

2 tablespoons dark red miso

4½ cups Roasted Vegetable Stock (page 46), kept at a simmer [1.15L]

1 cup grated Swiss Gruyère cheese [80g]

4 slices of Italian or other rustic bread, thickly sliced and lightly toasted

1. In large heavy-bottomed pot, cook the onions in the olive oil over medium heat, covered, for 5 minutes. Uncover and cook, stirring occasionally, until the onions are very brown and soft, 35 to 40 minutes longer. Don't rush them; this is the key to this soup: onions that have become tender and sweet, not burned or bitter. Season lightly with salt and pepper.

2. Add the caraway seeds and cook, stirring, for a few seconds. Pour in the port and bring to a simmer. With a wooden spoon, scrape up all the caramelized onion bits stuck to the bottom of the pot so they can dissolve in the liquid. Continue to cook, stirring often, until most of the liquid is evaporated and you are left with a pot of glazed caramelized onions.

3. Put the miso in a small bowl and stir in about ½ cup [125ml] of the stock. Stir until the paste is completely incorporated into the liquid. Add to the onions and sim-

mer until the liquid is reduced by half. Add the remaining stock and simmer for 15 minutes.

4. Preheat the oven to 400°F [200°C]. Place 4 ovenproof bowls on a baking sheet. Pour about 1 cup [250ml] of soup into each bowl, leaving room on top for cheese and bread. Add 2 tablespoons of the grated cheese to each bowl, then a bread slice. If the bread is too big for the bowl, cut it into 3 smaller pieces and wedge them in. Top with 2 more tablespoons cheese. Bake for 10 minutes, or until the cheese is browned and bubbly. Serve piping hot.

SERVES 4

Cashew potato leek soup

This soup has made an impressive transformation from a vichyssoise, made with dairy cream, to an even richer, creamier soup, made with cashew cream. Its pale green color contrasts subtly with the cashew cream.

If you're ambitious and want to really dress up the soup, make some crispy fried leeks or shallots and sprinkle them on top when serving (see page 6). The effect is very much worth the effort.

3 to 4 leeks (white and light green parts), coarsely chopped and well rinsed (see *Note*)

2 tablespoons olive oil

3 medium baking potatoes, peeled and cut into large chunks

6 cups Basic Vegetable Stock (page 45) [1.5L]

1 teaspoon salt

¼ teaspoon freshly ground pepper

1 cup unsalted raw cashews [120g]

About 1 cup apple juice [250ml]

Chopped fresh chives, for garnish

1. **Soften** the leeks in the olive oil over medium-low heat in a covered soup pot without allowing them to brown, about 5 minutes. Stir occasionally. Add the potatoes, stock, salt, and pepper. Bring to a boil. Reduce the heat and cook for 30 minutes, or until the potatoes are very soft.

2. While the soup is cooking, **prepare** the cashew cream by pureeing the cashews and apple juice in a blender until very creamy. Add more juice or water if the cream is too thick. Set aside in a small bowl or measuring cup and rinse out the blender.

3. In small batches, **ladle** roughly equal amounts of potatoes, leeks, and stock into a blender or a food processor. Puree until very smooth. Serve warm or reheat.

4. **Decorate** the soup with the cashew cream or blend it in entirely. (It's completely up to you how you want to proceed with this part of the soup. Visually, the

off-white of the cream marked against the light green of the soup makes an excellent presentation. However, if you mix in the cream thoroughly, you will still have a deeply satisfying soup.) Season again with salt and pepper, if desired. Top with chopped chives or crispy leeks, if using.

SERVES 6 TO 8

note To clean leeks, which are usually layered with dirt, slice them in half lengthwise and then into half-moons. Soak in a large bowl or sink filled with cold water. Swish the leeks around with your hands, allowing any grit to settle to the bottom. Lift out the leeks and repeat, if necessary.

Fennel, tomato, and white bean soup

Tomato makes a wonderful, rich base with just enough **sweetness** to complement the licorice taste of fresh fennel beautifully. Any white bean—cannellini, Great Northern, or navy—will work here. If you can spare the time, let this soup stand for several hours or make it a day ahead, refrigerate, and reheat before serving.

1 large fennel bulb, coarsely chopped, tender leaves reserved for garnish

1 small onion, chopped

6 garlic cloves, thinly sliced

1½ teaspoons salt

¼ teaspoon freshly ground pepper

1½ tablespoons olive oil

1 pound ripe tomatoes, seeded and chopped [500g]

6 cups vegetable stock [1.5L]

3 cups cooked white beans [330g]

1 to 2 tablespoons fresh minced parsley

Splash of white wine vinegar or white wine

1. In a heavy-bottomed soup pot, **sauté** the chopped fennel, onion, garlic, salt, and pepper in the olive oil over medium heat until the vegetables are softened but not browned, about 7 minutes. Add the tomatoes and continue to cook another 2 to 3 minutes.

2. **Pour** in the stock and bring it to boil. Reduce the heat to a simmer and cook for 20 minutes.

3. Stir in the beans and parsley. **Simmer** for another 5 minutes or so. Season with additional salt and pepper to taste. Add the vinegar. Just before serving, garnish with the reserved fennel leaves.

SERVES 6

Savory harira soup

This Moroccan soup is so rich and delicious, your guests won't be able to get enough of it. Don't let the list of ingredients dissuade you: it's relatively **easy** to prepare, and the results are fabulous.

2 tablespoons olive oil

1 large onion, chopped

1 celery rib, chopped

½ cup minced parsley [125ml]

1 teaspoon turmeric

1 teaspoon salt

1 teaspoon freshly ground pepper

1 teaspoon paprika

1 teaspoon caraway seeds

½ teaspoon cinnamon

½ bay leaf

2 tablespoons chopped cilantro

½ cup dried lentils [100g]

1 can (28 ounces) crushed tomatoes [784g or 825ml]

1 tablespoon tomato paste

6 cups vegetable stock [1.5L]

3 tablespoons unbleached flour mixed to a paste with ½ cup cold water [125ml]

Lemon slices, for garnish

1. In a large soup pot, **heat** the olive oil over medium heat. Add the onion, celery, parsley, turmeric, salt, and pepper. Cook for 5 to 7 minutes, or until the onions are softened but not browned; stir often.

2. **Add** the paprika, caraway seeds, cinnamon, bay leaf, and cilantro and stir for about 15 seconds. Add the lentils, tomatoes, tomato paste, and stock. Bring to a boil. Reduce the heat to a simmer, cover, and cook for 20 minutes, or until the lentils are soft.

3. Just before serving, **whisk** in the flour mixture, blending thoroughly to avoid lumps. Bring to a boil, stirring until slightly thickened. Serve hot, with a slice of lemon in each bowl.

SERVES 8 TO 10

French lentil soup
with tarragon and lemon

This recipe calls for French lentils, which are smaller and darker—and hold their shape better—than their larger, greener cousins. It is a rich, hearty soup, perfect with sandwiches on a cool afternoon. The lemon juice and tart fresh sorrel garnish add just the right zing. On occasion, I've also added fresh tarragon as a garnish, which is another excellent complement to the soup.

1 medium onion, finely chopped	⅛ teaspoon freshly ground pepper
2 garlic cloves, minced	2 tablespoons olive oil
1 celery rib, finely chopped	1 cup lentils, preferably French [200g]
2 carrots, peeled and cut into ½-inch dice [1-cm]	6 cups vegetable stock or water [1.5L]
1 bay leaf	2 medium red potatoes, cut into ½-inch dice [1-cm]
1 tablespoon dried tarragon	4 to 5 tablespoons fresh lemon juice
1 teaspoon dried oregano	Chopped fresh tarragon or shredded sorrel for garnish
1 teaspoon salt	

1. In a large pot, cook the onion, garlic, celery, carrots, bay leaf, tarragon, oregano, salt, and pepper slowly in the olive oil over medium-low heat until the onion is soft but not brown, 7 to 9 minutes.

2. Add the lentils and stock and bring to a boil. Add the potatoes, reduce the heat, and simmer for 40 to 45 minutes, or until lentils are tender but not mushy.

3. Remove the soup from the heat. Stir in the lemon juice and season with additional salt and pepper to taste. Ladle the soup into bowls and garnish with tarragon or sorrel.

SERVES 6

Lentil ginger coconut soup

In my view, you can never have too many lentil soups. Lentils don't need soaking; they cook relatively quickly and work well with many flavor combinations. Lentil soups **taste great** in a light broth or in a thicker, heartier one, as in this soup. If you prefer, add an additional cup of stock for a lighter soup.

1 medium onion, finely chopped

1½ tablespoons olive oil

1 celery rib, finely chopped

1 carrot, peeled and chopped

1 tablespoon minced fresh ginger

1 teaspoon salt

⅛ teaspoon freshly ground pepper

2 tablespoons North African Spice Mix (page 158)

1½ cups lentils [300g]

1 can (14 ounces) unsweetened coconut milk [450ml]

4 cups vegetable stock [1L]

1 tablespoon tomato paste

1 tablespoon cider vinegar

1 tablespoon lemon juice

1 teaspoon hot sauce, or to taste

3 tablespoons unsweetened grated coconut

1. In a large soup pot, **cook** the onion in the olive oil over medium heat until very soft and lightly browned, 7 to 10 minutes. Add the celery, carrot, ginger, salt, and pepper. Continue to cook for another 2 minutes.

2. Add the spice mix and cook, **stirring,** 10 to 20 seconds, or until fragrant. Add the lentils, coconut milk, stock, and tomato paste. Cover and bring to a boil. Reduce the heat to a simmer and continue to cook, covered, for 30 to 40 minutes, or until the lentils are soft.

3. Stir in the vinegar, lemon juice, and hot sauce. **Simmer** for another 3 minutes. Season with additional salt and pepper to taste. Garnish the soup with grated coconut.

SERVES 6 TO 8

Pea and potato soup with smoky tempeh

I love the taste of smoke in pea soup and have found smoked tempeh—packaged as Fakin' Bacon—works with excellent results. In addition to the smoky flavor, you get soft crunch of the tempeh squares in the soup. If you can't find smoked tempeh, use plain tempeh, fried until crisp. You can't miss calling this soup a meal in a bowl. Serve with fresh bread and a salad.

2 packages (6 ounces each) Fakin' Bacon brand smoked tempeh [350g]

3 to 4 tablespoons vegetable oil

1¾ teaspoons salt

1 onion, finely chopped

2 carrots, peeled and finely chopped

3 garlic cloves, minced

4 medium white potatoes, diced

¼ teaspoon freshly ground pepper

2 cups split green peas [400g]

9 cups vegetable stock or water, or more as needed [2.25L]

1 to 2 tablespoons fresh lemon juice

Fresh mint, thinly sliced for garnish

1. In heavy-bottomed soup pot, fry the smoked tempeh strips in 2 tablespoons of the vegetable oil over medium-high heat, turning frequently, until lightly browned and crisp, 2 or 3 minutes per side. Drain on paper towels and season with ¼ teaspoon of the salt, then cut into squares.

2. In the same pot, sauté the onion in the remaining oil until soft and lightly browned, about 5 minutes. Add the carrots, garlic, and potatoes and cook for 1 or 2 minutes longer, until the garlic softens and becomes fragrant. Season with the pepper and remaining 1½ teaspoons salt.

3. Add the split peas and stock and bring to a boil. Reduce the heat, cover, and simmer for 45 minutes.

4. Stir in the lemon juice and fried tempeh. Cover and simmer for 15 minutes longer. Season with additional salt and pepper to taste. Garnish with mint just before serving.

SERVES 8 TO 10

Creamy red lentil chowder

Lentil chowder? Yes, but no corn in this one. I blend red lentils—which actually look orange—with silken tofu and miso to make a lively cream soup. This chowder offers an easy way to add soy to your diet, perfect for those who don't eat dairy.

1 tablespoon olive oil	¼ teaspoon freshly ground pepper
½ onion, finely chopped	1 large tomato, cut into medium dice
1 carrot, finely chopped	1½ cups red lentils [300g]
1 celery rib, finely chopped	5 cups vegetable stock or water [1.25L]
2 garlic cloves, minced	1 cup dry white wine [250ml]
1 bay leaf	6 ounces silken tofu [180g]
2 teaspoons dried oregano	1 tablespoon chickpea miso or white miso
2 teaspoons dried basil	2 tablespoons fresh lemon juice
1 cinnamon stick	1 tablespoon cider vinegar
1 teaspoon salt	Splash of hot sauce

1. In a heavy-bottomed soup pot, **heat** the olive oil over medium-low heat. Add the onion and cook until slightly softened, about 3 minutes. Add the carrot and celery and continue to cook for another few minutes until the vegetables soften. Add the garlic, bay leaf, oregano, basil, and cinnamon stick. Sauté for 1 to 2 minutes, stirring often, until the garlic is fragrant. Season with the salt and pepper.

2. Add the tomato and cook for 1 minute. **Stir** in the lentils, stock, and wine. Cover and bring to a boil. Reduce to a simmer and cook, partially covered, for 15 to 20 minutes, or until the lentils are soft. Remove and discard the bay leaf and cinnamon stick.

3. Put the tofu, miso, and 2 cups of the soup in a blender or food processor. **Puree** until very well mixed. Stir into the rest of the soup in the pot. Add the lemon juice, vinegar, and hot sauce. Season with additional salt and pepper to taste.

SERVES 8 TO 10

Corn tempeh chowder

Oats and soy milk make this soup creamy without the addition of dairy products. The dried mushrooms, arame, and grated tempeh provide a hint of both earth and sea, which gives this soup a comforting, chowder-like taste.

½ ounce dried mushrooms (chanterelle, shiitake, or mixed) [15g]

3 tablespoons arame sea vegetable

1 medium onion, chopped

2 celery ribs, finely chopped, leaves reserved for garnish

2 tablespoons olive oil

1 package (8 ounces) tempeh, grated [250g]

Salt and freshly ground pepper

3 cups fresh or frozen corn kernels [375g]

4 cups plain soy milk [1L]

½ cup rolled oats [50g]

2 cups vegetable stock or water [.5L]

1 tablespoon chickpea miso or white miso

1. In a small bowl, soak the dried mushrooms and arame in enough hot water to cover. Cover the bowl and set it aside until the vegetables are softened, about 30 minutes. Drain, reserving the soaking water. Coarsely chop both the mushrooms and the arame. Strain the soaking water through a paper coffee filter and set it aside.

2. In a heavy-bottomed soup pot, cook the onion and celery in the olive oil over medium heat until the onion is soft and translucent, about 5 minutes. Add the grated tempeh and cook for 2 minutes longer, stirring frequently. Season lightly with salt and pepper.

3. Stir in the corn and chopped mushrooms and arame. Add the soy milk and reserved soaking water and bring to a simmer. In the meantime, puree the oats with the vegetable stock in a blender or food processor. Stir into the soup and simmer, partially covered, for 30 minutes. Stir often, as oats tend to stick.

4. In a small bowl, blend the miso with a small amount of the soup until well mixed. Stir into the rest of the soup in the pot. Season generously with salt and pepper. Garnish with celery leaves when serving.

SERVES 8 TO 10

Barley mushroom seitan soup

We look at barley today and see a simple, hearty, and nutritious grain. Yet, a look back reveals a fascinating history. It has been revered for thousands of years by virtually all the great civilizations, from the Hebrews, Greeks, and Romans, to the Hindus and Chinese. It's been used for currency in all kinds of rites and celebrations, and as training food for athletes. Traditional mushroom barley soup has a deep, dark, meaty base. My healthful vegetarian version uses lots of tomato and chunks of seitan to produce a hearty, nutritious broth.

1 medium onion, finely chopped

1 celery rib, finely chopped

1 large carrot, peeled and finely chopped

1 parsnip, peeled and finely chopped

2 teaspoons dill seeds, crushed in a mortar and pestle

2 garlic cloves, minced

½ pound cremini mushrooms, thinly sliced [250g]

½ pound prepared seitan, cut into ½-inch [1-cm] chunks [250g]

1½ teaspoons salt

¼ teaspoon freshly ground pepper

5 cups vegetable stock or water [1.25L]

2 cups crushed tomatoes [500ml]

1 cup hulled barley [180g]

2 tablespoons coarsely chopped fresh dill

1. In a soup pot, heat the olive oil over medium heat. Add the onion, celery, carrot, and parsnip. Cook, stirring occasionally, until soft, 7 to 10 minutes.

2. Add the dill seeds, garlic, and mushrooms. Continue to cook until the mushrooms are tender and lightly browned, 5 to 7 minutes.

3. Stir in the seitan and season with the salt and pepper. Add the stock, tomatoes, and barley; bring to a boil. Reduce the heat and simmer, stirring occasionally, for 1½ hours, or until the barley is tender. Stir in the dill just before serving.

SERVES 10 TO 12

Fat elbow tomato soup with ginger and sherry vinegar

This soup originated when I was trying to create a dish without having many ingredients to work with. Consequently, it is simple and very fast. Lightly spiced tomatoes with pasta—you don't need much more than that.

¼ pound chiocciole or large elbow pasta [125g]

1 large onion, chopped

3 tablespoons olive oil

1½ teaspoons minced fresh ginger

3 garlic cloves, minced

2 tablespoons unrefined cane sugar

1 tablespoon ground cumin

1 teaspoon paprika

1 teaspoon salt

⅛ teaspoon freshly ground pepper

2 tablespoons sherry vinegar or cider vinegar

1 can (32 ounces) crushed tomatoes [900ml]

4 cups vegetable stock [1L]

Slivered fresh basil, for garnish

1. Cook the pasta in a large pot of boiling salted water until barely tender and still slightly undercooked, 8 to 9 minutes. Drain the cooked pasta and run under cold water until completely cooled; drain well. Set aside in a bowl.

2. In a soup pot, cook the onion in 1½ tablespoons of the olive oil over medium heat, stirring occasionally, until softened and slightly browned, 5 to 7 minutes. Add the ginger, garlic, sugar, cumin, and paprika. Cook, stirring often, 1 to 2 minutes. Season with the salt and pepper.

3. Stir in the vinegar and cook until it evaporates and the onion mixture is thick, 1 to 2 minutes. Add the tomatoes and stir to mix all the ingredients thoroughly. Add the stock and bring to a simmer. Simmer, uncovered, for 10 to 15 minutes.

4. Add the pasta and cook, stirring occasionally, until heated through and tender, 3 to 5 minutes. Stir in the remaining 1½ tablespoons oil. Season again with additional salt and pepper and a splash of vinegar, if desired. If you have time, let the soup stand for about an hour to let the flavors fully develop; then reheat. Garnish with basil before serving.

SERVES 8 TO 10

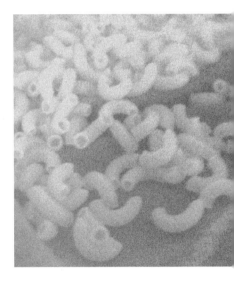

Roasted butternut squash and shallot soup

Beautiful and extremely nutritious, this soup has it all: color, consistency, and flavor as well as an OUTStanding garnish. The soup is easy to make and can be prepared ahead of time and reheated. A sweet apple or a couple of potatoes can easily be substituted for or added to the pear. The garnishes require a little more work, but they make the soup unforgettable.

4 large shallots, coarsely chopped

1 Bosc pear, peeled, cored, and coarsely chopped

2 teaspoons olive oil

2 teaspoons dried rubbed sage

Salt and freshly ground pepper

1 large butternut squash, 3 to 3½ pounds [1.5 to 1.75kg]

6 ounces silken tofu [180g]

½ cup dry white wine [125ml]

4 cups vegetable stock or water [1L]

3 tablespoons fresh lemon juice

3 to 4 tablespoons canola or safflower oil

36 fresh sage leaves

1. **Preheat** the oven to 375°F [190°C]. Line 2 large baking sheets with aluminum foil or parchment paper. In a bowl, toss the shallots and pear with 1 teaspoon of the olive oil and the dried sage. Season lightly with salt and pepper. Spread over one of the baking sheets. Bake for 20 to 30 minutes, or until the shallots and pear are soft and lightly browned.

2. **Split** the squash with a large knife; scoop out and reserve the seeds. Lightly coat the cut sides of the squash with the remaining olive oil and place it face down on the other baking sheet. Bake for 35 minutes, or until a sharp knife slips through the squash like butter.

3. Rinse the reserved squash seeds under cold running water, removing any orange fibers; drain and let dry. Coat the seeds lightly with olive oil and a sprinkling of salt. Scatter them over the same baking sheet and return to the oven until well browned, 10 to 15 minutes. Set aside.

4. Scoop the meat from the squash or simply peel off the skin. In a blender, puree the squash, shallots, pear, tofu, wine, and stock in batches. If desired, add additional liquid to attain a lighter consistency. Pour into a soup pot and bring to a boil. Reduce the heat and simmer for 10 minutes. Season generously with salt and pepper. Add the lemon juice and cook over low heat for another 5 minutes.

5. While the soup is cooking, in a medium frying pan heat the canola oil over medium-high heat until almost smoking. (Test the oil to make sure it's hot enough by dropping one sage leaf into it. If the sage sizzles immediately, the oil is ready.) In small batches, fry the fresh sage leaves until crisp and lightly browned, 15 to 20 seconds. Remove with a slotted spoon and drain on paper towels.

6. To serve, ladle the soup into bowls and float 2 to 3 sage leaves on top. Place a few toasted squash seeds in the middle of each. Serve immediately.

SERVES 10 TO 12

Chilled summer fruit soup with berry-wine swirl

I was never a big fan of chilled soup until I made this one. The Berry-Wine Swirl brings alive an already luscious soup. What a great way to start a summer lunch or end light supper on a hot summer evening. Use the freshest, sweetest fruit you can find.

1 medium cantaloupe—seeded, rind removed, melon coarsely chopped

1 peach—skinned, pitted, and coarsely chopped

1 mango—skinned, seeded, and coarsely chopped

2 to 3 tablespoons honey

Juice of 1 large orange

Juice of 1 lime

Pinch of salt

Berry-Wine Swirl (recipe below)

1. In a blender or food processor, combine all the ingredients except the Berry-Wine Swirl. Puree until smooth. Transfer to a bowl, cover, and refrigerate until well chilled, at least 2 hours.

2. Ladle the cold soup into bowls. Drizzle Berry-Wine Swirl on top, decorating the soup with Jackson Pollock squiggles or Zen-like swirls.

SERVES 4

Berry-wine swirl

1 tablespoon minced fresh ginger

½ cup blueberries [65g]

1 teaspoon tamarind paste

¼ cup dry red wine [60ml]

2½ tablespoons maple syrup

Splash of red wine vinegar

Puree all the ingredients in a blender or food processor. Adjust the sweetness or tartness to reach desired taste.

MAKES ABOUT ¼ CUP (60ML)

BREAKFAST LUNCH, and BRUNCH: From Scrambles to Sandwiches

There's nothing like a good breakfast, especially when you have the time and the mood is right. A solid start in the morning definitely sets the tone for the rest of the day. But how many of us have time for a gourmet breakfast? Or simply a satisfying one? Isn't it cereal and fruit or toast for most of us—or a bagel or muffin to go? And don't get me started with the espresso and latte shops on every corner. . . .

chef talk

Breakfast really is a luxury, isn't it? So, luxurious breakfasts (or at least deeply satisfying and comforting ones) are the stars of this chapter. When you're ready to enjoy a Sunday off or serve breakfast in bed or celebrate an anniversary or birthday, I think you will find some unusually interesting vegetarian and vegan breakfast and brunch ideas here to do it right.

One classic breakfast that sticks out in my mind is Marmalade-Almond Stuffed French Toast. Featuring a creamy tofu filling, this is an attention-getter if ever there was one. I offer both a vegan and a vegetarian version. The Sun Lake Eggs are homey because they are scrambled eggs, but not just any scrambled eggs. Their untamed flavor bites back with chiles, lime juice, shiitake mushrooms, and feta cheese. And, of course, The Ultimate Tofu Scramble . . . well, you'll just have to try it to believe it.

Lunch has always been one of my favorite meals. I guess I associate it with sandwiches. And I *love* sandwiches: the crunch of the bread, the delicate and bold flavors, the spicy spreads. Sandwiches have got it all—and I've got a couple in this chapter that are outrageous. But if you're not partial to sandwiches, that's okay. You can pass up the Hummus Jarlsburg Roasted Cayenne Sandwich and try the Spicy Tofu Chipotle Enchiladas or Cheryl's Frittata, filled with tomatoes, garlic, and shredded kale and topped with macadamia nuts.

As it happens, the enchiladas are one of those dishes that easily defy limitations and expectations. In my view, the label of *vegetarian* is meaningless for the enchiladas, as for so many dishes in this book. The dish satisfies the vegetarian and the meat-eater alike. The filling is tasty, feisty, and satisfying—no label necessary. And with that, enjoy breakfast and lunch like a king or queen!

Cinnamon polenta porridge with bananas and almonds

Often overlooked, polenta is a great meal idea for breakfast. Embellish with strawberries, apples, and/or melted butter if you like.

2 cups vanilla rice milk or soy milk [500ml]

3 cups water [750ml]

2 tablespoons maple syrup

½ teaspoon salt

1 cup coarsely ground polenta [125g]

2 bananas, sliced into rounds

¼ cup honey [100g]

½ cup slivered blanched almonds, toasted* [40g]

1 to 2 teaspoons ground cinnamon

1. In a heavy saucepan, **combine** the milk, water, maple syrup, and salt. Bring to a boil over medium heat.

2. **Drizzle** the polenta into the pot in a slow, thin stream, stirring as you add it. Whisk constantly until all the grains have been absorbed. Reduce the heat to medium-low.

3. Switch to a wooden spatula and continue to cook, **stirring,** for 15 to 20 minutes, until the polenta is very creamy and pulls away from the sides of the pot. Add more milk or water if the mixture becomes too thick.

4. Ladle the polenta into bowls. **Top** with bananas, honey, almonds, and cinnamon.

SERVES 6

* To toast almonds, preheat the oven to 300°F [150°C]. Place almonds on a baking sheet and toast for 7 to 10 minutes, watching carefully so they don't burn. Mix and move them around every few minutes until they start to brown slightly.

Oatmeal with dried cherries, apples, and nuts

Okay, I admit, this recipe has many **health** benefits. It's loaded with protein, fiber, vitamins, and minerals. But who can complain about starting the day with such abundance. This oatmeal is very **thick** and porridgy—the way I like it. If you prefer a softer consistency, add more liquid.

1½ cups plain or vanilla rice milk [375ml]	1 teaspoon flax seeds
¼ cup apple juice [60ml]	1 teaspoon brown or white sesame seeds
¼ teaspoon salt	1 teaspoon raw, hulled sunflower seeds
1 cinnamon stick	½ tart apple, seeded and finely diced
⅔ cup rolled thick-cut rolled oats [70g]	1 tablespoon maple syrup
3 tablespoons dried cherries	½ teaspoon vanilla extract
2 teaspoons sliced almonds	

1. In a large saucepan, **combine** the milk, apple juice, salt, and cinnamon stick. Bring to a boil.

2. Add the rolled oats and reduce the heat to a bare simmer. **Cook,** stirring often to prevent sticking, for 10 minutes, or until the oats are as soft as you desire.

3. **Stir** in the dried cherries, almonds, flax seeds, sesame seeds, sunflower seeds, apple, maple syrup, and vanilla. If the cereal is too thick, add more milk; if too loose, cook for another 1 to 2 minutes.

4. Remove from the heat, **cover,** and let the oatmeal stand for 5 minutes before serving.

SERVES 2

The ultimate tofu scramble

A tasty dish with zing and a mysterious resemblance to scrambled eggs, this **vegan delight** is the real deal when it comes to tofu scrambles—don't accept substitutes. It is excellent topped with fresh salsa or Worcestershire sauce. Add dried or fresh herbs, or substitute chipotle or regular chile powder for the mustard to spice up the scramble.

2 tablespoons yellow miso or chickpea miso

½ teaspoon turmeric

2 teaspoons yellow powdered mustard

Dash of wasabi powder (optional)

1 tablespoon nutritional yeast

1 teaspoon salt

¼ teaspoon freshly ground pepper

⅓ cup vegetable stock or water [75ml]

1 pound firm or soft (not silken) tofu, drained and pressed of water [500g]

2 tablespoons extra virgin olive oil

3 medium shallots or ½ onion, finely chopped

1 red bell pepper, diced

2 tablespoons chopped chives or scallions

Salsa or vegetarian Worcestershire sauce

1. In a medium bowl, **combine** the miso, turmeric, powdered mustard, wasabi, yeast, salt, pepper, and stock. Mix to a smooth paste.

2. **Crumble** the tofu into the miso mixture and blend well. Add 1 tablespoon of the olive oil and mix again until very well incorporated. Set aside.

3. In a medium skillet, preferably nonstick, **cook** the shallots in the remaining oil over medium heat until softened, 2 to 3 minutes. Add the red pepper and sauté an additional 1 to 2 minutes.

4. Add the tofu mixture and cook, **stirring** constantly, until the tofu is just heated through and the shallots and bell pepper are mixed in. Remove from the heat. Garnish with chives and top with salsa or Worcestershire sauce.

MAKES 2 LARGE OR 3 MEDIUM-SIZE PORTIONS

Spicy tofu chipotle enchiladas

This dish is fun to cook, it makes an excellent presentation, and it is perfect for a bold brunch. What's more fun, it will shock people who thought tofu was, well, just tofu. This recipe derives from The Ultimate Tofu Scramble (page 73) and shows you how, with a little creativity and improvisation, you can fashion tofu into many amazing dishes.

Make this dish as hot or as mild as you like. I prefer chipotle chile powder to regular chile powder but substituting is okay. Look for jarred enchilada sauce, preferably organic, as opposed to the canned with preservatives and little flavor.

The preferred method of preparing tortillas is on a flattop grill, but a skillet will work as well. Serve with Mexican Brown Rice with Jalapeños and Tomatillos (page 268), and a tossed salad.

2 tablespoons yellow miso or chickpea miso

1 teaspoon chipotle or regular chile powder

½ teaspoon turmeric

2 teaspoons nutritional yeast

3 tablespoons olive oil

1 teaspoon salt

⅛ teaspoon freshly ground pepper

⅓ cup vegetable stock or water [75ml]

1 pound soft or firm (not silken) tofu, drained and pressed of water [500g]

1 jar (16 ounces) enchilada sauce [500ml]

12 corn tortillas, at room temperature

Nonstick vegetable oil spray

½ cup coarsely chopped cilantro [125ml]

1. **Preheat** the oven to 350°F [175°C]. Line a large baking dish with parchment paper and set aside.

2. In a medium bowl, **combine** the miso, chile powder, turmeric, yeast, olive oil, salt, pepper, and stock. Stir until all the ingredients are well mixed and smooth. Crumble the tofu into the miso mixture and mix well. Set aside.

3. Create plenty of workspace for yourself. **Pour** the enchilada sauce into a bowl. With a pastry brush, brush sauce onto both sides of the tortillas and stack them on a plate.

4. **Heat** a heavy skillet or flattop grill over medium heat and spray with oil. Fry the tortillas for a few seconds on each side until just softened, 10 to 15 seconds. Flip using a spatula; tongs may tear the tortillas. Add more oil for each tortilla.

5. Spoon approximately 2 teaspoons tofu filling onto the middle of a cooked tortilla. Roll up and place seam side down in the lined baking pan. **Drizzle** any remaining enchilada sauce on top of the rolled tortillas.

6. **Bake** in the oven for 3 to 5 minutes, until just hot. Take care not to cook too long, as the tortillas will toughen. Let the enchiladas rest for a few minutes to set up. Garnish with cilantro just before serving.

SERVES 6

Frittata with oven-dried tomatoes and Cheddar cheese

Boldly flavored tomatoes, fresh basil, and Cheddar cheese on top make this frittata a **masterful** presentation. The key to a successful frittata is to cook the eggs nice and slowly, so that they set before the bottom browns too much.

N O T E The exact number of servings depends on the size of the crowd and on whether you're offering this as a main dish along with several other items in a buffet brunch.

1 red onion, thinly sliced

3 tablespoons olive oil

4 garlic cloves, minced

¼ teaspoon crushed hot red pepper

8 free-range eggs

4 large oven-dried plum tomatoes (recipe follows), cut into quarters

½ cup grated sharp Cheddar cheese [50g]

8 or 10 fresh basil leaves, torn into small pieces

½ teaspoon salt

Freshly ground pepper

Salsa

1. In a 10- to 12-inch [26- to 30-cm] cast-iron skillet, cook the red onion in 1½ tablespoons of the olive oil over medium heat until very soft and lightly browned, about 10 minutes. **Stir** in the garlic and hot pepper and cook for 1 minute longer. Transfer to a bowl and let cool to room temperature. If you're in a rush, put in the fridge for 5 or 10 minutes.

2. Break the eggs into a large bowl and whisk until well blended. **Add** the tomatoes, Cheddar cheese, basil, salt, and a generous grinding of black pepper. Mix the ingredients thoroughly. Add the cooled onion and garlic to the eggs and mix again.

3. Preheat the broiler with the oven rack set 5 to 6 inches [13 to 15cm] from the heat. In the same cast-iron skillet, **heat** the remaining 1½ tablespoons oil over medium heat. Add the egg mixture and evenly distribute in the pan with a fork. Lift the edges several times with a spatula and tilt the pan to let the uncooked egg run underneath. Reduce the heat to medium-low and cook for 8 to 10 minutes, or until the frittata is set around the edges but still a little wobbly in the center. Place the pan under the broiler for about 2 minutes, until lightly browned and firm on top.

4. Let the finished dish set for 5 to 10 minutes before serving. **Remove** with a spatula, carefully dislodging the egg from around the inside edge of the pan first. The frittata should slip right out onto a large plate. If it does not, slice it into quarters first. Pass a bowl of salsa on the side.

SERVES 4 TO 6

Oven-dried tomatoes

Preheat the oven to 175°F (80°C). Slice plum tomatoes lengthwise in half. Place face down on a parchment paper-lined heavy-duty baking sheet and bake at for at least 6 to 8 hours. Sun-dried tomatoes can be substituted but will not carry the day as your own freshly dried tomatoes will.

Cheryl's frittata with macadamia nuts, feta cheese, and shiitake mushrooms

My wife, Cheryl, was the inspiration for this frittata. My favorite part of the dish is the toasted macadamia nuts. Use high-quality, **tangy** feta for this dish, perhaps French or Israeli.

½ cup raw macadamia nuts [50g]

1 medium onion, thinly sliced

3½ tablespoons olive oil

3 garlic cloves, minced

¼ pound shiitake mushrooms, stemmed, caps thinly sliced [125g]

2 cups packed shredded kale [500ml]

8 free-range eggs

2 fresh ripe plum tomatoes, seeded and diced

4 ounces crumbled feta cheese (about 1 cup) [125g]

½ teaspoon salt

Freshly ground pepper

Tabasco sauce (optional)

1. In a dry 10- to 12-inch [26- to 30-cm] cast-iron skillet set over medium heat, **toast** the macadamia nuts, shaking and moving the pan continuously, until they start to brown lightly, about 5 minutes. Let cool, then crush into smaller pieces, making sure to keep any crumbs as well.

2. In the same pan, **cook** the onion in 1½ tablespoons of the olive oil over medium heat until very soft and lightly browned, 5 to 7 minutes. Add the garlic and mushrooms; raise the heat to medium-high and cook, tossing often, until the mushrooms are tender and lightly browned, about 7 minutes. Add the kale and cook for 1 to 2 minutes, until the leaves are soft and have cooked down considerably. Transfer the ingredients to a bowl and let cool to room temperature.

3. **Break** the eggs into a bowl and whisk until well blended. Add the tomatoes, feta cheese, salt, and a generous grinding of pepper. Mix well.

4. Preheat the broiler with the oven rack set 5 to 6 inches [13 to 15cm] from the heat. Add the cooled vegetables and mushrooms to the eggs and **mix** lightly.

5. In the same skillet, **heat** the remaining 2 tablespoons olive oil over medium heat. Add the egg mixture and evenly distribute the ingredients in the pan with a fork. Lift the edges several times with a spatula and tilt the pan to let uncooked egg run underneath. Reduce the heat to medium-low and cook for 8 to 10 minutes, or until the frittata is set around the edges but still a little wobbly in the center.

6. Quickly sprinkle the macadamia nuts on top of the eggs and transfer the pan to the broiler. **Broil** about 2 minutes, or until the frittata is lightly browned and firm on top.

7. Let the finished dish rest and cool for 5 to 10 minutes before serving. **Remove** the frittata with a spatula, carefully dislodging the egg from around the inside of pan first. The frittata should slip right out onto a large plate. If it does not, slice it into quarters first. Pass a bottle of Tabasco sauce on the side, if you like.

SERVES 4 TO 6

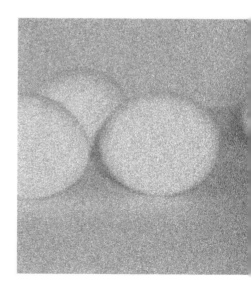

Marmalade-almond stuffed french toast

Here is proof a prolific breakfast dish can be made with or without dairy or eggs. The tofu filling is simple and creamy; the batter contains flax seeds, banana, and soy milk or rice milk. Choose between vegan batter and the more traditional egg batter that follows.

TOAST

1 pound [500g] stale or lightly toasted semolina, French, or Italian bread, or enough to make 8 slices, cut 1 inch thick [2.5cm]

6 ounces soft tofu, drained and pressed of water [180g]

3 tablespoons orange marmalade

2 tablespoons maple syrup

½ teaspoon almond extract

Pinch of salt

VEGAN BATTER

1½ cups plain or vanilla rice milk or soy milk [375ml]

1 tablespoon plus 1 teaspoon flax seeds

½ teaspoon vanilla extract

1 ripe banana, sliced

1 tablespoon maple syrup

½ teaspoon cinnamon, plus more for dusting

Pinch of salt

Vegetable oil, for frying

TRADITIONAL EGG BATTER

8 egg whites or whole free-range eggs

1 cup vanilla soy milk or rice milk [250ml]

4 tablespoons butter [60g]

½ teaspoon cinnamon

Maple syrup, cinnamon, and/or fresh fruit, as accompaniment

1. Using a sharp paring knife, gently cut out a center block from the flat crust side of each bread slice. Set aside.

2. In a food processor, combine the tofu, marmalade, maple syrup, almond extract, and salt. Blend until very smooth, 2 to 3 minutes, scraping down the sides once or twice. If you have time, prepare the tofu filling ahead and let it rest an hour or so to pick up more flavor.

3. With a pastry bag or a small spoon, **pipe** about 1 tablespoon tofu mixture into each bread hollow. Smooth out with the back of the spoon.

preparing vegan batter

1. In a blender, **combine** ½ cup [125ml] of the milk and the flax seeds and blend until the seeds break apart and are very well dispersed, about 3 minutes. Be patient with this. Scrape down the sides several times. The finished product will be somewhat like egg whites: thick and foamy.

2. **Add** the remaining milk, vanilla extract, banana, maple syrup, cinnamon, and salt and blend again for another 30 seconds or so. Follow the same procedures as below for dipping, cooking, and garnishing, except use oil instead of butter.

preparing traditional egg batter

1. **Whisk** the eggs and milk in a bowl until blended.

2. Heat half of the butter in a large frying pan over medium heat. **Dip** each slice of bread in the egg-milk mixture, coating both sides generously.

3. Arrange 3 or 4 slices of bread in the pan and **cook** until golden brown on both sides, 2 to 3 minutes for each side. Repeat procedure with remaining butter and bread. Serve warm with maple syrup. Garnish with cinnamon and fruit.

SERVES 4

note For best results when using vegan batter, use a nonstick pan. Regular soft or even firm tofu is probably your best bet for the filling. Silken is a little too soft and will spill out more easily. A pastry bag works best for piping in the filling. Buy disposable bags if you don't have a regular pastry bag.

Sun lake scrambled eggs

Interesting ingredients make these eggs uncommonly good. This recipe, born on a camping trip over an open fire and then refined in the kitchen, still makes good use of the cast-iron skillet. The use and quantity of the jalapeño pepper depends on your love of heat.

1 to 2 jalapeño peppers, seeds and ribs removed, sliced lengthwise in quarters or eighths

8 free-range eggs

¼ cup plain soy milk or dairy milk [60ml]

Juice of ½ lime

1 tablespoon maple syrup

1 tablespoon soy sauce

2 to 3 drops of hot pepper oil (optional)

½ teaspoon salt

⅛ teaspoon freshly ground pepper

2 teaspoons olive oil

1 small red bell pepper, cut into thick strips

6 ounces shiitake mushrooms, stemmed, caps thinly sliced [180g]

2 to 3 tablespoons feta cheese

Shredded fresh basil leaves, for garnish

1. In a small, very hot dry skillet, **cook** the jalapeño peppers until blistered and slightly withered. Remove to a plate.

2. **Heat** half of the olive oil in a large nonstick or well-seasoned cast-iron skillet. Add the red bell pepper and cook over medium-high heat until softened, 2 to 3 minutes. Remove with tongs or a slotted spoon and add to the jalapeño peppers on the plate.

3. Add the mushrooms to the skillet and cook until tender and lightly browned, 3 to 5 minutes. **Add** to the other vegetables.

4. In a medium bowl, **beat** the eggs with the milk, lime juice, maple syrup, soy sauce, hot oil, salt, and pepper. Heat the remaining olive oil in the skillet, add the egg mixture, and reduce the heat to medium. As the eggs start to set, move them with a wooden spoon, repeating as they set again. Just before they are done to a medium firmness, add the vegetables and fold over to mix the ingredients. Add the feta cheese just as the desired firmness is achieved. Top with basil and serve at once, right from the skillet.

SERVES 4

Herbed potatoes, corn, and zucchini

Herbed potatoes make a good side dish for almost any breakfast, but of course they work especially well with eggs. Sometimes I am reluctant to use the word *healthy,* even though it might be true of some of my recipes. I think it's overused and too subjectively understood, but what the hay— let's call this dish a healthy version of hash browns. There. I said it. And they taste good, too.

4 small red potatoes, 1½ to 2 inches in diameter [4 to 5cm]

½ medium onion, finely chopped

1 tablespoon vegetable oil

1 teaspoon dried fennel seeds

1 teaspoon dried thyme

1 teaspoon dried basil

1 cup fresh or frozen corn kernels [120g]

½ medium zucchini, cut lengthwise in half and sliced crosswise ¼ inch thick [.5cm]

Salt and freshly ground pepper

Extra virgin olive oil

1. **Cut** the potatoes into eighths and steam or boil them until tender but still firm.

2. In a hot wok or large skillet, **cook** the onion in the vegetable oil over medium-high heat until soft and lightly browned, about 5 minutes. Season with the fennel seeds, thyme, and basil and cook, tossing, for 15 to 30 seconds.

3. Add the potatoes and stir until they are well coated with onions and herbs. **Add** the corn and then the zucchini. Cook for 2 to 3 minutes, or until the vegetables are crisp-tender. Season generously with salt and pepper and drizzle with olive oil.

SERVES 4 TO 6

Maple-glazed potatoes with garlic and soy sauce

Sweet and savory potatoes, lightly crisped in a very hot oven, are soul-satisfying. Serve with spicy eggs and a salad.

8 medium-size red potatoes, scrubbed and sliced into eighths

1½ tablespoons olive oil

Salt and freshly ground black pepper

¼ cup maple syrup [60ml]

2 teaspoons soy sauce

2 garlic cloves, minced

½ teaspoon crushed hot red pepper

1. **Preheat** the oven to 450°F [230°C]. In a large bowl, toss the potatoes with the olive oil and salt and black pepper to taste. Transfer to a baking dish, tent with foil, and roast for 15 minutes. Set the used bowl aside.

2. Meanwhile, in a small bowl, **stir** together the maple syrup, soy sauce, and garlic.

3. After 15 minutes, **remove** the roasted potatoes from the oven and spoon them back into the same large bowl. Pour in half of the maple syrup mixture. Toss to coat the potatoes well. Return them to the baking dish and bake, uncovered, for 10 minutes.

4. Remove the potatoes from the oven and return them to the bowl. **Add** the remaining maple syrup mixture plus the hot pepper and toss to coat well. Season again with salt and black pepper and return to the oven for 10 minutes longer, or until the potatoes are browned and lightly crisped.

SERVES 4

Roasted pear sandwich with walnut pesto

Pears and walnuts are a classic duo, more familiar in salads than between two slices of bread. This gourmet sandwich offers a variety of contrasting tastes and textures: sweet and savory, soft and crunchy. There's plenty of room to improvise with your own additions, if you like. I add roasted red bell peppers to mine. You could use a different-flavored pesto or spread or substitute an apple for the pear.

1 firm ripe pear, halved lengthwise, cored and cut lengthwise into slices about ¼ inch [.5cm] thick

1 teaspoon olive oil

3 tablespoons Walnut Pesto (recipe follows)

4 slices of whole-grain bread, toasted

6 slices of smoked or regular mozzarella cheese

4 leaves of crisp lettuce

Roasted red bell peppers, cut into strips (optional)

Salt and freshly ground pepper

1. **Preheat** the oven to 400°F [200°C]. Lightly coat the pear slices with the olive oil. Spread out in a single layer in a small baking dish and roast for 20 minutes, or until softened and lightly browned.

2. Spread the pesto on one side of each slice of toast. **Layer** the remaining ingredients on half the slices and season with salt and pepper to taste. Sandwich with the second slice of bread, pesto side down, and press down firmly. Serve at once or wrap tightly in plastic and refrigerate for up to 3 hours.

MAKES 2 SANDWICHES

Walnut pesto

¾ cup walnut pieces [75g]

3 garlic cloves

¼ cup coarsely chopped parsley [60ml]

¼ cup extra virgin olive oil [60ml]

1 tablespoon lemon juice

2 teaspoons maple syrup

Salt and freshly ground pepper

In a food processor, **combine** the walnuts, garlic, parsley, olive oil, lemon juice, and maple syrup. Puree to a paste. Season with salt and pepper to taste. Set aside for at least 1 hour before serving.

MAKES ABOUT 1 CUP [250ML]

Sun-dried tomato pesto

If you are old fashioned or just prefer using a little muscle, use a large marble mortar and pestle to prepare this rather than a food processor. Start by grinding the sun-dried tomatoes and move on down the list until you get a nice thick paste. Slowly add the oil and lemon juice and season with salt and pepper.

1 ounce sun-dried tomatoes, soaked in hot water until soft, chopped [30g]

1 roasted red pepper, coarsely chopped

3 garlic cloves, coarsely chopped

2 tablespoons pine nuts

¼ cup coarsely chopped fresh basil [60ml]

2 tablespoons nutritional yeast

1 teaspoon paprika

2 tablespoons extra virgin olive oil

2 tablespoons lemon juice

Salt and freshly ground pepper

1. In food processor, **pulse** the sun-dried tomatoes, roasted pepper, garlic, pine nuts, basil, yeast, and paprika until a thick, chunky paste forms.

2. Add the olive oil and lemon juice and pulse again once or twice. **Season** with salt and pepper to taste. Set aside for at least 1 hour before serving.

MAKES ABOUT 1 CUP [250ML]

Hummus, jarlsburg, and roasted hot pepper sandwich

Garlic from the hummus, a bite from the pepper, and a smoky, savory sensation from the cheese work beautifully together to create what is possibly one of the greatest vegetarian sandwiches I have ever tasted. Yes, I know that's a bold statement, but most chefs love their own cooking, so what can I say?

Fresh cayenne peppers are exquisite, one of those ingredients worth going out of your way to find. Many large gourmet supermarkets or small Mexican or Asian markets will have a variety of peppers during the season. If you cannot find a fresh cayenne, substitute another hot pepper, such as a serrano or jalapeño. If you prefer milder food, use a roasted red bell pepper.

2 tablespoons Roasted Pepper Hummus (page 20)

2 slices of whole grain bread, toasted

Store-bought or homemade seitan slices (see page 230)

2 slices of roasted cayenne, serrano, or other hot pepper

½ avocado, sliced

2 slices of Jarlsburg cheese

4 or 5 thinly sliced cucumber rounds

Salt and freshly ground pepper

1 teaspoon extra virgin olive oil

1. **Spread** the hummus over one side of both pieces of toast.

2. On one slice, layer the seitan, roasted hot pepper, avocado, Jarlsburg cheese, and cucumber rounds. Season lightly with salt and pepper. **Drizzle** the olive oil over the cucumbers.

3. Top with the remaining slice of toast, hummus side down. **Press** down firmly and cut in half.

MAKES 1 SANDWICH

Tempeh reuben

Virtually every time I see a recipe for a vegetarian Reuben I am disappointed, because often the tofu or tempeh is left as is, unseasoned, as if that part of the sandwich were unimportant. Oh, yes, sometimes there is a cursory marinade, but nothing much of any merit. I, of course, call for the sauerkraut, cheese, and rye bread; they are givens with a Reuben. But this tempeh is marinated overnight in flavors that are interesting, compelling you to actually taste the tempeh, not just the condiments.

1 package (8 ounces) tempeh [250g]

2 tablespoons vegetarian Worcestershire sauce

1 tablespoon minced fresh dill or 2 teaspoons dried dill

2 teaspoons nutritional yeast

1 teaspoon onion powder

½ teaspoon caraway seed

½ teaspoon celery seed

1 tablespoon red wine vinegar

1 teaspoon salt

¼ teaspoon freshly ground pepper

1 cup vegetable stock or water [250ml]

Russian Dressing with Sun-Dried Tomatoes (recipe follows) or mustard

4 or 8 slices of rye bread

1 cup jarred sauerkraut, rinsed and drained [125g]

4 slices of Swiss cheese

4 to 6 tablespoons vegetable oil (if pan-frying)

1. Split the tempeh in half horizontally to create 2 equal pieces half as thick; cut each piece crosswise to create 4 squares or rectangles.

2. In a large sealable plastic bag, combine the Worcestershire sauce, dill, yeast, onion powder, caraway seed, celery seed, vinegar, salt, pepper, and vegetable stock. Add the tempeh to the bag and seal, squeezing out as much air as possible. Turn the bag over a few times to make sure all the pieces are coated with marinade. Refrigerate 8 hours or overnight, turning the bag 2 or 3 times.

3. To bake tempeh: Preheat the oven to 350°F [175°C]. Arrange tempeh pieces in a small baking dish in a single layer. Coat with 3 or 4 tablespoons of the marinade and cover with aluminum foil. Bake for 15 minutes.

4. To pan-fry tempeh: In a large nonstick skillet, heat the oil over medium-high heat. Add the tempeh and fry, turning once, until golden brown, 2 to 3 minutes on each side. Remove and drain on paper towels.

5. To assemble the sandwich, spread the Russian dressing or mustard on bread. Add tempeh, sauerkraut, Swiss cheese, and a second slice of bread. Grill or serve as is.

MAKES 4 MEDIUM-SIZE OR 2 VERY HEARTY SANDWICHES

chef talk

The difference between baking and frying tempeh is significant. Frying tempeh gives it a crispy texture and alters the taste, sort of like the coating for fried chicken or even French fries. For sandwiches, or to present a sauce, I like this technique best. However, you do lose some of the flavor in the cooking pan of any marinade you used.

Baking tempeh, on the other hand, allows you to fully taste the mushroom or nutty tempeh flavor as well as the marinade. And little or no oil is used, which may be important to some. If well coated in liquid and covered, baked tempeh will be moister than fried—meaning, working with tempeh properly is key to the best taste sensations. See the pages 119–120 for details.

Both techniques are good, and each has its own place. Try both methods and see for yourself.

Russian dressing with sun-dried tomatoes

This dressing is especially thick—a bold dressing for a hearty salad of greens and tomatoes. It also doubles beautifully as a spread over tempeh and sauerkraut for a Reuben sandwich. Add more soaking liquid if you prefer a thinner dressing.

4 ounces silken tofu [125g]

2 teaspoons bottled plain (not creamed) horseradish (red or white)

5 sun-dried tomatoes soaked in 1 cup [250ml] hot water until soft, coarsely chopped, soaking liquid reserved

1 tablespoon ketchup

1 small shallot, minced

1 teaspoon vegetarian Worcestershire sauce

½ teaspoon salt

Pinch of freshly ground pepper

Mix all the ingredients in a blender, gradually adding the reserved tomato soaking liquid (anywhere from 2 to 4 tablespoons) until the dressing reaches the desired thickness. Scrape down the sides of the blender two or three times until the dressing is very well mixed. Adjust seasoning, if necessary. Let stand at least 1 hour before serving.

MAKES ABOUT ½ CUP [125ML]

Tempeh-mushroom joe

To my mind, there's no Joe like a tempeh Joe. Trying to get your children to eat soy may be difficult, but not with this dish. They'll enjoy it just as they would a meat-based sloppy Joe—and chances are they won't notice the difference. By the way, you'll like it, too. As a change, consider ladling the savory topping over spaghetti or linguine instead of buns.

1 medium onion, chopped

2 tablespoons canola or olive oil

3 garlic cloves, minced

½ pound cremini or white button mushrooms, thinly sliced [250g]

½ green bell pepper, chopped

½ red bell pepper, chopped

8 ounces tempeh, shredded or crumbled [250g]

1 teaspoon salt

¼ teaspoon freshly ground pepper

1 can (28 ounces) crushed tomatoes [875ml]

1 tablespoon unrefined cane sugar or honey

1 tablespoon vegetarian Worcestershire sauce

2 tablespoons tomato paste

1½ tablespoons cider vinegar

8 hamburger buns

1. In a large skillet, cook the onion in the olive oil over medium heat until very soft, about 5 minutes. Add the garlic, mushrooms, green and red peppers, and tempeh. Season with the salt and pepper. Cook until the vegetables are softened, stirring several times, 5 to 7 minutes longer.

2. Add the crushed tomatoes. Bring to a boil. Stir in the sugar or honey, Worcestershire sauce, tomato paste, and vinegar. Reduce the heat to medium-low and simmer for 5 to 10 minutes. Serve hot between split hamburger buns.

SERVES 8

Open-faced focaccia with fava bean spread and tofu

This sandwich uses a wonderfully mellow but richly flavored spread made with fava beans. Fresh fava beans require a bit of work with the shelling and peeling, but they are worth it. If you are reading this and it's not late spring or summer, you probably won't be able to get fresh fava beans—or broad beans, as they are also called. Out of season, look for frozen, peeled, and blanched fava beans in Asian or specialty/gourmet grocery stores.

You will have plenty of leftover spread here; save it for crostini or mix it into pasta or risotto. The tofu is very simple. Not all tofu needs to be marinated; in fact, some people are so used to it that they eat it plain, out of the box. In this recipe I recommend a cast-iron skillet to quickly brown the tofu. For even more flavor, grill the tofu, if you have the opportunity, as well as the focaccia.

3 pounds fava beans, shelled [1.5kg] (about 1 pound [500g] shelled beans)

½ cup extra virgin olive oil [125ml]

2 tablespoons lemon juice

½ sheet nori, toasted and crumbled*

1 teaspoon salt

⅛ teaspoon freshly ground pepper

2 garlic cloves, minced

1 tablespoon chopped fresh basil plus 2 or 3 fresh leaves, thinly sliced

1 to 2 tablespoons vegetable oil

½ pound firm tofu, pressed of water, sliced into 4 cutlets [250g]

1 piece of focaccia, approximately 6 x 4 inches [15 x 10cm], sliced horizontally into 2 thinner pieces

A few thinly shaved slices of pecorino Romano cheese

4 to 6 fresh ripe tomato slices

Salt and freshly ground pepper (optional)

Extra virgin olive oil

1. Fill a bowl with ice water and set aside. **Cook** the shelled fava beans in a large saucepan of boiling water until just cooked through, 2 to 3 minutes; or 30 seconds to 1 minute if they are very small. Drain the beans and plunge into the ice bath. Drain again, then immediately peel the beans by pinching off a small piece of skin and popping the naked bean out.

2. In a food processor, **puree** the beans along with the olive oil, lemon juice, nori, salt, pepper, garlic, and 1 tablespoon chopped basil. Scrape down the sides a few times. Puree until very creamy. Pour into a bowl and set aside.

3. **Heat** the vegetable oil in a large cast-iron skillet over high heat. Add the tofu and quickly sear for about 2 minutes on each side, or until lightly browned.

4. Spread half of the fava bean puree over each cut side of focaccia. **Layer** on the tofu, Romano cheese, tomato slices, and remaining basil leaves, dividing evenly between the sandwiches. Season with a dusting of salt and pepper, if you desire. Drizzle on additional extra virgin olive oil for an authentic touch.

MAKES 2 OPEN-FACED SANDWICHES

*If the nori is not already toasted, place the sheet in a dry skillet over medium-low heat for 1 to 2 minutes, turning several times until the sheet turns a brighter green.

chef's tip

If fresh fava beans are not in season, substitute 1 pound [500g] frozen broad, fava, or lima beans and skip Step 1. Run the frozen beans under warm water just to thaw.

4 BURGERS, FRITTERS, and LOAVES: Stars of Vegetarian Cuisine

The veggie burger is probably the best-known and most popular product of the vegetarian world. It was one of the first foods—albeit frozen—that crossed over and was accepted by meat eaters. People thinking of vegetarian food are now as likely to think of veggie burgers as a staple of a vegetarian's diet as they might have thought of tofu and sprouts years ago. Today it is not uncommon to find restaurants—from the local tavern to the higher-end bistro—with veggie burgers on the menu. They are no longer weird or fascinating to the meat-eating world. Not to mention, many meat eaters actually enjoy them.

That said, in my opinion, most of the dozens of frozen burgers on the market lack zip and flavor. After all, the prime business of frozen foods is simply convenience. Frozen veggie burgers come in handy on many occasions for millions of hungry folks, myself included.

Even restaurants that offer handmade burgers, while certainly much better than the commercial variety, lack the full body and zing you get from making them at home. Most restaurants simply don't have the time or the creativity to make a veggie burger that is special. Some are admittedly good, but they always seem to be missing something.

Let's be clear. Fresh vegetarian burgers are not meat burgers—and they don't pretend to be. If you are not a meat eater, you may not care, but some folks may be looking for the old familiar look, taste, and feel of a hamburger. Move on, I say, and try something completely new. Veggie burgers designed from an almost infinite array of vegetables, beans, grains, nuts, and spices offer a whole new culinary experience with the same pack-it-between-a-bun-and-eat-it-with-your-hands convenience as conventional burgers. The variety and flavors you choose are limited only by your imagination. Oh, and they taste great, too.

General burger tips and techniques

When assembling a veggie burger, exact amounts are usually not critical—although *ratios* are, to create the right balance of textures and to make sure the patties hold together. If you don't like curry, substitute fennel, oregano, or cumin. If buckwheat doesn't do it for you, use brown rice or tofu. Add wine or stock when sautéing; or add Worcestershire or hot sauce to finish the burger. As long as the whole mixture sticks together in the end and ingredients are cut into relatively small pieces, you're in business. Once you've made the burgers offered in this chapter once or twice, you'll get the hang of how they should feel before you cook them.

All the burgers do fantastically well sautéed in oil. Taste and texture dictates this as the number-one choice for best overall cooking method. There simply is no substitute for frying in oil. The crisp outer texture, the moist middle—the snap and crackle, if you will—is sorely missed without this technique. It cannot be achieved by baking or barbecuing. Sautéed in oil, the burgers hold together and make a beautiful presentation.

I recommend buying a box of thin latex gloves. They are invaluable when mixing and forming burgers as well as when working with very hot peppers. Of course, you can mix with a spoon, but to truly feel the burger take shape and know when it's ready, you need to get your hands in there.

Making burgers is an inexact science. I have created these burgers many times over. Most days, they hold together beautifully; yet on occasion they are soft and have a hard time keeping their shape. Maybe there's more pan liquid than the time before, perhaps the bread crumbs have more or less moisture in them, or maybe one too many potatoes was added to the mix. How hot you heat your oil or the quality of your skillet can also make a big difference. The bottom line here is to stay relaxed and keep an open mind when making your burgers, and you'll do just fine.

To make burgers work well nearly every time, keep in mind the following tips

- Let ingredients cool down before shaping them into patties. Hot ingredients tend to fall apart.

- Make sure the oil you fry in is canola, high-oleic safflower, peanut, or other vegetable oil that can withstand high heat without burning.

- Make sure the oil is sufficiently hot before adding the burgers. If the oil is only minimally hot, the patty will quickly absorb the oil and become soggy. The oil is hot enough when its consistency changes and it begins to shimmer and smoke slightly. This is something you will learn to recognize quickly with practice. If you plan to make a whole batch of burgers, you will probably need to change the oil after cooking six or eight burgers. (This number will vary.)

- Bread crumbs and cornmeal will naturally fall from the burger into the oil. These crumbs will start to burn as well as prohibit the burger from having direct contact with the oil—two no-nos you want to avoid. Either strain the oil or remove it entirely and replenish.

Even more tips

- Use two spatulas to flip patties in bread crumbs or cornmeal and when removing them from the pan. This makes a world of difference.

- Place paper towels (to absorb excess oil) on a plate *before* you start cooking. It's often awkward to start fishing around for towels once the burgers are frying.

- In the recipes, I have indicated the amount of oil you will need to use when frying veggie burgers. You may want to start with less, but on occasion you may need more. Much depends on the quality and type of pan you use as well as the type of stove you have. There is a certain degree of difference in heat efficiency based on the type of equipment you use.

- I have also indicated how many burgers each recipe will make. Generally, I would not make bigger burgers from the same amount (as they might not hold together), but you definitely can make smaller or thinner burgers as you see fit.

- To grill burgers on the barbecue, you need to line the grill with heavy-duty aluminum foil. Poke a few holes in the foil and place it over hot but not burning coals. In this instance, rather than coating burgers with bread crumbs or cornmeal, I recommend brushing them with oil. Cover and cook for a few minutes on each side. Veggie burgers are not likely to hold well directly on a metal grid.

- To broil burgers, coat lightly with bread crumbs or brush lightly with oil. I don't recommend cornmeal for broiling, as it will probably burn. Keep a very close watch on broiling burgers. Flip after 2 or 3 minutes.

- Baking works well with loaves (see page 106), but it tends to dry out burgers. The goal, with most burgers, is to produce a crisp exterior and a moist, tender interior. For the most part, the veggie burger's ingredients are already cooked. Baking will then recook them—and possibly dry them out—in the 15 to 20 minutes you must keep them in the oven in order to heat them through.

- To freeze burgers, form patties and wrap them in plastic. Defrost before proceeding to desired cooking method. Already cooked, they also taste good the next day; just reheat or eat cold in a sandwich.

Sweet potato and black bean burger with roasted yellow pepper sauce

These gourmand burgers have a rich, interesting flavor; the cornmeal gives them a beautiful crispy coating. I would have to say that of all the recipes in this book, this burger stands out as my signature dish. The recipe combines an extremely nutritious yet diverse selection of ingredients. The sweet and savory flavors make a triumphant blend. The number-one choice to top these burgers can only be Roasted Yellow Pepper Sauce (page 100); the flavors and colors shine together.

Shortly after graduating from cooking school, I made this dish whenever I cooked for family or friends. My parents were hooked immediately, which of course obligated me to make them every time I saw them. Which then encouraged me to start thinking of new recipes. And so a book was born.

1 medium onion, finely chopped

1½ tablespoons olive oil

3 garlic cloves, minced

1 carrot, peeled and finely grated

2 cups cooked black beans [330g]

½ ounce dried shiitake mushrooms, soaked in hot water until soft, stemmed, caps coarsely chopped [15g]

2 tablespoons tomato paste

1 teaspoon salt

¼ teaspoon freshly ground pepper

½ cup peeled and mashed cooked sweet potato [120g]

1 cup cooked quinoa [160g]*

1 tablespoon caraway seeds

3 tablespoons chopped cilantro

1 teaspoon hot sauce and/or 1 tablespoon vegetarian Worcestershire sauce

1 tablespoon balsamic vinegar

1½ to 2 cups dried bread crumbs [100 to 140g]

1 cup coarse ground cornmeal [125g]

½ cup safflower or canola oil, for frying [125ml]

1. In a large skillet, **cook** the onion in the olive oil over medium heat until soft and nicely browned, 7 to 10 minutes. Add the garlic, carrot, black beans, and mushrooms to the pan and cook for 2 to 3 minutes, stirring occasionally, until the garlic is softened and fragrant.

2. Remove from the heat. With a potato masher or large fork, **mash** until the beans are about half crushed. Stir in the tomato paste. Season with the salt and pepper.

3. Place the bean mixture in a large bowl. **Add** the sweet potato, quinoa, caraway seeds, and cilantro. Mix thoroughly. Season with hot sauce and/or Worcestershire sauce, vinegar, and additional salt and pepper to taste. Gradually add enough bread crumbs to produce a mixture firm enough to hold together. Let cool.

4. **Form** the bean mixture into 8 burgers about 3 inches [8cm] in diameter. Spread out the cornmeal on a clean plate.

5. One at a time, **dredge** the burgers in the cornmeal, using your hands to carefully coat both sides. Place on another plate or clean surface. Finish all 8 burgers and set aside. Use extra cornmeal, if necessary, to coat them all.

6. In a large skillet, heat ¼ cup [60ml] of the oil over medium-high heat. When the oil begins to shimmer, add 3 or 4 of the burgers and **fry**, turning once with a wide spatula, holding a second spatula perpendicular to the burger to "catch" it and let the burger down easy on the other side. (This prevents splashing.) Cook until crispy and brown outside and heated through, about 2 minutes per side. Add the remaining oil and, when it returns to temperature, cook the remaining burgers. Drain on paper towels. Serve with Roasted Yellow Pepper Sauce.

MAKES 8 BURGERS

*Quinoa (pronounced KEEN-wah) is called a super-grain because of its nutritious qualities. It is extremely high in protein and cooks in just about 15 minutes. To end up with 1 cup cooked quinoa, start with ⅓ cup [60g] raw.

Roasted yellow pepper sauce

While this recipe calls for a fairly hot pepper, you can step it up even higher by using a fresh habañero pepper—the boldest of the bold. The combined sweetness of the bell pepper, banana, and caramelized onion will tone down the heat and bring out the citrus overtones of the habeñero. I do suggest, however, that unless you are a real chile head, use just a small piece of the habañero to start with; add more only after you have tasted the sauce. The habañero generally has thin skin, which is why I roast only the bell peppers.

2 yellow bell peppers

1 medium onion, coarsely chopped

2 tablespoons olive oil

½ to 1 fresh hot pepper (jalapeño, Serrano, or habañero), minced

½ banana

¼ to ½ cup dry white wine or vegetable broth [60 to 125ml]

Salt and freshly ground pepper

1 or 2 splashes of peach, mango, white wine, or cider vinegar

1. Preheat the broiler. Cut the bell peppers lengthwise in half; remove the stems, seeds, and excess ribs. Slit the ends slightly so you can flatten them out. Place the peppers stem side up under the broiler with the rack set about 4 inches [8 to 10cm] from the heat and broil until they are blackened, about 10 minutes. Let cool, then scrape off the blackened skin and cut the peppers into strips.

2. In a small skillet or saucepan, cook the onion in 1 tablespoon of the olive oil over medium heat until soft and lightly browned, 5 to 7 minutes.

3. In a food processor, combine the roasted bell peppers, cooked onion, hot pepper, banana, and remaining oil. Blend briefly. With the machine on, gradually add the wine, mixing until smooth and creamy.

4. Strain the sauce through a food mill or fine mesh strainer and scrape into a medium saucepan. Bring to a simmer and cook until reduced slightly. The sauce should be a bit thick, but not heavy. Season with salt, pepper, and vinegar to taste.

MAKES ABOUT 1 CUP [250ML]

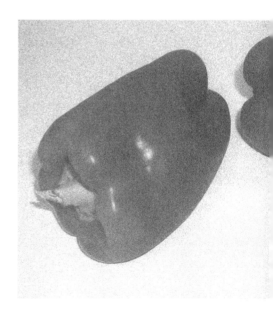

Curried potato, chickpea, and corn burgers

You may flavor these burgers delicately or strongly depending on your taste for curry. They are a little on the soft side, compared to some of the other burgers, but their taste is remarkable. And they make an excellent introductory veggie burger for those who usually eat meat. Top with Mango Salsa (page 35) or Spicy Yogurt Sauce (page 111).

2 cups cooked chickpeas [320g]

1 pound red potatoes, scrubbed, cut into quarters [500g]

1 medium onion, finely chopped

1 tablespoon vegetable oil

2 garlic cloves, minced

1 large tomato, coarsely chopped

1 small hot chile pepper, minced

1 cup fresh or frozen corn kernels [120g]

2 tablespoons curry powder

1 teaspoon salt

Freshly ground pepper

2 tablespoons dry white wine or vegetable stock

1½ to 2 cups dried bread crumbs [100 to 140g]

1½ teaspoons rice vinegar

½ cup canola or safflower oil, for frying [125ml]

1. Mash the chickpeas in a large bowl or pulse in a food processor until a chunky paste is formed. Set aside.

2. Steam the potatoes for about 10 minutes, or until soft.

3. Meanwhile, in a large skillet, cook the onion in the vegetable oil over medium heat until golden, 5 to 7 minutes. Add the garlic, tomato, chile, and corn. Raise the heat to medium-high and cook, stirring frequently, until the tomato is soft, 2 to 3 minutes. Add the curry powder, salt, and a generous grinding of pepper. Stir and cook for an additional minute or so. When the mixture begins to stick slightly, add

the wine. Cook until the mixture has reduced slightly to a thick sauce. Remove from the heat.

4. Add the curry mixture and steamed potatoes to the chickpeas. Mash the potatoes while mixing them in well. **Mix** in ½ cup [35g] bread crumbs. Add the vinegar and additional salt and pepper to taste. If you feel the mixture is too wet, add more bread crumbs. Let cool completely, then form into 8 patties about 3 inches [8cm] in diameter.

5. **Spread** out the remaining bread crumbs on a clean plate. One at a time, place the burgers on the bread crumbs. Use your hands to carefully coat both sides. Set aside on another plate or clean surface.

6. In a large skillet, heat ¼ cup [60ml] of the canola oil over medium-high heat. When the oil begins to shimmer, **fry** 3 or 4 burgers until crispy, 1 to 2 minutes on each side. Look for burgers to be crispy brown on the outside and heated through. Add the remaining oil and, when it returns to temperature, cook the remaining burgers. Drain on paper towels and serve.

MAKES 8 BURGERS

Sage, mushroom, buckwheat, and tempeh burgers

These extremely nutritious and uniquely flavored burgers actually look a lot like beef burgers—and, coincidentally, **taste great** topped with ketchup. Look for toasted buckwheat, which has more flavor than regular buckwheat, in your natural foods store and supermarkets.

6 to 8 dried shiitake or porcini mushrooms

¼ cup toasted buckwheat [40g]

1 tablespoon soy sauce

½ onion, minced

1 tablespoon olive oil

1 medium-large portobello mushroom, cut into cubes

3 garlic cloves, minced

2 teaspoons dried sage

¼ teaspoon crushed hot red pepper

4 ounces tempeh, shredded [125g]

½ teaspoon salt

¼ teaspoon freshly ground black pepper

¼ cup lemon juice [60ml]

3 tablespoons sunflower seeds

¼ cup shredded smoked Cheddar cheese [20g]*

Coarsely ground cornmeal or dried bread crumbs, for coating

½ cup canola or safflower oil, for frying [125ml]

1. **Soak** the dried shiitake or porcini mushrooms in 2 cups [500ml] hot water until soft, about 20 minutes. Lift out and squeeze excess liquid back into the bowl. If using shiitakes, remove and discard the stems. Coarsely chop the mushrooms. Strain and reserve the soaking water.

2. Meanwhile, **cook** the buckwheat in ⅔ cup [150ml] water and the soy sauce for about 10 minutes, until just tender. Buckwheat cooks quickly, so keep an eye on it. Place the buckwheat in a large bowl and set aside.

*If you can't find smoked, use regular sharp Cheddar or a cheese of your choice.

3. In a large skillet, cook the onion in the olive oil over medium heat, stirring occasionally, until softened, about 3 minutes. **Add** the portobello mushroom, shiitake or porcini mushrooms, garlic, sage, and hot pepper. Continue to cook, stirring often, until the portobello is soft. Add the tempeh and season with the salt and pepper.

4. As soon as the ingredients in the pan start to stick slightly, **stir** in the lemon juice and 2 tablespoons of the reserved mushroom soaking water. Simmer for 1 to 2 minutes, or until the liquid is absorbed.

5. Remove from the heat and add to the buckwheat. Add the sunflower seeds and cheese and mix well. **Season** with additional salt and pepper to taste. Let cool, then form into 6 patties, about 3 inches [8cm] in diameter.

6. **Spread** out the cornmeal or bread crumbs on a plate. One at a time, place the burgers on the cornmeal or bread crumbs and use your hands to carefully coat both sides. Set aside on another plate or clean surface. Finish all 6 burgers and set aside.

7. In a large skillet, **heat** ¼ cup [60ml] of the canola oil over medium-high heat. When the oil begins to shimmer, add 3 burgers and fry until crispy outside and heated through, about 2 minutes on each side. Add the remaining oil and when it returns to temperature, cook the remaining burgers. Drain on paper towels and serve.

MAKES 6 BURGERS

Mushroom walnut roast

Walnuts, tofu, and oats make for a familiar yet **distinctive** taste that resembles a traditional meatloaf. Like meatloaf, this tastes great hot or cold. Serve with mashed potatoes and a vegetable and top with Chipotle Mushroom Ragout (page 220) or Rustic Creamy Tomato Sauce (page 226).

3 tablespoons olive oil

1 large onion, finely chopped

3 garlic cloves, minced

½ cup coarsely chopped walnuts, toasted [50g]

½ cup rolled oats (regular or instant) [50g]

¼ pound fresh shiitake mushrooms, stemmed, caps thinly sliced [125g]

About 2 cups vegetable stock or water [500ml]

1 tablespoon soy sauce

3 tablespoons Dijon mustard

2 tablespoons tomato paste

2 tablespoons red wine or red wine vinegar

1 tablespoon vegetarian Worcestershire sauce

Salt and freshly ground pepper

1 pound firm tofu, pressed of excess water, crumbled [500g]

3 tablespoons arrowroot

1 to 1½ cups dried whole wheat or white bread crumbs [100 to 140g]

1. **Preheat** the oven to 350°F [175°C]. In a large nonstick skillet, heat half the olive oil over medium heat. Add the onion and cook, stirring occasionally, until soft and golden brown, 7 to 10 minutes. Add the garlic and cook for 1 to 2 minutes longer, until fragrant. Set aside in large bowl.

2. In the same skillet, **heat** the remaining oil over medium heat. Add the walnuts, oats, and mushrooms. Sauté for a few minutes, stirring frequently, until the mushrooms are tender. Add a splash of stock or water if the ingredients stick too much.

3. **Stir** in a small amount of stock, turn up the heat, and deglaze the pan (deglazing means loosening stuck-on bits of the good stuff with a hot liquid). Add the remaining stock and cook for 10 minutes. Add the soy sauce, mustard, tomato paste, red wine, and hot sauce. Continue to cook until the mixture is thick, 2 to 3 minutes. Add to the bowl with the onions and set aside. Season generously with salt and pepper to taste.

4. Add the tofu and arrowroot to a food processor; puree until smooth. Add to the onion mixture and blend in enough bread crumbs to make a thick paste; mix well. Pour into a nonstick or lightly oiled loaf pan measuring 9 by 5 by 3 inches [about 23 by 12 by 8cm]. Press down firmly to pack the mixture into the pan.

5. Bake for 40 minutes. For optimal results, let the loaf cool for 2 hours before slicing it, or make a day ahead and reheat.

SERVES 6 TO 8

chef's tip

For a perfect crispy top, place an additional pan of water in the oven while you bake the loaf.

Roasted corn and ancho plantain cakes topped with red pepper chipotle cream

Take advantage of fresh corn in season. When it is not available, substitute frozen corn kernels. Plantains, referred to as *cooking bananas*, are blander and less sweet than bananas and are eaten only when cooked. They make an excellent base for many dishes and can be fried, baked, sautéed, and boiled. For this recipe, choose a firm plantain, not an overly soft one.

Red Pepper Chipotle Cream (recipe follows)

4 large ancho chiles

2 cups fresh or frozen corn kernels [250g]

1 tablespoon olive oil

1 small onion, finely chopped

1 large ripe plantain, thinly sliced

1½ cups soy milk or rice milk [375ml]

1 teaspoon salt

Freshly ground pepper

Juice of 1 lime

1 tablespoon unrefined cane sugar

2 tablespoons unbleached white flour

6 tablespoons canola or safflower oil, for frying

1. **Make** the Red Pepper Chipotle Cream 2 hours ahead or the night before.

2. Start a kettle of water boiling. **Crack** open the chiles and remove the seeds and stems. Place in a heatproof bowl and cover with boiling water. Cover and let stand until the chiles are soft, 20 to 30 minutes. Scrape the meat off the pepper from the inside with the back edge of a knife, leaving the skin behind. Scrape onto a small plate and set aside.

3. In a large dry cast-iron skillet, **toast** the corn over medium-high heat, stirring often, until the kernels are lightly browned, 2 to 3 minutes. Set aside in large bowl.

4. In the same pan, heat the olive oil over medium heat. **Add** the onion and cook until soft and lightly browned, about 5 minutes. Add the plantain and milk and bring to a boil. Reduce the heat to a simmer and cook for 5 minutes. Mash the plantain in the pan with a potato masher until the sauce is thick and chunky. Stir in the chile. Season with the salt and pepper to taste. Continue to simmer 5 minutes longer, stirring occasionally.

5. **Stir** in the lime juice, sugar, and flour; mix well. Add the corn and cook 1 more minute. You should end up with a nice thick batter. Return to a bowl and let cool, then form the batter into 6 equal cakes, about 3 inches [8cm] in diameter.

6. Heat 2 tablespoons of the canola oil in the cast-iron skillet over medium-high heat. **Cook** 2 cakes at a time until browned and crisp on both sides. Repeat the process with 2 more cakes, and so on. You may not need to use all 6 tablespoons of the oil. If you use less oil, you will get a more blackened cake. Serve hot, topped with the chipotle cream.

MAKES 6 CAKES

Red pepper chipotle chile cream

This is a multipurpose topping for almost any burger or fritter. It also makes a great dressing for a crunchy salad and a fine sauce for Cajun Tempeh (page 146).

N O T E As with many tofu spreads, the possible alternatives here are infinite. Substitute sun-dried tomatoes or prepared sun-dried tomato pesto for the red pepper. Or try cilantro, lime, or pesto as flavor ingredients.

1 dried chipotle chile

2 garlic cloves, minced

1 red bell pepper, roasted and coarsely chopped

8 to 10 ounces silken tofu [250 to 300g]

1 tablespoon extra virgin olive oil

1 teaspoon ground cumin

½ teaspoon paprika

2 teaspoons red wine vinegar or sherry vinegar

1 teaspoon maple syrup

Salt

1. Start a kettle of hot water boiling. Remove the stem from the chipotle chile. Crack open the chile and remove the majority of the seeds. Soak the chile in about 2 cups [500ml] of the boiling water until soft. Drain and finely chop or mince.

2. Puree the garlic, bell pepper, and chile in a food processor until very smooth, scraping down the sides once or twice. Add the tofu and blend well again. With the machine on, add the olive oil, cumin, paprika, vinegar, and maple syrup, processing until very smooth and creamy. Season with salt to taste.

3. Cover and refrigerate 2 hours or overnight.

MAKES ABOUT 1 CUP [250ML]

Spicy yogurt sauce

The technique of making "cheese" out of yogurt is quite appealing. It thickens the yogurt and concentrates the flavors. Use as a dip or topping or even as a side dish. At parties I've watched people who stand by the table and keep eating it until it's all gone. It's perfect as a sauce for the Lentil Scallion Fritters that follow. Other ideas for using Spicy Yogurt Sauce include as a topping for Curried Corn Burgers (page 102), or as a dip for Pita Chips (page 34).

3 cups plain yogurt, preferably organic [750ml]

1 cup sour cream, preferably organic [250ml]

3 tablespoons crushed peanuts

3 garlic cloves, minced

1 small red onion, finely chopped

1 or 2 fresh serrano pepper, minced

Salt

½ cup unrefined cane sugar [100g]

1½ teaspoons ground cumin

1. **Line** a fine mesh strainer with a double layer of cheesecloth, using enough cloth so that it hangs over the sides. Set the strainer over a bowl so there is 1 to 2 inches [3 to 5cm] of space between the bottom of strainer and the bottom of bowl. Pour the yogurt into the strainer and cover it with plastic wrap or a plate. Refrigerate overnight.

2. When done, the yogurt should be very thick, like sour cream. Discard the water in the bowl. Place the thickened yogurt and remaining ingredients in a clean bowl. **Add** the peanuts, garlic, red onion, serrano peppers, sugar, and cumin. Fold to mix well. Season with salt to taste. Let stand for about 1 hour to allow flavors to develop. Serve cool or at room temperature.

MAKES ABOUT 3 CUPS [750ML]

Lentil-scallion fritters with feta cheese

These are very simple fritters, yet they have a fresh, lively taste. Make into 1- or 2-ounce [30- to 60-g] patties and serve as appetizers, or make larger patties and serve as a main course. For maximum flavor, don't skip the final step of spritzing each fritter with fresh lemon juice.

The Spicy Yogurt Sauce (page 111) is a phenomenal topping as well as an outrageous stand-alone dip. I highly recommend serving it alongside this dish. You will, however, have to make it ahead of time. Alternatively, you may want to try topping the fritters with Horseradish-Mustard Dip (page 25).

½ cup lentils [100g]

2 large shallots, minced

2 tablespoons extra virgin olive oil

1 bunch of scallions, coarsely chopped

3 garlic cloves, minced

1 tablespoon coarse ground mustard

2 tablespoons fresh lemon juice

4 ounces feta cheese, crumbled (about 1 cup) [125g]

¼ to ⅓ cup dried bread crumbs [20 to 35g]

Several drops of hot sauce, or more to taste

Salt and freshly ground pepper

About ½ cup canola or safflower oil, for frying [125ml]

Lemon wedges

Spicy Yogurt Sauce (recipe on page 111)

1. In a saucepan of salted boiling water, cook the lentils over medium heat until soft, 25 to 30 minutes. Drain well, transfer to a large bowl, and let cool.

2. Meanwhile, in a medium skillet, cook the shallots in 1 tablespoon of the olive oil over medium-low heat until softened and just beginning to color, 2 to 3 minutes. Add the scallions and garlic and cook for another 2 minutes. Remove from the heat.

3. **Stir** the mustard, lemon juice, feta cheese, ¼ cup [60ml] of the shallot-scallion mixture, and the remaining olive oil into the lentils. Mash with a large fork until thoroughly blended. Add the bread crumbs and hot sauce. Mix well. Season with salt and pepper to taste. Add more bread crumbs, if necessary, to get the right consistency: a well-formed patty that holds together—not too dry, not too wet. Form into 16 small patties, about 2 inches [5cm] in diameter.

4. In a large skillet, **heat** 3 to 4 tablespoons of the canola oil over medium-high heat. Add as many patties as will fit in a single layer without crowding and fry until browned and crisp on both sides, 2 to 3 minutes. Fry the remaining fritters in batches, if necessary, adding more oil as needed to prevent sticking. Drain the fritters on paper towels.

5. **Serve** hot, with lemon wedges for spritzing. Pass the yogurt sauce on the side.

SERVES 4 (AS AN APPETIZER)

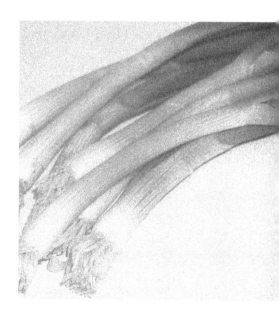

5 OUTRAGEOUS

SOY: Tempting Tofu and Tempeh

For me—given the often subjective nature and broad interpretation of cooking styles for tofu and tempeh—I have often felt more comfortable navigating my own way. Yes, I have picked up tips, techniques, and ideas from other cooks over the years, but ultimately experimenting time and again, until I found out for myself what worked and what didn't, seemed the best path for working with soy.

What this means to you is that a lot of work is already done for you. Simply follow the recipes, or variations of them, and discover the outrageous world of gourmet tofu and tempeh you may not have known existed before.

Tofu 101

Some 2000 years ago the Chinese invented *dow-foo,* or bean curd. They considered the vegetarian product, rightly so, to be "meat without bones." Monks brought it to Japan some 800 years later and called it tofu. Tofu is made by curdling fresh hot soy milk with a coagulant. Many varieties of tofu are available, including soft, firm, extra-firm, and silken. Soft and firm styles as especially appropriate for spreads; firm and extra-firm styles are more suitable for recipes where you would like the tofu to keep its shape.

Silken tofu is best used in desserts, such as puddings and pies, or in spreads and dressings. Note that even though some silken tofu packages say firm or extra-firm on the box, they are still very soft in comparison to regular (non-silken) tofu. Silken tofu is not pressed but allowed to solidify in its package. The packaging may be shelf-stable aseptic or a plastic boxlike tub. If you have trouble remembering the difference between silken tofu and regular, Japanese- or Chinese-style tofu, just think about the name—it really has a silky, lustrous feel. Generally speaking, whether regular or silken, the more water the tofu contains, the softer it is.

Most varieties and many brands of tofu are packed in a small tub of water. Unpack the tofu by first poking a hole in the top of the package over a sink and squeezing out excess water. Then cut open the remainder of the plastic, pour out any remaining water, and remove the tofu.

Pressing water out of tofu before you use it is important for one basic reason: The more water you squeeze out, the more flavor you can get in, as tofu is very much like a sponge. Begin by placing the tofu on a dinner plate and covering it with another plate. Set any relatively heavy object on top—a can of tomatoes, a teakettle half-filled with water, or a cast-iron skillet. If the object stays balanced and doesn't keel over but puts enough pressure on the tofu to elicit some water, you're doing fine. Weigh down the tofu for 15 to 30 minutes, but no more than an hour. Remove the weight and hold the two plates together, like a big sandwich, with the tofu as the fill-

chef talk

ing, then tilt to drain off the water. Repeat the process for an even firmer, drier tofu or proceed to marinating or freezing. If you are going to fry the tofu in oil, I recommend that you dry it off with a paper towel to limit splattering.

One important note: You should not try to press water from silken tofu. The small bit of water that disperses when you empty the package will be enough. Pressing will crush the tofu. I have found that to drain it in a colander, for example, is not worth the time and mess it makes.

Freezing tofu

Freezing alters the consistency of tofu, making it somewhat chewier and more absorbent. It may also help the tofu hold its shape, which is especially useful in dishes that may be mixed about a lot, such as stews and stir-fries. This aside, frozen tofu can be fickle. Even drained and pressed tofu may still have excess water inside, which may lead to the tofu cracking after thawing. And unless you're going to deep-fry it, cracked tofu is something you don't want to work with. Don't freeze any tofu you plan on pureeing. When frozen, tofu turns slightly yellow, but it quickly becomes white again after thawing. To freeze: Drain, then press a block of firm or extra-firm tofu, as described above. Slice in half lengthwise; wrap each piece several times over with plastic wrap. Freeze at least overnight or 24 to 48 hours, if possible.

When ready to thaw, unwrap from the plastic and seal the tofu block in a sandwich bag, pressing out the air. Place the bag directly in a bowl of hot tap water. Remove after 30 to 60 minutes, or when the tofu is thawed all the way through. You will probably have to change the water a couple of times with fresh hot water. Remove the tofu from the bag, squeeze out excess water with your hands (between your palms), and set aside for the next step.

Marinating tofu (the longer version)

Drain and press a block of tofu. Cut it into the desired shape and place in a sealable plastic bag (the very best way) or in a shallow pan or pie dish (the okay way). The plastic bag is best because it enables you to flip it over or press down and disseminate the marinade without having to splash or use any utensils. As with any marinated food, the flavoring possibilities are limitless. (See marinade chart, page 8 for details.) Ideally, marinate the tofu overnight. That said, you can have success marinating for only 4 to 8 hours, depending on the ingredients and the density of the tofu. For example, tofu tends to suck up citrus especially quickly. If the tofu is not completely covered in marinade, turn the pieces over once or twice. Once marinated, the tofu is ready for grilling, broiling, or pan-frying.

IMPORTANT NOTE Marinades that are too thick will not penetrate tofu in the proper manner. They should not be like soup nor should they be like water but somewhere in the middle.

Marinating tofu (the shorter version)

Here is a quicker way to marinate tofu, which will still pack a punch of flavor. You might call this faux marinating, as the flavors are not completely absorbed into the tofu but wrapped tightly around it. While this shortcut is quite good, tofu will still taste better the next day after it has had more time to absorb the flavors around it.

1. Press and drain a block of tofu for 30 to 60 minutes. For this method, frozen tofu works nicely, as it holds together well under the strain of stirring and seems to absorb somewhat better, though some of this depends on the brand of tofu. Use frozen tofu if you have time (or have frozen tofu on hand), but don't feel obligated. Tofu that has not been frozen will work fine as long as it is firm. Fresh tofu will have a creamier mouthfeel, which many people seem to prefer. You'll have to try it to decide for yourself.

2. Pat the pressed tofu dry with paper towels. This will help keep water and hot oil from splattering excessively. You may choose to use a splatter guard if you have one on hand for the sake of safety and cleanliness. In a cast-iron or other heavy skillet, heat $1/4$ cup canola, high-oleic safflower, or peanut oil to a medium-high temperature. When the oil is very hot and shimmering, add the tofu and fry, turning once, until lightly browned. Ultimately, you will decide whether you like your tofu super-crisp or just a touch so. Drain on paper towels. Pour out excess oil from the pan.

chef talk

3. While still warm, slice or cube the tofu into pieces as specified in the recipe you are using. Add to a prepared marinade and mix until the tofu is well coated. You could proceed to Step 4 directly, but I recommend letting the tofu marinate for 30 to 60 minutes if you have time.

4. Pour the tofu and all the marinade back into a very hot skillet. Stir constantly until most of the liquid is absorbed. If you want a more browned look and crunchy texture, sprinkle a small amount of sugar on the tofu as it cooks.

Outdoor grilling with tofu

If done properly, which is not difficult in the least, barbecued marinated tofu offers the ultimate flavor. For best results, use only extra-firm or firm marinated tofu on the grill. Lightly oil your grill racks and let them heat up as you would with any grilling. Grill your tofu over a medium flame. If you have good control of your fire, let the flame lick the tofu slightly, blackening it lightly on both sides. Brush additional marinade on while it's cooking, then top the finished tofu with additional marinade. It's hard to put an exact time on how long to grill, as temperatures and types of barbecues vary widely. I estimate about 5 minutes per side for a piece of tofu ½ to ¾ inch [1 to 2cm] thick.

Tempeh 101

ORIGINALLY FROM INDONESIA, tempeh (pronounced *TEM-pay*) is a chunky cake made from partially cooked whole soybeans and a friendly culture, or tempeh starter. The ingredients are fermented and shaped into bricklike rectangles. Tempeh has a nutty, mushroom-like taste and a firm, chewy texture. It is available in a variety of flavors, which run the gamut from five-grain to sea vegetable to just plain soybean tempeh. Because tempeh is made from whole soybeans, nutritionally it makes an excellent meat substitute, especially when complemented with a grain dish. Tempeh can be marinated or seasoned and grilled, pan-fried, or grated and added to stews or chili.

Sauté it, fry it, bake it, steam it, you name it—you can do almost anything with tempeh if you do it right. Techniques are critically important to tempeh, more so than with tofu, to get a great taste and texture.

chef talk

In my cooking classes, I always ask students what their experiences with tempeh have been like. It's not uncommon to get a room half full of people who have never tried it. A few may have had unpleasant or indifferent experiences. After class, armed with a few easy techniques and recipes, much of that changes for many students. Usually, tasting Crisp Tempeh with Mango and Hot Pepper (page 145) or North African Tempeh Tagine (page 158) makes true believers and instant converts.

In the store, tempeh may come fresh or frozen. Fresh tempeh can be stored in the refrigerator for a week, and usually more, depending on the use-by date on the package. When it's on sale, I usually buy more than I need and freeze it. Tempeh lasts several months in the freezer. To thaw, soak in hot tap water for 30 to 45 minutes or so. It usually defrosts quickly. The package is typically well sealed, so it doesn't have to be covered or otherwise sealed when thawing. However, if the package is loosened or you opened it and then decided to freeze it for later, make sure to seal it very well. Freezer frost will ruin the taste.

For marinating, I like to cut the tempeh cake in half horizontally so that it is half as thick. (If the tempeh is too thick when you cook it, you will be left with a crisp outside and a raw inside.) Then I cut it crosswise in half to make 4 pieces and ensure that the marinade penetrates the tempeh cake. Follow the marinating instructions for tofu; the process is virtually the same.

chef talk

Frying gives tempeh a distinctive texture and taste. It is so different from steamed tempeh that you might think it was a different food. Frying gives tempeh a taste and texture somewhere between French fries and chicken-fried steak. Go figure.

Steaming plumps tempeh and moistens it slightly. However, I rarely steam it by itself. Instead, I prefer to simmer tempeh in a sauce or stew, which accomplishes the same thing but at the same time allows it to absorb all those other flavors. And as with tofu, marinating overnight enhances the taste tremendously. If you'll be steaming or baking tempeh for any extended period of time, simply cut the tempeh cake into cubes, allowing it to cook through faster.

The tofu and tempeh recipes included in this chapter represent many of my specialties; however, you will find more sprinkled throughout the book. No matter where you find them, try the recipes, play with them, experiment with them, and get to know them. Outrageous soy is a vital part of the bold vegetarian's diet.

Preparation and cooking

One of my favorite techniques is to pan-fry tempeh. Cut the tempeh into 4 thinner pieces. Heat enough oil (4 to 6 tablespoons) to cover the bottom of a skillet over medium-high heat. When the oil is very hot, fry the tempeh on both sides until golden brown, 2 to 3 minutes per side. Drain the tempeh on paper towels and sprinkle with salt while it's still hot.

NOTE Do not walk away from the stove when you are frying tempeh: a minute too long, and it's burned. Many sauces go beautifully over fried tempeh. Tempeh made this way and cut into cubes also makes excellent croutons for a green salad (see page 284).

Amazing tofu teriyaki

If you like teriyaki, you'll love this dish. The sugar gives it a nice gloss, and the flavor is intense. This very easy recipe makes use of the quick version of marinating tofu. It also works well with frozen tofu.

3 tablespoons sherry vinegar	4 to 5 dashes of Tabasco sauce
2 tablespoons toasted sesame oil	1 tablespoon minced fresh ginger
2 tablespoons mirin	Freshly ground pepper
1 tablespoon soy sauce	¼ cup vegetable oil [60ml]
2 tablespoons unrefined cane sugar	1 pound extra-firm tofu, sliced in half or thirds lengthwise [500g]

1. In a small bowl, **combine** the vinegar, sesame oil, mirin, soy sauce, sugar, Tabasco, ginger, and a light grinding of pepper. Stir to mix well.

2. In a large cast-iron skillet or heavy-duty frying pan, **heat** the vegetable oil over medium-high heat. When the oil is very hot and almost shimmering, fry the tofu, turning once, until lightly browned and crisp on both sides, 3 to 5 minutes. Drain on paper towels. Pour out excess oil from the pan and set aside.

3. While the tofu is still warm, **cut** it into cubes. Add the marinade and mix until very well coated. Set aside until ready to finish them off in the skillet. If you have the time, let the tofu marinate for 30 to 60 minutes.

4. Increase the heat to high. When the skillet is very hot, **pour** the marinated tofu and all the marinade back into the pan. (Use a rubber spatula to scrape all the marinade out of the bowl.) Fry, stirring constantly, until the marinade is completely absorbed and the tofu is well coated.

SERVES 2

Citrus-marinated tofu cutlets

These are crisp, crunchy cutlets, marinated with an **Asian**-inspired sauce, coated with bread crumbs, and quick-fried. They are equally as good grilled or broiled, without bread crumbs, or they can be baked. Serve with lightly sautéed spinach and a red and yellow pepper stir-fry.

Juice of ½ lime

Juice of ½ orange

Splash of hot sauce

½-inch piece of fresh ginger, minced or grated [1-cm]

2 garlic cloves, minced

1½ teaspoons chickpea miso or white miso

1 teaspoon brown rice vinegar

½ teaspoon soy sauce

1 teaspoon unrefined cane sugar

¼ teaspoon freshly ground pepper

1 pound extra-firm tofu, cut into 4 rectangles [500g]

½ cup unbleached all-purpose flour [60g]

¼ teaspoon salt

½ cup dried bread crumbs [35g]

About ⅓ cup canola or high-oleic safflower oil [60ml]

1. In a measuring cup, **mix** the lime juice, orange juice, hot sauce, ginger, garlic, miso, vinegar, soy sauce, sugar, and half the pepper. Mix well so the miso and sugar are well incorporated. Pour into a large sealable plastic bag or a shallow dish. Carefully place the tofu cutlets in the bag and seal, or put them in the dish and cover tightly with plastic wrap. For best results, marinate in the refrigerator 8 hours or overnight.

2. When ready to start cooking, **remove** the tofu cutlets from the marinade and pour the liquid into a shallow bowl.

3. **Season** the flour with the salt and remaining pepper and place on a dinner plate. Place the bread crumbs on a separate plate.

4. One by one, **dip** the cutlets into the marinade, then coat them in the seasoned flour. Return the cutlets to the marinade—dipping them individually very quickly—then coat with bread crumbs. Set aside on another clean plate or tray.

5. In a large skillet, **heat** the oil over medium-high heat. When it is very hot and slightly shimmering, fry the cutlets, turning once, until browned and crisp, about 1 minute on each side. Drain on paper towels. Serve warm.

SERVES 2

Charney's classic tofu with peanut sauce

This crowd-pleasing classic peanut sauce is loaded with flavor.
I recommend natural peanut butter (easy to find in health food stores and
many supermarkets), not the traditional type loaded with fillers, sugar,
and hydrogenated oils.

TIP This recipe makes a wonderful sauce for pasta salad and can be
used for cold Chinese sesame noodles as well. Serve with rice and a salad.

3 tablespoons natural peanut butter

3 garlic cloves, peeled and smashed

2 teaspoons minced fresh ginger

1 tablespoon molasses

1 tablespoon toasted sesame oil

2 teaspoons honey

1 teaspoon soy sauce

1 teaspoon balsamic vinegar

½ to 1 chile pepper, seeded and chopped, or
1 teaspoon crushed hot red pepper

1 teaspoon salt

1½ cups vegetable stock or water [325ml]

1 pound extra-firm or firm tofu, drained,
pressed, and cut into about 6 to 8 rectangles, 2 by 3 inches [5 by 8cm] [500g]

1. **Preheat** the oven to 400°F [200°C]. In a blender, mix all the ingredients except
the tofu. Set the peanut sauce aside.

2. Line a baking sheet with parchment paper or aluminum foil. **Pour** about ⅓ cup
[75ml] of the peanut sauce onto the baking sheet. Lay the tofu pieces on the sauce,
then pour the rest of the sauce over the tofu, reserving 2 or 3 tablespoons. Smooth
over with a butter knife to ensure all pieces are coated. Use the reserved sauce to top
the tofu once it's cooked and ready to serve.

3. **Bake** the tofu for 15 to 20 minutes, or until the peanut sauce has hardened and
darkened slightly.

SERVES 2 TO 4

variation If you prefer your tofu fried, with a light crunch, try this alternative. Fry the tofu until lightly browned, cut into cubes while still warm, and toss in the peanut sauce. Let the tofu marinate in the sauce for 30 to 60 minutes. Serve warm or at room temperature.

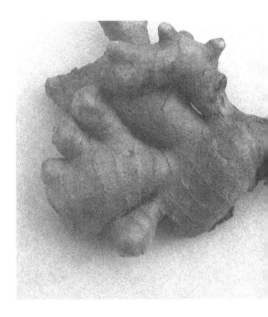

Roasted garlic–lemon tofu and broccoli

The flavors in this dish are a combination of savory with a touch of sweet and a dash of tang. The roasted garlic and lemon juice work beautifully together with the bite of the Tabasco and the brightness and crunch of the broccoli florets. While its flavors are rich, it's an easy dish to make.

2 heads of garlic

2 teaspoons olive oil

2 to 3 tablespoons lemon juice

1 tablespoon brown rice vinegar

Several dashes of Tabasco sauce

¼ cup vegetable stock [60ml]

½ teaspoon salt

Freshly ground pepper

¼ cup vegetable oil, for frying [60ml]

1 pound extra-firm tofu, preferably thawed frozen, pressed to remove excess water and sliced lengthwise in half [500g]

½ pound broccoli florets [250g]

1. Preheat the oven to 325°F [160°C]. Separate the heads of garlic into individual cloves. Skin them and cut off the hard bits on the ends. (It's okay if the cloves are slightly crushed as you get the skin off them.) Toss the garlic cloves with the olive oil to coat lightly and cook them in a covered baking dish for 30 to 40 minutes, or until lightly browned and very soft. You may toss them once or so while they are cooking.

2. In a medium bowl, mash the roasted garlic to a paste with a fork. Add 2 tablespoons of the lemon juice, the vinegar, Tabasco, vegetable stock, salt, and a generous grinding of pepper. Mix well.

3. In a large cast-iron skillet, heat the vegetable oil over medium-high heat until very hot. Fry the tofu, turning once, until lightly browned and crisp on both sides, 2 to 3 minutes. Drain the tofu on paper towels and lightly salt it. Pour out all but 1 to 2 tablespoons oil from the pan.

4. While the tofu is still warm, **cut** it into cubes and stir into the marinade. Toss until very well coated. Let marinate at room temperature for 15 minutes.

5. Heat the cast-iron skillet over high heat. **Pour** the tofu with all its marinade into the skillet. (Use a rubber spatula to scrape all the marinade out of bowl.) Cook, stirring constantly, until the marinade is completely absorbed and the tofu is well coated. I recommend preparing the tofu up to this point, where it can be set aside. Then cook the broccoli and mix it in when you are ready to eat.

6. **Steam** or blanch the broccoli until just tender, 3 to 5 minutes; drain. Reheat the tofu and marinade, if necessary. Add the broccoli and toss gently to mix. For best results, finish with a splash of lemon juice and a dash of Tabasco sauce.

SERVES 2

Creamed almond spinach and tofu

Indian-style is a wonderful way to prepare spinach, with chunks of tasty tofu instead of the traditional paneer, or homemade cheese. Paneer, also spelled panir, is a simple, unripened cheese, not unlike farmer's cheese. It's used in Indian dishes, often as an essential protein source. If you're vegan or serving one, here's your opportunity to shine with your alternative to dairy. The dish looks beautiful spooned over rice. Serve with Indian flatbread, potatoes, and a salad.

6 garlic cloves, minced

1 tablespoon nutritional yeast

1 teaspoon curry powder

1 tablespoon brown rice vinegar

2 tablespoons unrefined cane sugar

3½ tablespoons olive oil

¼ cup vegetable oil [60ml]

1 pound extra-firm tofu, pressed to remove excess water and sliced horizontally in half [500g]

Salt

1 small onion, chopped

1 tablespoon minced fresh ginger

1 fresh serrano or jalapeño pepper, minced

½ teaspoon black mustard seeds

1 teaspoon turmeric powder

1 teaspoon crushed coriander seed

1 bunch of fresh spinach (about 10 to 12 ounces), thoroughly washed, tough stems removed [300 to 350g]

½ cup almond milk [125ml]

1. **Mix** 3 cloves of the garlic with the nutritional yeast, curry powder, vinegar, and 1 tablespoon each sugar and olive oil in a large bowl. Set the marinade aside.

2. Heat the vegetable oil in a large cast-iron skillet over medium-high heat. When the oil is very hot and almost shimmering, fry the tofu, turning once, until lightly browned and crisp on both sides, 2 to 3 minutes. Drain on paper towels and season lightly with salt. Pour out excess oil from the pan and set pan aside.

3. As soon as the tofu is cool enough to handle, **cut** it into cubes and add to the marinade. Toss until very well coated.

4. In a separate large sauté pan, **heat** 1½ tablespoons of the olive oil over medium heat. Add the onion and cook until soft and translucent, 3 to 5 minutes. Add the remaining garlic, the ginger, and serrano pepper and cook for another minute or so, stirring constantly. Add the mustard seeds, turmeric, coriander, and ½ teaspoon salt and continue to cook for another 30 seconds, or until the spices are very fragrant.

5. **Add** half of the spinach to the pan. Raise the heat to medium-high. As soon as the spinach wilts and there is room, add the rest to the pan. Cook, stirring often, until all the spinach is reduced and is soft and tender, about 3 minutes.

6. Scrape the spinach mixture into a food processor and **blend** with the almond milk until smooth and creamy. Pour back into the pan and stir in the remaining 1 tablespoon each olive oil and sugar. Remove from the heat.

7. Heat the cast-iron skillet over high heat. **Pour** the tofu with all its marinade into the skillet. (Use a rubber spatula to scrape all the marinade out of bowl.) Cook, stirring constantly, until the marinade is completely absorbed and the tofu is well coated, about 1 to 2 minutes. Let the tofu cool slightly, then add to the spinach and stir well. Simmer over low heat for 5 minutes.

SERVES 2

Spinach and sun-dried tomato manicotti

Traditionally stuffed with three cheeses—Parmesan, ricotta, and mozzarella—plus herbs and spices, cheese manicotti is creamy, a little tangy, and always comforting. In this recipe, tofu replaces the cheese; nutritional yeast imparts a slight cheesy tang. For convenience, if you don't want to bake and eat the manicotti at once, cover and refrigerate or freeze to cook another time.

1 ounce sun-dried tomatoes [30g]

1 pound soft tofu, pressed to remove excess water [500g]

2 tablespoons lemon juice

1 tablespoon nutritional yeast

½ teaspoon salt

Freshly ground pepper

2 tablespoons olive oil

1 small onion, finely chopped

3 garlic cloves, minced

4 ounces fresh spinach, washed, tough stems removed, leaves coarsely chopped [125g]

2 cups homemade or jarred tomato pasta sauce [500ml]

10 manicotti shells, boiled until softened but not limp

1. Soak the sun-dried tomatoes in 2 cups [500ml] hot water until soft, about 30 minutes. Coarsely chop the tomatoes; reserve the soaking liquid.

2. In a food processor, blend the sun-dried tomatoes with 2 tablespoons of the soaking liquid until coarsely chopped. Crumble the tofu into the processor. Add the lemon juice, nutritional yeast, salt, and a generous grinding of pepper. Blend, scraping down the sides 2 or 3 times, until smooth. Set the filling aside.

3. In a large skillet, heat the olive oil over medium-low heat. Add the onion and cook until very soft and slightly browned, 7 to 9 minutes. Add the garlic and spinach to the skillet and cook for about a minute, until the spinach just wilts.

4. Add the spinach and onion mixture to the food processor with the tofu and **blend** until very smooth and creamy. Remove to a covered bowl for at least 1 hour or proceed to stuffing the manicotti shells. (This procedure can be done a day ahead or the morning you plan to serve.)

5. **Preheat** the oven to 325°F [160°C]. Lightly layer a baking dish with some of the tomato sauce. Fill a pastry bag with tofu filling. Gently fill each shell (or at least 8) until nearly full. If you don't have a pastry bag, use a small spoon. Arrange the stuffed shells side by side in the baking dish. Spoon the remainder of the tomato sauce on top.

6. Cover the dish with foil and **bake** for 30 to 40 minutes. To test for doneness, pierce the center of a shell for a couple of seconds with a small sharp knife. The knife tip should be hot.

SERVES 4

chef's tip

For best results, I strongly recommend purchasing a pastry bag, even if it is disposable, to stuff the manicotti shells.

Soft tofu tacos with tomatillo pumpkin seed sauce

A slightly spicy, wonderfully tart tomatillo sauce pairs with crunchy tofu to produce a traditional Mexican specialty you'll make over and over. Start with one of my guacamole recipes and serve Red Chile Roasted Tomato Rice (page 270) on the side. I highly recommend ice-cold beer to wash it all down. NOTE For this recipe you will need two pieces of equipment: a spice grinder and a steamer large enough to accommodate the tortillas.

¼ cup vegetable stock [60ml]

1 tablespoon olive oil

1 tablespoon sherry vinegar

1 tablespoon unrefined cane sugar

½ teaspoon salt

Freshly ground pepper

¼ cup vegetable oil, for frying [60ml]

1 pound extra-firm tofu, pressed to remove excess water, sliced in half [500g]

6 corn tortillas, steamed until soft

Tomatillo Pumpkin Seed Sauce (recipe follows)

1. In a medium bowl, mix together the vegetable stock, olive oil, vinegar, sugar, salt, and a generous grinding of pepper. Set the marinade aside.

2. In a large cast-iron skillet, heat the vegetable oil over medium-high heat until very hot and almost shimmering. Add the tofu and fry, turning once, until lightly browned and crisp on both sides, 3 to 4 minutes. Drain on paper towels. As soon as the tofu is cool enough to handle, cut it into thin strips 2 inches [5cm] long and add to the marinade. Stir gently until very well coated.

3. Pour out most of the oil from the skillet. Heat the skillet over medium-high heat. Pour the tofu strips with their marinade into the pan. Cook, stirring constantly, until the marinade is completely absorbed and the tofu is glazed with sauce.

5. Form each taco by placing tofu strips in the center of a tortilla. Spoon warm tomatil-lo pumpkin seed sauce over the tofu, and roll up the tortilla. **Serve** at once.

MAKES 6 TACOS (SERVES 2 OR 3)

Tomatillo pumpkin seed sauce

¼ cup raw pumpkin seeds [35g]

10 tomatillos (about ¾ pound), husked and rinsed [375g]

2 fresh serrano peppers

1½ tablespoons olive oil

1 small white onion, chopped

2 garlic cloves, minced

1 tablespoon unrefined cane sugar

½ cup vegetable stock [125ml]

Salt

1. **Preheat** the broiler with the rack set 4 to 5 inches [10 to 13cm] from the heat. In a hot dry skillet, toast the pumpkin seeds until they plump, 30 to 60 seconds. Let cool, then grind them to a powder in a spice grinder or mini food processor.

2. Put the tomatillos and serrano peppers on a baking sheet and **broil,** turning with tongs, until they are softened and their skins are lightly charred all over, 9 to 12 minutes. As soon as the tomatillos are cool enough to handle, coarsely chop them—skin and all—and set aside in a bowl along with their juices. Remove the stems and seeds from the serrano peppers, coarsely chop them, and add to the tomatillos.

3. In a large cast-iron skillet, **heat** the olive oil over medium heat. Add the onion and cook, stirring occasionally, until softened and lightly browned, 7 to 9 minutes. Add the garlic and cook for another minute.

4. In a blender or food processor, **combine** the tomatillos, peppers, onion, garlic, sugar, and pumpkin seed powder. Puree until smooth. Add 1 to 2 tablespoons vegetable stock or water if the mixture is not blending.

5. For a creamy smooth sauce, **press** through a mesh strainer with a rubber spatula or pass through a food mill into a medium saucepan. Bring to a boil and add the stock. Return to a simmer and cook for 15 to 20 minutes, uncovered, stirring frequently. Season with salt to taste.

MAKES ABOUT 1½ CUPS [375ML]

Roasted marinated Mexican tofu steaks

Chiles add an intense and authentic depth to the flavor of this Mexican-inspired marinade. When different types of chiles are toasted and hydrated, their flavor profiles run the gamut from hot and smoky to grassy, fruity, and woody. The ideal way to cook this dish is over a hot barbecue. Obviously, this may not always be an option. Second-best choice is to roast at a high heat. Serve with one of my tasty rice side dishes and a salad.

2 pounds tofu, pressed to remove excess water [1kg]

3 ancho chiles

2 New Mexican chiles

1 guajillo chile or 3 New Mexican chiles instead of 2

4 plum tomatoes

2 fresh jalapeño or serrano peppers

1 red bell pepper

3 garlic cloves, minced

2 tablespoons coarsely chopped cilantro, plus more for garnish

Juice of ½ lime

1 teaspoon ground coriander

2 teaspoons unrefined cane sugar

¼ teaspoon cinnamon

1 teaspoon dried oregano, preferably Mexican

2 teaspoons ground cumin

2 teaspoons red wine vinegar

2 teaspoons extra virgin olive oil

1 teaspoon salt

About ¼ cup vegetable stock or water [60ml]

1. Preheat the broiler with the rack set 5 to 6 inches [13 to 15cm] from the heat. Slice the tofu into 8 cutlets.

2. In a large dry skillet, toast the chiles over medium heat, 1 or 2 at a time, by laying them flat in the pan and pressing down with a spatula for 15 to 30 seconds, until they crackle and give off a slight wisp of smoke. Be careful not to burn them. Flip

over and repeat on the other side. When the chiles are done, submerge them in hot water in a small bowl, cover, and soak until very soft, 30 to 60 minutes.

3. In the meantime, place the tomatoes, jalapeño or serrano peppers, and red bell pepper on a baking sheet. **Broil,** turning with tongs, until blackened all over. They will finish in varying degrees of time. The tomatoes and peppers will slightly char and their skins will blister in 5 to 7 minutes. The bell pepper will probably take 10 to 15 minutes. You want the bell pepper to blacken almost completely.

4. When done, let cool, then **remove** the skins from the tomatoes and the stems from the peppers. You may leave the charred skin on the hot peppers unless it is exceptionally burned. Coarsely chop the tomatoes and the hot peppers, retaining the juices. Scrape the charred skin off the bell pepper, remove the seeds and ribs, and coarsely chop the pepper.

5. In a blender or food processor, **combine** the chopped vegetables with all the remaining ingredients except the tofu and the stock. Puree until smooth, adding enough stock or water to achieve a sauce with the consistency of thick cream.

6. Put the tofu cutlets in 2 large heavy-duty, sealable freezer bags. **Divide** the sauce between the bags, making sure the tofu is well coated. Seal the bags and lay them on a platter or tray. Refrigerate overnight.

7. **Preheat** the oven to 450°F [230°C]. Place the tofu with about half its sauce in an oiled baking dish. Roast for 10 minutes on one side, then 5 minutes on the other. Meanwhile, heat the remaining sauce in a small saucepan on top of the stove or in a bowl in a microwave. Serve the tofu cutlets with the warm sauce. Garnish with chopped cilantro.

SERVES 4 TO 8

note This tofu marinates overnight for maximum flavor. For easier preparation, use canned peeled tomatoes and/or roasted peppers from the deli or your grocery store. Use this recipe to marinate tofu, or modify it slightly and make a sauce simply by omitting the water and pressing the liquid through a fine mesh strainer.

chef's alternative A recipe for Tamarind and Chipotle Sweet-Hot Sauce follows. If you choose, use it to marinate the tofu instead of the Mexican marinade. Cook in the same way.

Tamarind and chipotle sweet-hot sauce

One of my favorite chiles, the chipotle, adds heat and smokiness—a perfect combination for a barbecue-type sauce. Tamarind imparts a unique fruity-sweet tartness. This is an outstanding marinade for tofu. Marinate overnight, then grill on the barbecue. My trick is to let the flames lick the tofu and crisp it slightly, then continue to cook until heated through. Top with additional sauce, reduced until thickened.

2 large chipotle chiles or 1 teaspoon chipotle chile powder, or less to taste

1 cup canned peeled tomatoes [250g]

½ cup cider vinegar [125ml]

½ cup balsamic vinegar [125ml]

½ teaspoon cinnamon

½ teaspoon paprika

½ teaspoon ground coriander

½ teaspoon ground cumin

¼ teaspoon ground cloves

1 tablespoon olive oil

1 small onion, finely chopped

2 garlic cloves, minced

½ cup unrefined cane sugar [100g]

1 tablespoon molasses

1 tablespoon tamarind paste

1 tablespoon tomato paste

½ teaspoon salt

2 pounds extra-firm tofu, pressed to remove excess water [1kg]

1. **Crack** open the chipotle chiles and remove the seeds, ribs, and stems. Soak in 2 cups [500ml] hot water until soft, 45 minutes to 1 hour. Chop the chiles and set aside. Reserve the soaking liquid. In a blender or food processor, puree the chiles with the tomatoes.

2. Meanwhile, in a nonreactive medium saucepan, **combine** the cider vinegar, balsamic vinegar, cinnamon, paprika, coriander, cumin, and cloves. Bring to a boil, reduce the heat to medium-low, and simmer, uncovered, until reduced by half, 10 to 15 minutes.

3. In a large skillet, **heat** the olive oil over medium heat. Add the onion and cook until golden brown, 5 to 7 minutes. Add the garlic and cook another minute, or until soft and fragrant. Stir in the reduced vinegar mixture, sugar, molasses, tamarind paste, tomato paste, salt, chipotle-tomato puree, and ½ cup [125ml] of the reserved chile soaking liquid. Bring to a boil, stirring well. Reduce the heat to low, cover, and cook for 20 to 30 minutes, until thickened. For a thicker sauce, cook uncovered for the last 5 to 10 minutes. Strain the sauce through a fine-mesh strainer. Season with additional salt to taste.

4. **Cut** the tofu into 8 cutlets. Put the tofu cutlets in 2 large heavy-duty, sealable freezer bags. Divide the sauce between the bags, making sure the tofu is well coated. Seal the bags and lay them on a platter or tray. Refrigerate overnight.

5. Light a medium-hot fire in a barbecue grill or preheat the broiler with the rack set 5 to 6 inches [13 to 15 cm] from the heat. Grill or broil the tofu cutlets, turning once and **brushing** with sauce, until they are crisp and lightly charred on the outside, 3 to 5 minutes.

6. Quickly reheat the remaining sauce. **Spoon** some of it over the grilled tofu cutlets and pass the remainder on the side.

MAKES ABOUT 2 CUPS [500ML]

Tofu kebabs with cucumber-yogurt sauce

You'll need 4 wooden skewers for this recipe. Cut them, if necessary, to fit into a large skillet, leaving an inch [2.5cm] on each end to grab hold of. The recipe below cooks them easily in a large cast-iron skillet on top of the stove. If you prefer to grill the kebabs, soak the Skewers in a bowl of water for at least half an hour to prevent burning. The tofu is vastly tastier if marinated overnight, so plan accordingly.

1 pound extra-firm tofu, pressed for 1 hour to remove excess water [500g]

½ teaspoon caraway seeds

1 teaspoon fenugreek

¼ cup plain yogurt, preferably organic [60ml]

2 tablespoons olive oil

2 tablespoons fresh lemon juice

2 teaspoons tamarind paste

2 tablespoons minced cilantro

2 garlic cloves, minced

1 teaspoon powdered mustard

½ teaspoon turmeric

3 splashes of Tabasco sauce

1 tablespoon unrefined cane sugar

2 tablespoons vegetable oil

Cucumber-Yogurt Sauce (recipe follows)

1. Cut the tofu into 1-inch [2.5-cm] cubes. Place in a large sealable plastic bag.

2. In a spice grinder, finely grind the caraway and fenugreek. Turn into a medium bowl. Add the yogurt, olive oil, lemon juice, tamarind paste, cilantro, garlic, sugar, mustard, turmeric, and Tabasco. Whisk to blend well.

3. Pour the yogurt marinade into the bag with the tofu. Make sure the cubes are well coated. Press out any extra air, seal, and refrigerate overnight.

4. Remove the tofu, reserving the marinade. Skewer 4 cubes onto each wooden skewer, lining them up so that they lie flat. Heat 1 tablespoon of the vegetable oil in

a large cast-iron skillet over medium-high heat. When very hot, fry 2 skewers at a time, turning, for 20 to 30 seconds on each of 4 sides, until crisp and browned all over. You should be able to grab the ends of the skewers to turn them. If you can't, use tongs. Repeat with another tablespoon of the oil and 2 more skewers.

5. **Serve** the warm kebabs with the cool cucumber-yogurt sauce on the side.

MAKES 4 SKEWERS

note This recipe serves 4 as an appetizer or 2 as a main dish.

Cucumber-yogurt sauce

1 large cucumber

2 tablespoons minced cilantro

2 tablespoons finely diced red onion

2 garlic cloves, minced

1 fresh serrano or jalapeño pepper, seeded and minced (optional)

1 cup plain yogurt, preferably organic [250ml]

¼ teaspoon salt

⅛ teaspoon freshly ground pepper

1. **Peel** the cucumber. Cut it lengthwise in half and scoop out the seeds. Grate the cucumber on the large holes of a box grater.

2. In a medium bowl, **combine** the cucumber with all the remaining ingredients. Mix well. Cover and refrigerate for at least 30 minutes before serving.

MAKES ABOUT 2 CUPS [500ML]

Spicy tofu pineapple rice salad

This dish has a brilliant flavor and look to it. It can be served as a side dish, an entree, or a salad among many in a buffet. The pineapple and dark rice make an **excellent** combination.

½ cup Lundberg Japonica rice blend [100g]*

1 cup finely chopped fresh pineapple (a chunky mush) [180g]

5 tablespoons vegetable oil

1 tablespoon molasses

1 tablespoon unrefined cane sugar

2 teaspoons tomato paste

2 teaspoons balsamic vinegar

1 teaspoon tamarind paste

1 teaspoon chipotle chile powder

2 garlic cloves, minced

½ teaspoon salt

Freshly ground pepper

1 pound extra-firm tofu, pressed to remove excess water and sliced lengthwise in half [500g]

1 small onion, minced

1 carrot, thinly sliced on the diagonal

1 yellow bell pepper, cut into ½-inch [1-cm] squares

4 scallions, thinly sliced

¼ cup coarsely chopped cilantro [60ml]

1. **Cook** the rice as directed on the package. Meanwhile, in a medium bowl, mix half of the pineapple with 1 tablespoon of the vegetable oil, the molasses, sugar, tomato paste, vinegar, tamarind paste, chile powder, garlic, salt, and a light grinding of pepper. Set the marinade aside.

2. Heat the remaining oil in a large skillet over medium-high heat. When very hot and almost shimmering, **add** the tofu and fry, turning once, until lightly browned and crisp on both sides, 3 to 5 minutes. Drain on paper towels. As soon as the tofu is cool

*Lundberg brand sells a combination rice that includes a short-grain black and a medium-grain mahogany. If you can't find this, look for other interesting dark rice, either packaged or in the bulk section.

enough to handle, cut it into ¾-inch [2-cm] cubes. Add to the marinade and stir gently to coat.

3. **Pour** out all but 1 tablespoon or so of the oil from the skillet. Add the onion and cook over medium heat until softened and lightly browned, about 5 minutes. Add the carrot and yellow bell pepper and cook for another 2 or 3 minutes, until the vegetables are slightly softened. Add the scallions and cook for another 30 seconds, stirring frequently. Turn into a large bowl.

4. Pour the tofu with all its marinade into the skillet. (Use a rubber spatula to scrape all the marinade out of the bowl.) **Cook** over high heat, stirring constantly, until the marinade is completely absorbed and the tofu is nicely browned.

5. Add the tofu, cooked rice, remaining fresh pineapple, and the cilantro to the vegetables in the bowl. **Toss** to mix well. Season with additional salt and pepper to taste. Serve warm or at room temperature.

SERVES 4 TO 6

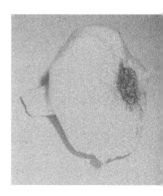

Tofu with shredded tempeh

Tofu *and* tempeh? This recipe may sound like a strange combination! In fact, I got the idea after reading a recipe for shredded pork and tofu. The Chinese integrate tofu into their diet, including it in dishes with or without meat. This may seem contrary to vegetarians, as it did to me, until I realized vegetarians are not the only ones to enjoy or desire tofu in their diet.

The bottom line? If you like spicy Chinese stir-fry, then this dish is for you. It calls for homemade chili paste, but if you prefer to use store-bought, that's okay. If you've never shredded tempeh, not to worry. Use the larger-size grater, about the size of a hole punch, as opposed to the very fine grater. Serve with plenty of steamed rice.

2 to 3 tablespoons Sweet and Hot Garlic Chili Paste (recipe follows) or jarred garlic chili paste

2 tablespoons plus 1 teaspoon vegetable oil

1 package (8 ounces) tempeh, shredded [250g]

1 teaspoon salt

About 6 tablespoons vegetable stock

1 large carrot, halved lengthwise and thinly sliced

2 celery ribs, thinly sliced on the diagonal

1 pound firm or extra-firm tofu, pressed of excess water, cut into 1-inch [2.5-cm] cubes [500g]

1 medium leek (tender white part), thinly sliced and well rinsed

Soy sauce (optional)

1. If making Sweet and Hot Garlic Chili Paste, do this first.

2. Heat 2 tablespoons of the oil in a wok or large nonstick skillet over medium-high heat. When the oil is very hot and almost shimmering, add the tempeh and sauté until golden brown, 3 to 5 minutes. Stir several times, but allow the tempeh to brown for several seconds on all sides before turning, much like making hash browns. Season with the salt.

3. Add 1 tablespoon of the chili paste and 3 tablespoons of the vegetable stock. Continue to **stir** until they are completely absorbed into the tempeh. Transfer the tempeh to a plate and set aside.

4. Heat the remaining oil in the pan. **Add** the carrot and celery and cook over medium-high heat, stirring often, until the vegetables are slightly softened but still crunchy, about 2 to 3 minutes.

5. Add the tofu and **cook** for another 1 to 2 minutes, until the tofu is lightly browned. Add the leek and continue to cook for another 30 seconds or so, just until the leek begins to soften.

6. Return the tempeh to the pan and **mix** well. Add another tablespoon of chili paste and the remaining stock. Increase the heat to high and stir constantly until the paste and stock are completely absorbed into the stir-fry. Splash with soy sauce, if desired. Serve at once.

SERVES 4 TO 6

Sweet and hot garlic chili paste

There's just something about making your own chili paste that's so satisfying. This is a good quick one for a stir-fry or any other dish you would like to spice up. If you want, make a big batch, seal it tightly in a covered container, and refrigerate. There are many chili pastes on the market; some are very good, but some have preservatives, and Thai and Vietnamese varieties are sometimes flavored with anchovy and/or shrimp.

8 garlic cloves, finely chopped

2½ tablespoons crushed hot red pepper

1½ tablespoons unrefined cane sugar

1½ tablespoons tamarind paste

2 teaspoons red miso

About 1 tablespoon extra virgin olive oil

1. **Crush** or pulse the garlic, hot pepper, and sugar into a paste. For authenticity's sake, a stone mortar and pestle or a *suribachi,* a ribbed ceramic Japanese bowl with a wooden pestle, offer the best results for this recipe (see page 13). If you don't have one, pulse in a food processor—a mini one, if available.

2. Add the tamarind paste and miso and **mix** until well blended. Gradually stir in enough olive oil, a few drops at a time, to make a thick paste. Store the chili paste in a covered jar in the refrigerator. It will keep well for up to 2 weeks.

MAKES ABOUT ½ CUP [125ML]

Crisp tempeh with mango and hot pepper

This is at once an outrageous, delightful, simple, and colorful dish. The beauty of fruit and hot peppers is how well they work together; the punch of the generally common jalapeño or even serrano chile is tamed when matched with the tender sweetness of the mango. Some of the heat is retained, of course, but some dissipates, leaving the dish to shine with color and gusto.

¼ cup vegetable oil [60ml]

1 package (8 ounces) tempeh, cut into 10 strips [250g]

Salt

1 medium onion, coarsely chopped

2 mangoes, peeled and cut into ½-inch [1-cm] dice

1 to 2 fresh jalapeño or serrano peppers, cut into very thin strips

3 tablespoons dry white wine

2 tablespoons plus ½ teaspoon unrefined cane sugar

1 tablespoon peach or red wine vinegar

Freshly ground pepper

2 tablespoons coarsely chopped cilantro

1. In a large skillet, **heat** the vegetable oil over medium-high. When the oil is very hot, add the tempeh strips and fry on both sides until lightly browned, about 2 to 3 minutes. Drain on paper towels, sprinkle lightly with salt, and set aside.

2. **Pour** all but 1 tablespoon of the oil from the pan. Add the onion to the skillet and cook, stirring often, until soft and nicely browned, about 7 to 10 minutes. Add the mangoes and hot peppers. Cook until the fruit is very soft, 3 to 5 minutes. Increase the heat slightly and add the wine. Boil until the wine is reduced by about two-thirds. Stir in the sugar and cook for an additional 30 seconds or so, until completely dissolved.

3. Top the tempeh strips with the fruit sauce. **Splash** with the vinegar, season with pepper, to taste, and garnish with the chopped cilantro.

SERVES 2

Cajun tempeh with roasted green beans and corn

This is a striking dish—colorful and packed with flavor. It makes great use of a dry rub that gives the tempeh a **brilliant** flavor and crisp texture. It's spicy, but not too hot. Interestingly, tempeh does not need any additional moisture (such as a marinade or an egg wash, for example) for the spice rub to adhere to it.

Tender asparagus in season works nicely as a substitute for the green beans. Try black Japonica or another mixed dark or red rice as an accompaniment to this dish. Top with a dollop of Simple Tofu Sour Cream.

1 cup fresh or frozen corn kernels [120g]

¼ pound fresh green beans, sliced in half if large [125g]

1 tablespoon olive oil

½ teaspoon dried thyme

½ teaspoon salt

Freshly ground pepper

1 package (8 ounces) tempeh [125g]

2½ tablespoons Cajun Spice Rub (recipe follows)

¼ cup vegetable oil [60ml]

1 large onion, thinly sliced

3 garlic cloves, minced

⅓ cup vegetable stock or water [75g]

Simple Tofu Sour Cream (recipe on page 148)

1. **Preheat** the oven to 425°F [220°C]. In a medium bowl, toss the corn and green beans with the olive oil to coat. Season with the thyme, salt, and a light grinding of pepper. Spread out on a baking sheet and roast for 20 to 25 minutes, tossing once or twice, until the corn is lightly browned around the edges and the beans are slightly wrinkled and a tad browned.

2. Meanwhile, **slice** the tempeh horizontally so it is half as thick, then cut it cross-wise in half so there are 4 squares. Rub both sides of the tempeh squares with enough of the spice rub to coat. Reserve any extra spice rub.

3. In a large cast-iron or nonstick skillet, **heat** the vegetable oil over medium-high heat. When very hot and just shimmering, add the tempeh squares and fry, turning once, until nicely browned—even a tad blackened—on both sides, 2 to 3 minutes. Remove from the pan and drain on paper towels. As soon as the tempeh is cool enough to handle, cut into 1-inch [2.5-cm] squares.

4. **Pour** off all but 1½ tablespoons of the oil from the skillet. Reduce the heat to medium, then add the onion and cook, stirring occasionally, until it is is soft and deeply browned, 10 to 15 minutes. About 2 minutes before the onion is done, add the garlic and any reserved spice rub.

5. Add the tempeh and the roasted corn and green beans. Increase the heat to high, add the stock, and bring to a boil. **Stir** gently but constantly for a minute or so, scraping up any browned bits from the bottom of the pan with a wooden spoon, until the liquid reduces and creates a light sauce. Serve the tempeh and vegetables topped with Simple Tofu Sour Cream.

SERVES 2

Cajun spice rub

1½ tablespoons unrefined cane sugar	2 teaspoons dried basil
2 teaspoons imported sweet paprika	1 teaspoon fennel seeds
2 teaspoons powdered mustard	1 teaspoon salt
2 teaspoons cumin seeds	1 teaspoon black peppercorns
2 teaspoon dried oregano	¼ teaspoon cayenne pepper

In a spice grinder, **whiz** all the rub ingredients to a fine powder. Transfer to a covered jar and store at cool room temperature for up to 1 month.

MAKES ABOUT ⅓ CUP [75ML]

Simple tofu sour cream

½ **pound firm tofu** [250g]

3 tablespoons fresh lemon juice

**2 tablespoons flavorless vegetable oil, such
as safflower or grapeseed**

2 teaspoons nutritional yeast

1 teaspoon brown rice vinegar

1. **Drain** the tofu and press to remove as much water as possible (If you are not familiar with this technique, see page 115).

2. Place the tofu in a blender or food processor with all the remaining ingredients and blend until completely pureed and very well incorporated, at least 2 minutes. **Scrape** down the sides 2 or 3 times.

3. When the "cream" is very smooth, place it in a bowl, cover, and **refrigerate** until chilled. For best results, let chill at least 2 hours or overnight before using.

MAKES ABOUT 1 CUP [250ML]

Thai tempeh red curry

In the old days, canned soups were available in limited flavors. These days, a wide variety of better-quality soups are now available in aseptic containers. The variety and taste level of packaged soups has improved considerably. For this recipe, the best choice is butternut squash soup, which adds a delicate color and substantial flavor. Corn or potato leek soup could also be used, or a canned cream soup, if you cannot find butternut. Serve with quinoa or rice.

1 small onion, chopped

1 tablespoon vegetable oil

8 fresh shiitake mushrooms, stemmed, caps thinly sliced

1 small red bell pepper, coarsely chopped

¾ teaspoon salt

Freshly ground pepper

1 cup butternut squash soup [250ml]

1 teaspoon Thai red curry paste

1 tablespoon unrefined cane sugar

1 can (15 ounces) unsweetened coconut milk [500ml]

4 medium-size red potatoes, peeled and cut into ½-inch [1-cm] dice

1 package (8 ounces) tempeh, cut into ¾-inch [1-cm] cubes [250g]

1 can (15 ounces) baby corn [240g]

1 small crisp apple, cut into ½-inch [1-cm] dice

1 tablespoon soy sauce

2 tablespoons shredded fresh basil, preferably Thai

1. In a large Dutch oven, **cook** the onion in the oil over medium heat until very soft but not brown, 3 to 5 minutes. Add the mushrooms and bell pepper; season with the salt and a grinding of pepper. Cook, stirring often, for 3 to 5 minutes, until slightly softened.

2. In a small bowl, create a wet paste by stirring together 3 tablespoons of the squash soup with the curry paste and sugar. **Stir** into the remaining soup and add to the pan. Stir in the coconut milk. Add the potatoes and tempeh and bring to a boil. Cover, reduce the heat to a simmer, and cook for 20 to 30 minutes, until the potatoes are tender. Stir occasionally to prevent the ingredients from sticking to the bottom of the pot.

3. Add the corn, apple, and soy sauce. **Simmer** for 2 minutes longer to heat through. Serve garnished with fresh basil.

SERVES 4

Blackened fruit jerk tempeh

Looking through cookbooks, you can find dozens of jerk recipes. I added mango to mine and, for the final bold touch, blackened the tempeh in a cast-iron skillet. I found out by accident—when ripe mangoes were not available—that fresh pineapple works equally as well as mango. As I mention every chance I get, a cast-iron skillet is indispensable in the bold cook's kitchen, not to mention on camping trips. This cooking technique really helps make the dish special. Serve with corn relish and mashed potatoes.

½ to 1 fresh Scotch bonnet or habañero pepper, ribs and seeds removed, or hot sauce, to taste

3 garlic cloves, minced

1 teaspoon grated fresh ginger

4 scallions, coarsely chopped

1 large mango, peeled, seeded, and coarsely chopped

2 tablespoons dark rum

1 tablespoon molasses

Juice of 1 lime

1 tablespoon balsamic vinegar

1 tablespoon olive oil

2 tablespoons unrefined cane sugar

1 teaspoon allspice

1 teaspoon dried thyme

½ teaspoon cinnamon

¼ teaspoon grated nutmeg

¼ teaspoon ground cloves

2 packages (8 ounces each) tempeh [500g total]

2 tablespoons vegetable oil

1. In a blender or food processor, puree the hot pepper, garlic, ginger, scallions, mango, rum, molasses, lime juice, vinegar, and olive oil. Add the sugar, allspice, thyme, cinnamon, nutmeg, and cloves. Blend well. Jerk sauce should be thick, but sometimes it can be hard to get the blender turning with all the thick ingredients. If this is the case, gradually add water, 1 tablespoon at a time, to get the blades moving.

2. **Slice** each cake of tempeh in half horizontally so that it is half as thick; then cut each piece in half crosswise so that you end up with 8 cutlets. Put 4 pieces of tempeh into each of 2 large heavy-duty, sealable freezer bags. Pour half the jerk sauce into each bag. Make sure the tempeh pieces are well coated. Seal the bags and lay them on a platter or tray. Refrigerate overnight.

3. Heat a large cast-iron skillet over high heat until very hot. Add 2 teaspoons of the vegetable oil to the pan and heat until beginning to smoke. Add as many cutlets as will fit in a single layer without crowding. **Fry** 1 to 2 minutes on each side, until crisp and blackened. Repeat with the remaining oil and tempeh. Serve immediately.

SERVES 4

Crisp tempeh with honey-mustard sauce

If you're looking for an effortless recipe to help get food on the table fast, this is it. Yet it boasts **a nice gourmet touch—with the flavor of honey, mustard, and wine, and the color of delicate julienne vegetables. I recommend serving this tempeh with quinoa and a salad. If you want, double the recipe and make sandwiches the next day.**

1½ tablespoons powdered mustard

1 tablespoon instant powdered vegetable soup base

1 large carrot, cut into thin matchsticks

1 celery rib, cut into thin matchsticks

½ red bell pepper, cut into thin matchsticks

1 package (8 ounces) tempeh [250g]

¼ cup vegetable oil, for frying [60ml]

Salt

1 cup dry white wine [250ml]

1½ tablespoons honey

½ teaspoon salt

Freshly ground pepper

1. In a small bowl, mix the mustard and vegetable soup base with just enough water to make a paste.

2. Steam the carrot, celery, and red bell pepper until tender but still slightly crunchy, 2 to 3 minutes. Set aside.

3. Slice the tempeh horizontally so that it is half as thick, then cut each piece crosswise in half to create 4 squares.

4. In a large skillet, heat the oil over medium-high until very hot and just shimmering. Add the tempeh squares and fry, turning once, until lightly browned and crisp, 2 to 3 minutes. Drain on paper towels. Season with salt to taste.

5. Discard any oil remaining in the pan. Pour in the wine, keeping a prudent distance; the pan will sizzle and spit a bit. Boil, stirring frequently, until the wine is reduced by half, 2 to 3 minutes. Spoon a couple of tablespoons of the hot wine into

the mustard paste and mix well. Pour the entire mustard sauce back into the pan. Let the liquid reduce for another minute or so, until the sauce begins to thicken.

6. Remove from the heat and stir in the honey. Season with the salt and pepper to taste. Arrange the tempeh on a plate, then drizzle the sauce over it. Top with the steamed vegetables.

SERVES 2

Tempeh buckwheat shepherd's pie

The secret to this savory pie lies in the trio of tempeh, buckwheat, and portobello mushrooms—artfully combined with a variety of flavorings. The result is an original, delicious, substantial meal in a dish. Made ahead, the tempeh filling will taste even better as the flavors combine.

¼ cup toasted buckwheat [60g]

3 large shallots, minced

2½ tablespoons olive oil

1 package (8 ounces) tempeh, shredded or crumbled [250g]

2 medium carrots, peeled and finely diced

1 celery rib, finely diced

2 garlic cloves, minced

1 large portobello mushroom, cut into ½-inch [1-cm] dice

½ teaspoon dried sage

½ teaspoon dried thyme

½ teaspoon dried oregano

½ teaspoon dried rosemary

2 cups vegetable stock or red wine [500ml]

1 tablespoon tomato paste

2 teaspoons barley miso or red miso

1 tablespoon molasses or maple syrup

1 tablespoon red wine vinegar

2 teaspoons soy sauce

2 teaspoons vegetarian Worcestershire sauce

2 teaspoons nutritional yeast powder

1 teaspoon salt

¼ teaspoon freshly ground pepper

Mustard Mashed Potato Topping (recipe follows)

1. **Preheat** the oven to 375°F [190°C]. In a small saucepan, bring ⅔ cup [150ml] water to a boil. Stir in the buckwheat, reduce the heat to medium-low, and cook, stirring occasionally, until just tender, about 10 minutes. Buckwheat cooks very quickly, so keep an eye on it.

2. In a large skillet, **cook** the shallots in 2 tablespoons of the olive oil over medium-low heat until softened and lightly browned, about 3 minutes. Add the tempeh, carrots, celery, garlic, and mushroom. Increase the heat slightly and cook for about 5

minutes, stirring frequently. Add the sage, thyme, oregano, and rosemary. Cook and stir for another minute, until very fragrant. When the mixture begins to stick slightly to the bottom of the pan, turn up the heat and pour in the vegetable stock or wine. Stir in the tomato paste. Bring to a boil and cook until the liquid reduces and the mixture thickens, 3 to 5 minutes.

3. Stir in the miso, molasses, vinegar, soy sauce, Worcestershire sauce, nutritional yeast, salt, pepper, and cooked buckwheat. Spoon into 4 individual gratin dishes or other ovenproof containers. Spread the mashed potato topping over the tempeh mixture and press down firmly. Brush with the remaining olive oil.

4. Bake for 5 to 10 minutes, until the potatoes are just a touch browned on top.

SERVES 4

Mustard mashed potato topping

3 pounds baking potatoes [1.5kg]

1 cup [250ml] plain yogurt, preferably organic, or ½ cup [125ml] plain soy milk or rice milk

1 to 2 tablespoons Dijon mustard, or to taste

1 teaspoon salt

Freshly ground pepper

1. Peel the potatoes and cut into large chunks. Cook in a large saucepan of salted boiling water until soft, 10 to 12 minutes; drain. Pass the potatoes through a ricer or mash with a potato masher until smooth.

2. Add the yogurt or soy milk and mustard to the mashed potatoes and blend very well. Season with the salt and a generous grinding of pepper.

MAKES ABOUT 4 CUPS [1ML]

Tempeh **potato** hash

Many taste sensations will travel through your mouth with each bite of this **bold** dish: sweet, sour, spicy, savory, and hot. It is a somewhat busy recipe, but put your mind at ease by setting yourself up with a lot of prep space and you'll sail right through it. Use Mexican oregano here, if you have it, as its more assertive flavor works nicely in concert with the other strong ingredients. Serve with eggs or rice and a salad. This hash also makes an excellent stuffing for bell peppers or acorn or delicata squash.

N O T E A large nonstick skillet with a lid works well for this dish. It will allow the tempeh to brown without sticking, which it tends to do when grated or crumbled, even with oil, in a regular pan.

About ¼ ounce dried shiitake or porcini mushrooms [7g]

1 chipotle chile, stemmed, cracked open, seeds removed

6 plum tomatoes, cut in half

3 tablespoons olive oil

1 package (8 ounces) tempeh, crumbled or shredded [250g]

1 medium white onion, chopped

1 small fennel bulb (about 6 ounces), cut into small dice [180g]

1 tablespoon dried oregano, preferably Mexican

4 small red potatoes, scrubbed and cut into small cubes

½ pound cremini mushrooms, thinly sliced [250g]

1 tablespoon unrefined cane sugar

½ teaspoon salt

Sprigs of cilantro, for garnish

1. **Preheat** the broiler with the rack set 4 to 6 inches [10 to 15cm] from the heat. In a medium bowl, soak the dried mushrooms and chipotle chile in 2 cups [500ml] hot water until soft, 30 to 45 minutes. Strain and reserve the soaking liquid. Coarsely chop the mushrooms; mince the chile.

2. Set the tomatoes, cut side down, on a baking sheet. **Broil** until the skins are cracked and lightly charred, 5 to 7 minutes. Let cool, then peel and coarsely chop the tomatoes, saving their juices.

3. In a large nonstick skillet, **heat** 2 tablespoons of the olive oil over medium-high heat. Add the tempeh and cook, stirring often, until golden brown, about 5 minutes. Remove from the pan and set aside.

4. Heat the remaining oil in the same skillet over medium heat. **Add** the onion and fennel and cook until soft and lightly browned, 5 to 7 minutes. Stir in the oregano and let cook for a few seconds, until fragrant. Add the potatoes, cremini mushrooms, and chopped dried mushrooms and chipotle chile. Cook until the fresh mushrooms are soft.

5. **Add** the tempeh, the tomatoes with their juices, and the salt to the skillet. Raise the heat to medium-high and cook until the liquid in the pan has evaporated. Add 1 cup [250ml] of the reserved soaking liquid.

6. Bring to a boil, reduce the heat to a simmer, cover, and cook, stirring occasionally, for 15 minutes, or until the potatoes are tender and most of the liquid is absorbed. Season with additional salt or more chiles, if desired. **Serve** hot, garnished with cilantro.

SERVES 4 TO 6

note The recipe calls for 1 dried chipotle chile. This works well, though I feel it only reaches the middle ground for full-on chile flavor. For a more in-depth flavor, use a combination of chiles, such as pasilla negro, ancho, and guajillo. You certainly won't use a whole one of each, but just a piece. (Start with a small amount, then add more as you see fit.) Remember to crack open the chiles first and remove excess seeds before soaking. When the chiles are soft, chop into a pulp. If you're ambitious, soak several, chop them, and use them in hummus or in other spreads, soups, or dips. Seal well and freeze what you can't use in a week.

North African tempeh tagine

I call this my vegetarian goulash, though the sweet-spicy flavors are closer to those of the Mediterranean, as the title implies. I like to serve it with eggs or with rice or couscous and a salad. As with many stews, this one tastes especially good the next day—and believe it or not, even better the day after that. The spices have an almost magical quality to them as they combine in a mouthwatering crescendo. If you don't already, I recommend buying fresh bulk spices rather than using jarred ones that have been in your cabinet for many weeks or months. Fresh spices mean the difference between a decent dish and an outstanding dish.

2 medium carrots, peeled and roll-cut or sliced diagonally into ½-inch [1-cm] pieces

1 teaspoon fenugreek

½ teaspoon cumin seeds

½ teaspoon whole black peppercorns

½ teaspoon coriander seeds

½ teaspoon caraway seeds

½ teaspoon paprika

¼ teaspoon black mustard seeds

2 whole cloves

1 small onion, finely chopped

1 tablespoon olive oil

4 garlic cloves, thinly sliced

6 dates, pitted and coarsely chopped

1 teaspoon tamarind paste

⅔ cup vegetable stock [150ml]

1 package (8 ounces) tempeh, cut into ¾-inch [2-cm] cubes [250g]

2 tomatoes, seeded and coarsely chopped

Salt and hot sauce

1. **Preheat** the oven to 375°F [190°C]. Steam or boil the carrots until they are bright orange and just barely tender, 4 to 5 minutes. Set aside.

2. In a large dry skillet, **toast** the fenugreek, cumin, peppercorns, coriander, caraway, paprika, mustard seeds, and cloves over medium heat until they turn a shade or two darker and become aromatic, 2 to 3 minutes. Stir constantly to prevent burn-

ing. Transfer the spices to a small plate and let cool; then grind to a fine powder in a spice grinder or mini food processor.

3. In the same skillet, **cook** the onion in the olive oil over medium heat until soft and lightly browned, 5 to 7 minutes. Add the garlic and cook for another 2 to 3 minutes, until the garlic is softened. Add the spice mixture and mix well. Cook for another minute or so, until fragrant.

4. In a small bowl, **mash** the chopped dates with a fork. Mix in the tamarind paste and 2 tablespoons of the stock with the back of a spoon until well blended and smooth. Add the remaining vegetable stock to the skillet and bring to a boil. Stir in the date-tamarind combination and mix well. Add the tempeh, tomatoes, and steamed carrots. Season with salt and hot sauce to taste. If the stew seems somewhat dry, add additional vegetable stock or water to make sure the ingredients are just barely covered with liquid. Bring to a boil.

5. Transfer the entire stew to a covered baking dish or casserole. **Bake** for 20 to 30 minutes, until the dish is hot and bubbling and the potatoes are tender.

SERVES 4

note I recommend adding a dash of medium-hot hot sauce to this recipe, not because it's not spicy enough, but because a little extra kick seems to do it just right. Another idea you might find helpful is to double the spice mix and store it for use in this or other recipes you might make in the near future. Sealed well and kept out of direct light, the spice mix will stay fresh for about 3 to 4 weeks.

Drunken tempeh by the sea

Have you ever imagined a vegetarian surf and turf? Well, here it is in concept, anyway—an all-in-one meal, **perfect** for a fall or winter evening. Serve with a side of crunchy green salad. This casserole features hijiki, a mild type of dried dark brown or black seaweed also known as sea vegetable. The hijiki is reconstituted in water before use and is a nutritious addition to salads, soups, and stews.

About 1 ounce hijiki [30g]

1 medium onion, chopped

1½ tablespoons olive oil

½ yellow bell pepper, chopped

½ red bell pepper, chopped

3 garlic cloves, minced

1 teaspoon chili powder

½ teaspoon paprika

½ teaspoon cinnamon

1½ cups Guinness Extra Stout or other dark beer [375ml]

1 tablespoon hearty mustard, such as Dijon or country-style

1 tablespoon tomato paste

1 teaspoon tamarind paste

1 tablespoon vegetarian Worcestershire sauce

½ teaspoon salt

⅛ teaspoon freshly ground pepper

½ cup Bhutanese red rice [100g]

1 package (8 ounces) tempeh, cut into ½-inch [1-cm] cubes [250g]

1. **Preheat** the oven to 375°F [190°C]. Soak the hijiki in 1 cup [250ml] warm water until softened, about 15 minutes. Drain, reserving the soaking water.

2. In a large skillet, **cook** the onion in the olive oil over medium heat until softened and lightly browned, 5 to 7 minutes. Add the bell peppers and garlic and cook until softened, another 2 to 3 minutes. Add the chili powder, paprika, and cinnamon, and cook until fragrant, about 1 minute. Pour in the Guinness and ½ cup [125ml] of the reserved soaking water.

3. Bring to a boil. **Stir** in the mustard, tomato paste, tamarind paste, Worcestershire sauce, salt, and pepper. Cook and stir for 1 minute, then add the rice and tempeh and mix well. Pour into a 2-quart [2L] casserole dish.

4. Cover and **bake** for 35 to 40 minutes, or until the casserole is hot and bubbling, the rice is tender, and most of the liquid is absorbed.

SERVES 4

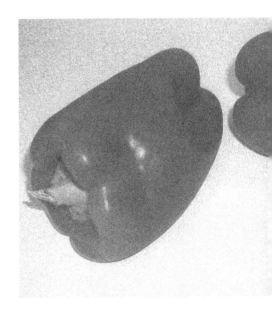

Jarlsburg tempeh casserole

The most comforting of comfort foods: the tuna casserole. But hold on. This is a tempeh casserole, made with crisp tempeh and Jarlsburg cheese and topped with cornflakes. I recommend using a high-quality natural foods cornflake or combination grain cornflake for the topping.

Vegetable cooking spray

1 package (8 ounces) tempeh [250g]

¼ cup canola or high-oleic safflower oil [60ml]

Salt

1 small onion, chopped

1 small red bell pepper, finely diced

3 tablespoons unbleached all-purpose flour [25ml]

2 cups plain soy milk [500ml]

1 tablespoon vegetarian Worcestershire sauce

1 cup grated Jarlsburg cheese [80g]

2 cups cooked egg noodles [280g]

1 cup frozen peas [120g]

Freshly ground pepper

½ cup crushed cornflakes or dry unseasoned bread crumbs [35g]

1. **Preheat** the oven to 375°F [190°C]. Coat a 2- to 3-quart [2- to 3-L] casserole dish with cooking spray. Split the tempeh cake horizontally so it is half as thick; then cut it crosswise in half to make 4 squares.

2. In a large deep skillet or flameproof casserole, **heat** the oil over medium-high heat until very hot. Add the tempeh squares and fry, turning once, until lightly browned on both sides, 2 to 3 minutes. Drain on paper towels and sprinkle with salt. As soon as the tempeh is cool enough to handle, cut it into ½-inch [1-cm] cubes.

3. Add the onion to the oil remaining in the pan and cook over medium heat, **stirring** several times, until lightly browned, 5 to 7 minutes. Add the bell pepper and cook until softened, about 3 minutes longer.

4. Add the flour and cook, stirring constantly, for 1 minute. **Whisk** in the soy milk and bring to a boil, stirring frequently until the sauce thickens. Reduce the heat and simmer about 3 minutes. Stir in the Worcestershire sauce.

5. **Remove** from the heat and stir in the Jarlsburg cheese until melted and smooth, then add the noodles and peas. Season with salt and pepper to taste. Transfer to the prepared baking dish.

6. Sprinkle the cornflakes or bread crumbs over all and **bake** for 25 to 30 minutes, until lightly browned and crisp on top.

SERVES 4 TO 6

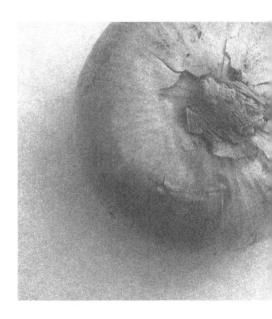

6 A BOLD WAY

with BEANS: Powerhouse Dishes

In this chapter I have herded together a stable of very compelling recipes that

cover a wide variety of beans, including lentils and chickpeas, also known as

garbanzo beans. A few titles may sound familiar, but I think you will find the taste

sensations and flavor combinations unique. And there are any number of new ideas for using this amazingly versatile and nutritious vegetarian staple. The recipes are substantial and interesting, and jammed with flavor.

Some of these dishes, such as the incredibly rich and intense Three-Bean, Three-Chile Chili and the spicy Black Bean Tacos, feature beans. Other recipes, like Spicy Bean Tamales and Moroccan Tagine with Chickpeas, Olives, and Prunes include beans as a small but integral part of the recipe.

Because they are relatively bland, beans and other legumes combine with many foods quite naturally. It's hard to find anything that doesn't go with them in one way or another. Beans in hot and cold salads, beans with pasta, beans with caramelized fennel, beans with plantains, beans with all kinds of savory sauces—the list goes on. Beans are rich in protein, calcium, phosphorus, and iron. They're also an excellent source of fiber. It's no coincidence that vegetarians have consistently found beans to be a central component of their food repertoire. Yet it's not uncommon to hear vegetarians complain about beans as well. "They're common; they're ordinary. Beans, beans, beans—I'm sick of them!"

Well, I feel your pain, which is why I have included this chapter just on beans. I think you will find plenty of new and special recipes to choose from. We'll start with what you should know.

Canned or dried is generally the first question about beans. They both have their advantages, and sometimes it doesn't make much, if any, difference which one you use. But there *are* differences, so let's discuss a few. Canned beans are often used simply as a matter of convenience, other times because they tend to keep their shape, giving them an advantage in certain salads. They also work well pureed—in hummus, for example—when texture is not essential. Dried beans are available in many dozens of varieties, while cans generally offer far fewer choices, though the list is growing. As a matter of expediency, it is difficult to beat a can of beans. You might compare them to frozen peas—no reason not to use them in many instances. Yet, when prepared properly, dried beans tend to be creamier, and there is no question as to what is in them. I like to use dried beans when making stews and soups.

A few bean basics

ALWAYS PICK THROUGH dried beans to make sure you have discarded any pebbles or other small objectionable tidbits that occasionally make their way into the mix.

Except for lentils and split peas, you will want to soak dried beans. This softens and rehydrates them, expediting the cooking process considerably. It also releases complex sugars that can cause gas. If you have the time, soak beans overnight. This creates anxiety for some people, who avoid a recipe altogether when they see "Soak overnight. . . ."

Here are ways to overcome that anxiety. Plan ahead. You may very well know beforehand when you will be cooking beans, so soaking the night before will not be a problem. Second, consider soaking first thing when you get up in the morning. Six or eight hours later, when you come home from work or are ready to cook, they will be softened and ready. And many times, because I forgot to do it earlier or felt it wasn't necessary, I have soaked beans for only the amount of time I had available. Meaning, if you have only four hours to soak beans, so be it. Your beans will cook up just fine; they may just take a little longer to cook.

To soak beans, cover them with several inches of cold water. Before cooking, discard the soaking water, rinse the beans, and cook them in a fresh pot of cold water. As a rule, keep the water level about 2 inches above the top of the beans. Add hot water as necessary when the water evaporates while cooking.

Cooking times vary based on how old the beans are and how long they've been soaked. Cooking very old beans may be an exercise in futility. Dried beans should be from a recent crop. Beans that have been sitting for many months (not to speak of years!) can lose flavor and become tough and very difficult to cook no matter how long you soak them. Because you will probably not know this information, buy where turnover is frequent. Generally, beans that have been soaked will cook in about 45 minutes to an hour, sometimes an hour and 15 minutes. Taste after 45 minutes to determine if they are ready.

Salt and acid slow and occasionally prohibit the cooking process of beans. Avoid adding salt or acidic ingredients like tomatoes or lemon juice until the beans have become as soft as you want them. Stir them in after the beans have almost reached their desired texture.

Very briefly, here are facts on the digestion of beans. Beans contain considerable amounts of indigestible sugars. Many people have a hard time digesting beans because they either eat them infrequently and their system has not adjusted or because the beans were not prepared properly beforehand. Soaking beans and changing the water before cooking them works wonders. So does adding a piece of kombu (a Japanese sea vegetable) during the cooking process or ¼ teaspoon of the Mexican herb epazote. The flavor of the kombu is minimal, and it tends to break apart. Any large pieces that remain can be removed. The epazote does add some flavor. It is reputed that cooking with certain other herbs and spices—ginger, thyme, caraway, coriander, fennel—also aids in digestion. Interestingly, some foods that are often cooked or eaten with beans, like onions, garlic, and peppers, can cause gas, and *they* in fact may be the gassy culprits.

Finally, when buying canned beans, look for organic. Generally, they contain only water, sea salt, and occasionally a sea vegetable. In most cases, they are actually a decent product and, when you just need a cup or two of cooked beans, are perfectly acceptable. Though canned beans are one of those store-bought ingredients that go a long way in terms of saving time, they don't save money as, ounce per ounce, dried beans are usually much less expensive. What is the bottom line? The type of recipe and the amount of time you have to cook will determine your use of canned or dried beans.

White bean and roasted fennel salad with honey-miso dressing

This salad speaks for itself, both visually and with its flavor. When roasted and browned, fresh fennel takes on a lovely nutty quality. Serve with a simple grain dish and a green salad.

½ pound dried white beans (1 cup) [250g]

1 large fennel bulb, trimmed and coarsely chopped, leaves reserved

½ red onion, thinly sliced

1 head of garlic, cloves separated and sliced into thick slivers

2 tablespoons olive oil

1 teaspoon salt

½ teaspoon freshly ground pepper

Honey-Miso Dressing (recipe follows)

8 large cherry tomatoes, quartered

1. **Place** the beans in a large pot with enough cold water to cover by about 2 inches [5cm]. Soak for 6 to 8 hours or overnight.

2. Drain the beans and cover again with fresh water. Bring to a **boil**; reduce the heat to a simmer and cook until the beans are tender but not falling apart, 45 to 60 minutes. Drain and rinse under cold running water until cool. Drain well.

3. While the beans are cooking, preheat the oven to 375°F [190°C]. In a medium bowl, **toss** the fennel, red onion, and garlic with the olive oil to coat. Season with ½ teaspoon of the salt and ¼ teaspoon of the pepper. Spread out in a baking dish or on a baking sheet and roast, stirring every 20 minutes, for 1 hour, or until the vegetables are lightly browned.

4. In a large bowl, **combine** the beans, roasted vegetables, and half the dressing. Toss to mix well. Add the cherry tomatoes and toss gently with the remaining dressing. Season with the remaining salt and pepper. Garnish with the reserved fennel leaves. If you have time, let the salad stand at room temperature for an hour before serving, tossing occasionally, to allow the flavors to develop.

SERVES 4 TO 6

Honey-miso dressing

¼ cup extra virgin olive oil [60ml]

2 tablespoons white wine vinegar

2 teaspoons honey

2 teaspoons chickpea miso or white miso

In a small bowl, whisk together all of the ingredients until well blended.

MAKES ABOUT ½ CUP [125ML]

Fava bean and artichoke salad with mint and feta cheese

It takes many favas to make a hill of beans. That's no joke. Three pounds [1.5kg] in the pod may easily yield less than a pound [500g] of edible beans. But because they are so large, favas are fun to shuck, and because of their subtle flavor, delicious to eat. This is a very attractive, enticing salad, definitely worth the preparation. Because the fava bean season is so short—spring and summer—at other times of the year, I suggest you substitute a pound [500g] of frozen baby lima beans.

Canned artichoke hearts are used here because they save so much work, but if you are so inclined, cook 3 fresh artichoke bottoms until just tender and slice them or cut them into eighths.

3 pounds fresh fava beans, shelled [1.5kg]

1 can (16 ounces) artichoke hearts, drained and quartered [500g]

1 ounce sun-dried tomatoes, softened in hot water if dry, cut into strips [30g]

2 tablespoons shredded fresh mint

2 medium shallots, thinly sliced

2 garlic cloves, minced

⅓ cup extra virgin olive oil [75ml]

3 tablespoons fresh lemon juice

½ teaspoon salt

¼ teaspoon freshly ground pepper

2 ounces feta cheese, crumbled (about ½ cup) [60g]

1. **Fill** a bowl with ice water and set aside. In a large saucepan of boiling salted water, cook the beans for 2 to 3 minutes, depending upon their size. Fava beans soften very quickly, so do not overcook. Drain and immediately plunge the beans into the ice water. Drain again, then peel the outer opaque skin off to reveal the bright green bean inside. Do this by pinching off a small piece of the skin at an edge and then squeezing gently to pop the naked bean out.

2. In a mixing bowl, **combine** the beans with the artichokes, sun-dried tomatoes, 1 tablespoon of the mint, the shallots, and the garlic. Toss gently.

3. **Drizzle** on the olive oil and lemon juice. Season with the salt and pepper. Toss again to coat. Transfer to a serving dish and sprinkle the feta cheese and remaining mint on top. Serve at room temperature.

SERVES 4 TO 6

Mung bean and caramelized fennel salad

I prefer a cast-iron skillet for this dish because it works so well with the **rich** caramelizing effects of the sugar. If you don't have one, substitute a sauté pan or other skillet.

Fennel varies greatly in size, so you may buy one large or two smaller bulbs to yield 2 cups [250g]. In either case, it doesn't matter much. You can always have more or less fennel in your salad. I prefer more. Serve with a side of Spicy Yogurt Sauce (page 111).

1 cup dried mung beans [200g]

2 cups coarsely chopped fennel bulb, excluding stems and leaves [250g]

3 tablespoons extra virgin olive oil

2 tablespoons unrefined cane sugar

1 teaspoon crushed hot red pepper

2 garlic cloves, minced

2 tablespoons lemon juice

2 teaspoons soy sauce

¾ cup shredded radicchio [175ml]

4 scallions, thinly sliced

Salt and freshly ground pepper

2 tablespoons balsamic vinegar

1 cup bean sprouts [250ml]

1. **Soak** the mung beans in a large saucepan of cold water to cover for 6 to 8 hours or overnight. Drain and cover again with fresh water. Bring to a boil, reduce the heat to a simmer, and cook the beans until just tender, 45 to 60 minutes. If they get too soft, they tend to split open and make a less aesthetically pleasing salad. Drain and rinse the beans under cold water until the heat is completely dissipated. Drain well. Set aside in a large bowl.

2. In a large cast-iron skillet, **sauté** the fennel in 1½ tablespoons of the olive oil over medium heat, stirring occasionally, until lightly browned, about 10 minutes.

3. **Add** the sugar, hot pepper, and garlic. Raise the heat a spot so the sugar melts and bubbles, then return to medium heat and cook, stirring often, until the sugar caramelizes and coats the fennel, about 5 minutes.

4. Add 1 tablespoon of the lemon juice and 1 teaspoon of the soy sauce and cook, **stirring,** for another minute. Remove from the heat; add the fennel to the mung beans along with the radicchio and scallions. Toss with the remaining 1½ tablespoons olive oil, 1 tablespoon lemon juice, and 1 teaspoon soy sauce and the balsamic vinegar. Season with salt and pepper to taste.

5. Serve at room temperature. **Top** each plate with a small handful of bean sprouts.

SERVES 4 TO 6

Black bean and
plantain salad

This is a very hearty salad featuring plantains, which are a starchy, mild type of banana used predominately in Latin American cuisine. As an ingredient, plantains might compare to America's potato. They must be cooked and are not eaten raw, which is why they are also referred to as *cooking bananas*. The salad's lively flavor and aroma make an appealing presentation.

½ pound (1 cup) dried black beans [180g]

1 cup long-grain white rice [200g]

1 teaspoon salt

¼ teaspoon freshly ground pepper

6 tablespoons vegetable oil

2 plantains, peeled and cut diagonally into ¼-inch [.5-cm] slices

1 large red bell pepper, cut into ½-inch [1-cm] dice

1 fresh jalapeño pepper, seeded and minced

3 garlic cloves, minced

1½ tablespoons cumin seeds

2 tablespoons unrefined sugar cane

2 to 3 tablespoons extra virgin oil

6 tablespoons lime juice

¼ cup coarsely chopped cilantro [60ml]

Hot sauce

1. Place the beans in a large saucepan and add enough cold water to cover by 2 inches [5cm]. Let stand 6 to 8 hours or overnight. **Drain,** return the beans to the pan, and cover them with fresh water. Bring to a boil, reduce the heat to a simmer, and cook until the beans are tender but not falling apart, 45 to 60 minutes. Drain and rinse under cold running water until cool. Drain well.

2. In a medium saucepan, **cook** the rice in 2 cups [500ml] lightly salted water, covered, until the rice is tender and liquid is absorbed, 15 to 18 minutes. Transfer the cooked rice to a large bowl and fluff with a fork. Season with ½ teaspoon of the salt and ⅛ teaspoon of the pepper.

3. **Heat** the vegetable oil in a large heavy skillet, preferably cast-iron, over medium-high heat. Add the plantain slices, in batches if necessary, and fry, pressing down gently with a spatula from time to time, until golden brown on both sides, about 2 to 3 minutes. Reduce the heat slightly if the plantains brown too quickly. Drain on paper towels and sprinkle with salt. Pour all but 2 tablespoons oil from the pan.

4. Add the bell pepper to the skillet and sauté over medium-high heat until softened and slightly browned around the edges, 3 to 4 minutes. **Add** the jalapeño pepper, garlic, cumin seeds, and sugar and sauté 1 minute longer, stirring constantly.

5. Add the cooked beans, fried plantains, and sautéed pepper mixture to the rice. Add the olive oil, lime juice, and cilantro. Mix well. **Season** with additional salt and pepper to taste. Serve at room temperature. Pass a bottle of hot sauce on the side.

SERVES 6

Adzuki bean and
butternut squash stew

Many people are not familiar with adzuki beans, though they are popular in Chinese and Japanese cooking. Adzuki beans are quick cooking and extremely **nutritious,** and they have a more distinctive, somewhat nuttier taste than most beans. They make a good substitute for lentils in soups, salads, and stews. Serve this recipe with brown or wild rice.

½ to ¾ cup vegetable stock [125 to 200ml]

1 tablespoon minced fresh ginger

1 tablespoon soy sauce

1 tablespoon toasted sesame oil

1 small butternut squash, peeled, seeded, and cut into small chunks

2 cans (15 ounces each) [850g total] adzuki beans, drained, or 1 cup [180g] dried adzuki beans, soaked, and cooked until tender

1 tablespoon red miso or barley miso

Salt and freshly ground pepper

1. In a large pot or saucepan, bring the stock, ginger, soy sauce, and sesame oil to a **simmer.** Add the squash and cook, covered, for 10 to 15 minutes, or until the squash is soft.

2. Add the beans and mix well, continuing to cook for another 2 to 3 minutes. Stir in the miso and season with salt and pepper, if it's needed. Add additional stock if the stew becomes too dry.

SERVES 4 TO 6

Almond coconut dal

Lentils are high in protein, fiber, and complex carbohydrates. They also provide an excellent source of folic acid. By the way, did you know that in the Old Testament, Esau sold his birthright for a pot of lentils? Needless to say, you don't have to go that far; just enjoy them. Serve with warm pitas, as salad, and with Roasted Root Vegetables (page 257).

1½ tablespoons olive oil

10 fresh chanterelle or shiitake mushrooms, thinly sliced

2 large shallots, coarsely chopped

¼ teaspoon salt

Freshly ground pepper

1 cup dried lentils [200g]

1 can (15 ounces) unsweetened coconut milk [450ml]

2½ cups vegetable stock or water [675ml]

2 tablespoons almond butter

2 tablespoons tomato paste

Hot sauce

1. In a large heavy saucepan or Dutch oven, **heat** the olive oil over medium heat. Add the mushrooms and shallots and cook until the mushrooms are tender, about 5 minutes. Season with the salt and a generous grinding of pepper.

2. **Add** the lentils, half the coconut milk, and 2 cups [375ml] of the stock. Cover, bring to a boil, and reduce the heat to low. Simmer for about 40 minutes, or until the lentils are softened and the liquid is mostly absorbed.

3. Add the remaining coconut milk and continue to **cook** over low heat for another 10 minutes.

4. While the lentils are cooking, **mix** the almond butter and tomato paste in a small bowl with the remaining ½ cup [125ml] of the stock until smooth. Stir into the pot of lentils. Season with additional salt and pepper if needed.

5. In a blender or food processor, **puree** 1 to 2 cups [250 to 500ml] of the cooked lentils with some of the liquid and return to the pot. Remove from the heat, stir in hot sauce to taste, and serve.

SERVES 4 TO 6

Roasted potatoes, chickpeas, and spinach with spicy cashew sauce

This is an exceptionally flavorful, quick meal-in-a-pot. I like to use nut butters other than peanut when I can. Cashew butter is an excellent vehicle for flavor, and it has a silky consistency. Cashew butter is, in fact, very creamy, almost luscious, not unlike dairy butter. Serve with a bowl of plain yogurt, warm bread, and your favorite chutney.

2 pounds small red potatoes, scrubbed and quartered [1kg]

¼ cup peanut oil [60ml]

¾ teaspoon salt

1 tablespoon fennel seeds

1 tablespoon ground cumin

1 teaspoon turmeric

1 cinnamon stick

1 medium onion, coarsely chopped

1 fresh jalapeño pepper, minced

1½ inches of fresh ginger, peeled and minced [4cm]

2 garlic cloves, minced

2 cans (15 ounces each) chickpeas, drained [850g total]

½ cup cashew butter [120g]

2 tablespoons tomato paste

¾ cup vegetable stock or water [200ml]

1 bunch of spinach (about 4 ounces), washed, thick stems discarded, leaves coarsely chopped or left whole if baby leaves [125g]

¼ teaspoon freshly ground pepper

1. **Preheat** the oven to 400°F [200°C]. Toss the quartered potatoes with 1 tablespoon of the peanut oil and ¼ teaspoon of the salt. Spread out on a baking sheet and roast 35 to 45 minutes, or until tender and nicely browned. Turn the potatoes once while they roast for even browning.

2. In a large dry skillet, **toast** the fennel seeds, cumin, turmeric, and cinnamon stick over medium heat, stirring, until fragrant and a shade or two darker, 1 to 2 minutes.

3. Add the remaining oil, the onion, jalapeño pepper, ginger, and garlic to the spices. **Cook,** stirring occasionally, until the onion is very soft and a touch browned, about 5 minutes. Add the chickpeas, cashew butter, tomato paste, and vegetable stock, stirring to blend. Bring to a boil, reduce the heat to a simmer, and cook until the sauce thickens, 5 to 7 minutes.

4. Stir in the roasted potatoes and the spinach. Cook just until the spinach wilts, 1 to 2 minutes. **Season** with the remaining salt and the pepper. Discard the cinnamon stick before serving.

SERVES 6

Moroccan tagine with chickpeas, olives, and prunes

A tagine, a stew named for the conical earthenware vessel it is traditionally cooked in, is a richly flavored dish loaded with herbs, spices, and perfectly cooked vegetables. In traditional Moroccan restaurants, the stew is slowly simmered on the bottom of a couscousier while the couscous steams above. To simplify, I bake this stew with excellent results. Dried or canned beans work equally well in this dish, but given all the other ingredients and prep work involved, I recommend canned beans to make your life easier.

4 shallots, coarsely chopped

1 celery rib, chopped

1 inch of fresh ginger, peeled and slivered [2.5cm]

2 garlic cloves, slivered

1 cinnamon stick

2 tablespoons olive oil

2 teaspoons paprika

2 teaspoons ground cumin

2 teaspoons ground coriander

1 teaspoon salt

1 teaspoon freshly ground black pepper

1/4 teaspoon cayenne pepper

1 can (32 ounces) crushed tomatoes [1 L]

1 can (15 ounces) cooked chickpeas [425g]

1 small butternut squash or sweet potato, peeled and cut into bite-size chunks

1 large carrot, peeled and cut into small bite-size chunks

1/2 fennel bulb, cut into 1-inch [2.5-cm] pieces

1/2 to 1 cup vegetable stock or water [125 to 250ml]

1/2 teaspoon saffron threads, crushed

1/2 head of cauliflower, cut into bite-size florets

6 ounces green beans, steamed until tender [180g]

3 ounces pitted kalamata olives [90g]

4 ounces pitted prunes, cut in half [120g]

3 tablespoons coarsely chopped parsley

1. **Preheat** the oven to 350°F [175°C]. In a large flameproof casserole, cook the shallots, celery, ginger, garlic, and cinnamon stick in the olive oil over medium-low heat for 5 to 7 minutes, stirring often, until the vegetables are softened but not browned.

2. Add the paprika, cumin, coriander, salt, black pepper, and cayenne. **Cook,** stirring, for about 1 minute, until the spices are nicely fragrant. Stir in the crushed tomatoes, then add the chickpeas, squash, carrots, and fennel. Pour in just enough vegetable stock to cover. Mix well and add the saffron. Cover and bring to a boil.

3. Transfer to the oven and **bake** for 20 minutes. Add the cauliflower and return to the oven for 10 to 20 minutes, or until the vegetables are just tender.

4. About 5 minutes before the tagine is done, stir in the green beans, olives, and prunes. **Garnish** with the parsley and serve hot over couscous.

SERVES 6 TO 8

Black bean tofu tacos

Black bean tacos are a special favorite of mine. It's the cooking techniques and special care you put into preparing this dish that make it simply exquisite—roasting the chiles, roasting and peeling the tomatoes, cooking the thinly sliced onion until it is soft and sweet. There are a few steps, yes, but they are not complicated. The recipe calls for a cast-iron skillet; I find it's the best tool for roasting garlic and chiles on the stovetop.

1¼ pound ripe tomatoes, cored and cut horizontally in half [625g]

4 garlic cloves, unpeeled

2 small serrano peppers or 1 jalapeño pepper, stems removed

1 large white onion, thinly sliced

2 tablespoons olive oil

2½ teaspoons oregano, preferably Mexican

1¼ teaspoon cumin seeds, lightly crushed

2 teaspoons unrefined cane sugar

1 teaspoon salt

2 to 2½ cups cooked black beans [330 to 400g]

½ to ⅔ pound firm tofu, pressed dry, cut into ½" cubes [300g]*

1½ ripe avocados

8 corn tortillas, steamed until hot and tender

Your favorite salsa (or one of mine), for topping

1. **Preheat** the broiler with the rack set 5 to 6 inches [13 to 15cm] from the heat. Set out the tomatoes, skin side up, on a baking pan. Broil until the tomatoes are slightly charred and the skins are wrinkled and peeling off, 3 to 5 minutes. When cool, pull off the skins. Coarsely chop the tomatoes, saving the juice.

2. In a medium-size cast-iron skillet set over medium heat, **dry-roast** the garlic and hot peppers, turning until the garlic skins are browned in spots, 5 to 7 minutes, and the peppers are blistered and soft, 10 to 15 minutes. When cool, peel the garlic and smash into a paste or coarsely chop. Stem and seed the peppers and coarsely chop them.

*Tofu is usually sold in 16-ounce [500-g] packages. For this recipe, you will need less than that amount. If you are not doubling the recipe, cover the remaining tofu in cold water and refrigerate.

3. In the same pan over medium-high heat, **sauté** the onion in the olive oil until very soft and lightly browned, 7 to 9 minutes.

4. Add the toasted garlic and peppers and the oregano, cumin seeds, sugar, and salt to the onion. **Cook,** stirring, for 1 minute. Add the cooked beans and the chopped tomatoes with their juices. Cook, stirring often, until the mixture begins to thicken slightly. If you like, mash some of the beans in the pan.

5. **Fold** in the tofu cubes and reduce the heat to medium-low. Simmer the bean filling for a few minutes before serving.

6. Peel and mash the avocado. To make tacos, spread a tablespoon or so of avocado over each warm tortilla. **Top** with the black bean filling and salsa to taste. Roll up and eat.

MAKES 8 TACOS; SERVES 4

note   If you have a lower-quality pan that is thin and tends to burn easily, I recommend spreading out aluminum foil in the pan to roast the garlic and chiles. It will help diffuse the heat.

Spicy bean tamales

Traditional tamales are made with pork or beef, not to mention animal lard. This vegetarian version is relatively easy once you locate two key ingredients: masa harina, which is made from dried corn that is boiled in lime, then hulled and finely ground, and dried corn husks. Both can be found in Mexican specialty stores, *bodegas*, and many supermarkets.

Serve your tamales warm, topped with salsa or fresh guacamole and a salad or with rice and beans. A large bamboo steamer is ideal for this recipe or a two-steamer insert. I made the recipe easier by using organic canned beans but, as always, dried can be used if that is your preference.

16 dried cornhusks

Spicy Two-Bean Filling (recipe follows)

2 cups [250 g] fresh or frozen corn kernels

1 cup masa harina [130g]

1 teaspoon baking powder

1 teaspoon salt

½ teaspoon freshly ground pepper

2 teaspoons maple syrup

½ to ⅔ cup water [125 to 150ml]

1. **Sort** through the cornhusks and pick out the largest ones; try to get them approximately the same size. Clean them of any debris, tie them with a string, and submerge completely in a bowl of warm water. Soak for about 1 hour, or until pliable. The recipe makes 8 tamales, but you'll want to have a few extra husks on hand in case you need to double-wrap some.

2. While the husks are softening, **prepare** the bean filling.

3. **Puree** the corn in a food processor. Add the masa harina, baking powder, salt, pepper, and maple syrup. Turn the machine on and gradually add enough water to form a thick paste, spreadable but not too loose.

4. Dry the softened cornhusks and begin to fill them as follows: **Spread** one out on a clean cutting board with the narrower end facing you. (If the husks are small, dou-

ble them up side by side, overlapping slightly and placing the narrow end of one next to the wide end of the other.) Spoon 2 generous tablespoons of corn filling on the upper third of the husk (toward the thicker end). With a butter knife, spread the filling into a rectangular shape, leaving a ¾-inch [2-cm] margin around the top and sides and plenty of room on the bottom third of the husk. Line 1 tablespoon of bean filling down the middle of the corn mixture and gently roll or fold in the sides to form a cone shape. Fold the narrow end up over the seam.

5. **Arrange** the tamales, seam side down, in a steamer. Cover with extra husks and steam for about 1 hour. Let the tamales rest for 3 to 5 minutes before serving.

MAKES 8 TAMALES; SERVES 4

Spicy two-bean filling

1 small onion, minced

2 garlic cloves, minced

½ fresh hot pepper (your choice), seeded and minced

1 tablespoon olive oil

1 cup cooked or canned adzuki beans [170g]

1 cup cooked or canned kidney beans [160g]

½ tablespoon chili powder or 1 teaspoon chipotle chile powder

2 teaspoons molasses

1 tablespoon coarsely chopped cilantro

Salt and freshly ground pepper

Cook the onion, garlic, and hot pepper in the olive oil over low heat until soft, about 5 to 7 minutes. Add the adzuki and kidney beans and continue to cook for another minute or so. With a potato masher or large wooden spoon, **mash** the beans until about half are mashed (this should take only 2 or 3 mashes). Add the chili powder, molasses, and cilantro. Season with salt and pepper to taste.

MAKES ABOUT 2½ CUPS [325ML]

Three-bean, three-chile chili with seitan and sun-dried tomatoes

I take my chili seriously, which is why I am often disappointed with the industrial sludge that passes for the real thing in many restaurants. Such chilis are either too soupy or lack any kind of vigor or character. A lot of interesting things are going on in this chili. The fusion of different dried chiles plus the sun-dried tomatoes and an interesting variety of spices and beans Because the flavors will triumphantly build as the hours go by, I highly recommend that you make this in advance.

½ cup dried adzuki beans [90g]

½ cup dried black beans [90g]

½ cup dried white cannellini beans [90g]

3 ounces sun-dried tomatoes [90g]

3 dried pasilla chiles

2 dried mulato or ancho chiles

1 dried chipotle chile

6 garlic cloves, unpeeled

2 tablespoons olive oil

2 medium onions, coarsely chopped

1 celery rib, chopped

1 large red bell pepper, cut into thin strips

1 large yellow bell pepper, cut into thin strips

1 tablespoon cumin seeds, lightly crushed

1 tablespoon dried basil

1 tablespoon dried Mexican oregano

1 teaspoon salt

2 cinnamon sticks

1 cup apple juice [250ml]

1 cup dark beer or vegetable stock [250ml]

3 tablespoons balsamic vinegar

1 tablespoon soy sauce

1 tablespoon molasses

1 pound [500g] packaged seitan, cut into ½-inch [1-cm] chunks

1 bunch of scallions, thinly sliced

1 cup Mexican queso a ñejo or feta cheese, or more to taste [125g]

1. **Rinse** all the beans and pick them over to remove any grit. Place them in a large pot and add enough cold water to cover by 2 inches [5cm]. Let stand for 6 to 8 hours or overnight. Drain, return the beans to the pan, and cover them with fresh water. Bring to a boil, reduce the heat to a simmer, and cook until the beans are tender but not falling apart, 45 to 60 minutes. Drain, reserving 1 cup [250ml] of the bean liquid, rinse briefly, and drain well. Return the beans to the cooking pot.

2. While the beans are cooking, soak the tomatoes in hot water to cover until they are soft, about 15 minutes. **Drain** and coarsely chop the tomatoes.

3. In a dry cast-iron skillet, **toast** the chiles over medium heat, 2 or 3 at a time, by laying them flat on the pan and pressing down with a spatula for 15 to 30 seconds, until they crackle and give off a slight wisp of smoke. Be careful not to burn them. Flip over and repeat on the other side. Transfer to a medium bowl. When all the chiles are toasted, cover them with very hot water and let soak until very soft, about 30 minutes.

4. In the same cast-iron skillet, toast the unpeeled garlic, stirring occasionally, until lightly browned, 7 to 10 minutes. Set aside and let cool, then peel. **Place** in a blender or food processor. Add the softened chiles and ½ cup [125ml] of the reserved soaking liquid. Puree until smooth. Add a little more liquid if the mixture is too thick.

5. In the same skillet, **heat** the olive oil over medium-high heat. Add the onions and cook, stirring often, until very soft and lightly browned, 7 to 9 minutes. Add the celery and the bell peppers and cook until tender, about 3 minutes. Add the cumin, basil, oregano, salt, and cinnamon sticks and cook, stirring, for about 1 minute, until the spices are fragrant and begin sticking to the bottom of the pan. Add the chile-garlic puree and cook, stirring constantly, for 1 to 2 minutes.

7. Immediately pour in the apple juice and beer or broth. **Stir** in the vinegar, soy sauce, and molasses. Add the cooked beans, seitan, and half the scallions. Bring to a boil, reduce the heat to a simmer, and cook, partially covered, until the chili is thick and rich-tasting, 45 to 60 minutes. Add more reserved bean liquid if you think the chili needs more moisture. Season with additional salt and pepper to taste. Serve in bowls with the cheese and remaining scallions sprinkled on top.

SERVE 6 TO 8

note This recipe calls for seitan, either homemade or store-bought. If making home-made, you will need to prepare it ahead of time. However, because there are already several steps in making this recipe, I think using store-bought seitan is perfectly acceptable.

7

PASTA, RISOTTO, and POLENTA:

Comfort Carbos

The triumphant Italian trio of pasta, risotto, and polenta has been effortlessly

assimilated into America's gourmet cuisine. These three primary carbohydrates

and quintessential comfort foods all have the easy distinction of *not* being food

especially for vegetarians *or* meat-eaters. They belong on everyone's plate

and thus form a significant 1-2-3 punch as part of a bold vegetarian chef's cooking repertoire. Most of us have eaten pasta throughout our lives in one fashion or another, as has the world for at least 1,000 years or so. Risotto, made from certain types of Italian rice (like Arborio) is a creamy, luxurious treat that has been served in many restaurants for quite some time now. Making it at home is easy if you follow a few simple techniques. Polenta, or Italian cornmeal, has a rich and remarkable culinary history. Interestingly enough, however, many people are only vaguely aware of what polenta is or how to cook it.

The recipes in this chapter reflect a range of flavors and techniques. Nonetheless, most don't stray too far from their roots, often showcasing the beauty of simplicity. I also cover culinary ground that you might not have trod before. Bow Tie Pasta with Roasted Asparagus, Oven-Dried Tomatoes, and Crisp Sage Leaves in Vegetable Broth takes pasta to a special place, both aesthetically and at a down-to-earth level. Asparagus and Fennel Risotto has an interesting kick and polish to it. And Broiled Polenta with Chipotle–Mushroom Ragout highlights a beautiful smoky, savory sauce that complements the polenta, broiled to browned perfection.

Pasta

When it comes to pasta, everyone seems to prefer a particular shape. While it's a whim, I personally think bow ties taste better than ziti, for example, even though they are made from essentially the same ingredients. Actually, textures and shapes *do* make a difference, though, in semi-essential matters, like how sauce clings, how the dish is plated, and how it appears next to other foods on the plate.

When eating in exceptional restaurants, I still find myself amazed at how such an apparently simple dish—pasta with smoked eggplant and fresh tomato, for example—is so touching, so perfectly appealing. The pasta is neither too soft nor too hard. The sauce covers every strand of pasta. It's piping hot. And it's just wheat and water, for crying out loud. But each bite is the way it should be, different from the one before, yet still the same. It reminds me of my checkered record in the boxing ring: I am lulled into a sense of false security, thinking this is just a little sparring, nice and easy. Jab—cross—hook. Ooops—forgot to duck! The lesson? What appears easy is in fact easy, but it clearly requires skill and thoroughness.

Here's what you need to know to avoid the knockout. For each pound [500g] of pasta, boil at least 4 quarts [4L] salted water vigorously. Add 1 to 2 tablespoons salt. Return the water to a boil, add the pasta, and stir immediately and often until the water returns to a boil. Cook until the pasta is al dente (slightly resistant to the bite), then drain it quickly in a ready colander. Shake out the water completely and toss thoroughly with your waiting sauce. Serve immediately.

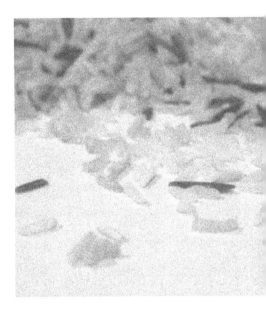

Spaghetti with sweet pepper and extra virgin olive oil sauce

Take advantage of the sweetest, plumpest bell peppers and seasonal ripe tomatoes you can find. When beefsteaks are red and juicy, they're **wonderful.** If you have access to any variety—or a mix—of heirloom tomatoes, consider yourself blessed. And when all the others look a little peaked, chances are the plum tomatoes will make a tasty sauce. Use your best extra virgin olive oil as well.

2½ pounds fresh ripe tomatoes [2.25kg]

1½ teaspoons salt

1 large onion, thinly sliced

¼ cup extra virgin olive oil [60ml]

3 garlic cloves, minced

1 celery rib, chopped

½ red bell pepper, thinly sliced

½ yellow pepper, thinly sliced

1 carrot, halved lengthwise, thinly sliced

1 tablespoon dried oregano

1 teaspoon cinnamon

1 teaspoon fennel seeds

½ teaspoon crushed hot red pepper

¼ teaspoon freshly ground black pepper

1 tablespoon unrefined cane sugar

1 pound spaghetti [500g]

Handful of fresh basil leaves, thinly sliced

Freshly grated Parmesan cheese

1. **Score** a shallow X with a sharp paring knife along the bottom of each tomato. Drop in boiling water for 30 to 60 seconds. Remove with a slotted spoon and run under cold water or drop in a bowl of ice water. Peel off the skin. Coarsely chop the tomatoes and set aside with their juices.

2. In a large flameproof casserole, **simmer** the tomatoes uncovered with 1 teaspoon of the salt for about 45 minutes, stirring occasionally, mashing down chunky pieces with the back of a spoon. The tomatoes will reduce and sweeten during this time.

3. Meanwhile, in another skillet, **cook** the onion in 2 tablespoons of the olive oil over medium heat until soft but not brown, about 5 minutes. Add the garlic, celery, bell peppers, and carrot and continue to cook for another 3 or 4 minutes, or until the vegetables are very soft and the onion is golden.

4. **Add** the oregano, cinnamon, fennel seeds, hot pepper, ½ teaspoon salt, black pepper, and sugar. Cook, stirring, for an additional 1 to 2 minutes, or until the spices are very fragrant.

5. Add the onion and vegetables to the simmering tomato sauce. Continue to cook, **stirring** occasionally, for another 20 minutes, or until the flavors are just right for you. Season with additional salt and pepper to taste. Remove from the heat and stir in the remaining 2 tablespoons oil.

6. While the sauce is cooking, bring at least 4 quarts [4L] salted water to a vigorous boil. **Add** the pasta and stir immediately and often until the water returns to a boil. Cook until the pasta is al dente (slightly resistant to the bite), then drain it quickly into a colander. Shake out the water completely and transfer to plates. Immediately top with the sauce, garnish with fresh basil, and pass the cheese on the side.

SERVES 4

Penne with roasted eggplant, peppers, and feta cheese

This is a small dish, perfect for an intimate dinner for two. Eggplant makes an outstanding ingredient in pasta sauce. It's smoky, silky, and has an excellent mouthfeel. This sauce is made with roasted red peppers, feta cheese, and oregano. Roasting eggplant is surprisingly easy and creates a taste that I find more **appealing** than many other methods of cooking eggplant.

1 pound eggplant [500g]

¼ cup pine nuts [30g]

1 medium onion, chopped

3 tablespoons olive oil

2 garlic cloves, minced

2 roasted red peppers, homemade or jarred

½ pound penne [250g]

¼ cup crumbled feta cheese [30g]

2 tablespoons coarsely chopped fresh oregano

Salt and freshly ground pepper

Splash of fresh lemon juice

1. Preheat the oven to 400°F [200°C]. **Pierce** the eggplant several times with the tip of sharp knife. Place in an uncovered baking dish and roast for 45 to 60 minutes, or until the eggplant is very fragrant and collapses on its own or easily with a squeeze. Slice in half and let cool, then scoop out the meat and coarsely chop it.

2. While the eggplant is cooking, in a large dry skillet, **toast** the pine nuts over medium heat, tossing constantly, until they are lightly browned, about 3 minutes. Remove and set aside.

3. In the same pan, **cook** the onion in 1½ tablespoons of the olive oil over medium-high heat until lightly browned, 5 to 7 minutes.

4. Put the onion, garlic, roasted peppers, cooked eggplant, and remaining oil in a food processor. **Pulse** several times until you achieve a nice chunky consistency. Return the sauce to the pan.

5. Bring at least 4 quarts [4L] salted water to a vigorous boil. **Add** the pasta and stir immediately and often until the water returns to a boil. Cook until the pasta is al dente (slightly resistant to the bite), then drain quickly into a colander. Shake out the water completely.

6. When the pasta is nearly done, **reheat** the sauce over very low heat. Stir in the feta cheese and oregano. Season generously with salt and pepper. Add a splash of lemon juice and toss with the warm pasta.

SERVES 2

Bow tie pasta with roasted asparagus, oven-dried tomatoes, and crisp sage leaves in vegetable broth

This is a magnificent gourmet pasta dish, perfect for spring and summer, when fresh asparagus is at its peak. It's inundated with bold flavors, wonderful colors, and interesting textures. Homemade oven-dried tomatoes, grilled asparagus, and lemon juice are its key components. Fried sage leaves complete the dish; as they melt in your mouth, they provide a very special treat.

Essentially, this dish is about prepping, then assembling. You will use several techniques from the bold vegetarian chef's repertoire, but I promise, it is well worth the effort. That said, however, here are two shortcuts: To save time, use store-bought organic vegetable broth instead of homemade stock, and use store-bought sun-dried tomatoes, softened in hot water, instead of oven-dried.

1 bunch of fresh sage

2 cups Basic Vegetable Stock (page 45) [500ml]

10 asparagus spears, tough ends removed

¼ cup plus 1 teaspoon extra virgin olive oil [60ml]

4 garlic cloves, thinly sliced

1 large carrot, thinly slivered

1 teaspoon crushed hot red pepper, or less to taste

1 pound bow tie pasta

8 oven-dried plum tomatoes (see page 10)

Salt and freshly ground black pepper

¼ to ⅓ cup fresh lemon juice [60 to 75ml]

1. **Drop** several stems of sage leaves into a saucepan with the vegetable stock. Bring to a simmer, cover, remove from the heat, and let steep while preparing the rest of the dish.

2. Preheat the oven to 400°F [200°C]. Lightly **coat** the asparagus with 1 teaspoon of the olive oil. Place on a small baking sheet and roast for 8 to 10 minutes, or until lightly browned, not blackened.

3. Remove 16 of the remaining sage leaves from their stems, choosing the largest, without blemishes. In a medium skillet, **heat** the remaining ¼ cup olive oil over medium heat. Add the sage leaves and fry until just crisp and lightly browned, 1 to 2 minutes. Remove with a slotted spoon. Set aside on paper towels.

4. Reduce the heat to medium-low. **Add** the garlic, carrot, and hot pepper. Cook until the garlic is golden and the carrots have softened slightly. Set aside.

5. Bring to vigorous boil at least 4 quarts [4L] salted water. Add the pasta and stir immediately and often until the water returns to a boil. **Cook** until the pasta is al dente (slightly resistant to the bite), then drain quickly into a colander. Shake out the water completely.

6. Divide the cooked pasta, carrot-garlic-oil mixture, and tomatoes among 4 pasta bowls. **Top** with the asparagus spears.

7. Remove the sage leaves from the saucepan and ladle ¼ to ½ cup [60 to 125ml] of the stock into each bowl. **Season** generously with salt and black pepper and pour 1 to 1½ tablespoons of the lemon juice into each bowl. Lightly toss the ingredients, top with the crisp sage leaves, and serve immediately.

SERVES 4

Ziti with walnut pesto, zucchini, and red pepper

Classic pesto is made with basil, garlic, pine nuts, Parmesan cheese, and olive oil. As you may know, however, the word *pesto* has taken on new meanings in the kitchens and restaurants of America. Versions abound with all kinds of ingredients. Different nuts are used; sun-dried tomatoes, parsley, cilantro, and mint can all be found in interesting recipes called *pesto*. Try my version of walnut pesto or use your own favorite pesto recipe. Serve this dish cold or warm.

1 pound ziti [500g]

½ cup pine nuts [60g]

1 large red bell pepper, cut into strips

1½ tablespoons olive oil

½ green zucchini, cut lengthwise in half, sliced diagonally into half-moons

½ yellow zucchini, cut lengthwise in half, sliced diagonally into half-moons

1 cup vegetable stock [250ml]

1 cup Walnut Pesto (page 86) [250ml]

1 cup cooked chickpeas [150g]

1 to 2 tablespoons fresh lemon juice

Salt and freshly ground pepper

10 fresh basil leaves, slivered

Freshly grated Parmesan cheese

1. Bring at least 4 quarts [4L] salted water to a vigorous boil. Add the pasta and stir immediately and often until the water returns to a boil. Cook until the pasta is al dente (slightly resistant to the bite), 10 to 12 minutes. Drain quickly into a colander. Run the pasta under cold water until the heat is completely dissipated and the pasta is cold to the touch. Shake out the water completely.

2. While the pasta is cooking, in a large dry skillet toast the pine nuts over medium heat, stirring often, until lightly browned, 3 to 4 minutes. Transfer to a bowl and set aside.

3. In the same pan, **cook** the red bell pepper in the olive oil over medium-high heat for 3 to 5 minutes, or until the peppers are soft and slightly blackened around the edges. Add the zucchini slices and cook for another 1 to 2 minutes, until just tender. Set the vegetables aside with the pine nuts.

4. Add the vegetable stock to the same pan and bring to a boil. **Boil** until the stock is reduced by half. Stir in the pesto and cook for 30 seconds. Add the cooked pasta and toss to mix. Reduce the heat to low and fold in the chickpeas, vegetables, and pine nuts. Season with the lemon juice and salt and pepper to taste. Garnish with the basil. Pass a bowl of Parmesan cheese on the side.

SERVES 4

Orzo with fresh tomatoes and mozzarella

This is one of those special dishes that are simple yet **bursting** with flavor. It's best made during the summer months when tomatoes are at their peak and a light dish is welcome. Fresh tomato sauce here means no cooking is involved. That's why it is critical to make the effort to find the freshest, ripest tomatoes as well as fresh mozzarella. And, of course, use your best olive oil. IMPORTANT . . . prepare all your ingredients before you cook the pasta.

1 pound orzo [500g]

1½ to 2 pounds ripe, seasonal tomatoes, cut into ½-inch [1-cm] dice [750g to 1kg]

3 garlic cloves, minced

½ to ¾ pound fresh mozzarella cheese, finely diced [250 to 375g]

Salt and freshly ground pepper

¼ cup extra virgin olive oil [60ml]

½ cup shelled raw pistachios [55g]

¾ cup shredded basil leaves [200ml]

1. Bring at least 4 quarts [4L] salted water to a vigorous boil. **Add** the orzo and stir immediately and often until the water returns to a boil. Cook until the pasta is al dente (slightly resistant to the bite), then drain quickly into a colander. Shake out the water completely.

2. Put the hot, drained pasta into a large bowl. Add the tomatoes, garlic, and mozzarella; **toss** to mix well. Season generously with salt and pepper. Add the olive oil and pistachios and mix. Toss in the basil and mix once again. Serve at once.

SERVES 4 TO 6

Rosemary mushroom white bean pasta

The combination of beans and pasta is a classic Italian favorite. It's homey, comforting, and very easy to prepare. NOTE: This is a thick, chunky sauce. If you want more liquid in your pasta sauce, add a ½ cup [125 ml] or so pasta cooking water, vegetable stock, or white wine when you add the beans.

½ pound penne [250g]

1½ tablespoons olive oil

1 small onion, chopped

1 pound cremini mushrooms, sliced [500g]

1 tablespoon fresh rosemary, minced

2 garlic cloves, minced

1 teaspoon crushed hot red pepper

Salt and freshly ground black pepper

1 can (15 ounces) organic white beans, liquid reserved [300g (drained)]

1 tablespoon tomato paste

1 tablespoon red wine vinegar

2 tablespoons coarsely chopped fresh parsley

1. Bring at least 4 quarts [4L] salted water to a vigorous boil. **Add** the pasta and stir immediately and often until the water returns to a boil. Cook until the pasta is al dente (slightly resistant to the bite), then drain quickly into a colander. Shake out the water completely.

2. While pasta is cooking, **heat** the olive oil in a large skillet over medium heat. Add the onion and cook until softened and slightly browned, about 5 minutes. Add the mushrooms, rosemary, garlic, and hot pepper. Season with salt and black pepper. Cook until the mushrooms are tender, about 5 minutes.

3. Add the beans with their reserved liquid and the tomato paste; stir well. Bring to a boil. Reduce the heat and simmer 2 to 3 minutes. **Season** again, if necessary, with salt and pepper. Remove from the heat and add the vinegar. Stir in the cooked pasta. Toss to coat evenly. Garnish with parsley and serve.

SERVES 2

Roasted pepper and chanterelle mushroom pasta

This is a colorful dish with a deep complexity of character and flavor. You can make this dish all year, of course, but there is something special about the fall, when chanterelle mushrooms and hot chiles are abundant and at their peak. Chanterelle mushrooms are extra-special, so I encourage you to seek them out. You can use other mushrooms or a combination of fresh and dried as well. As for the hot peppers, look for a variety from sweet to mild to hot; combining them works beautifully here.

1 head of garlic

2 tablespoons extra virgin olive oil

1 pound penne [500g]

4 fresh mild to hot peppers (red and/or yellow sweet bell, cayenne, green and/or red jalapeño, güero or banana, and the like)

3 large tomatoes

1 large yellow onion, thinly sliced

½ pound fresh chanterelle mushrooms, sliced [250g]

Salt and freshly ground pepper

Splash of balsamic vinegar

1. Preheat the oven to 325°F [160°C]. Separate the head of garlic into individual cloves. Skin them and cut off the hard bits on the ends. (It's okay if the cloves get crushed while you peel the skin off them.) Toss with 1½ teaspoons of the olive oil to coat lightly. Roast in a small covered baking dish for 30 to 40 minutes, or until lightly browned and very soft. Toss them once or twice while they are cooking.

2. Bring at least 4 quarts [4L] salted water to a vigorous boil. Add the pasta and stir immediately and often until the water returns to a boil. Cook until the pasta is al dente (slightly resistant to the bite), then drain it quickly in a ready colander. Shake out the water completely. Run under cold water until the heat is completely dissipated and the pasta is cold to the touch. Toss with 1½ teaspoons of the olive oil and set aside.

3. While the pasta and garlic are cooking, prepare the peppers. Make sure the kitchen is well ventilated before heating a cast-iron skillet to medium-hot. Slice the peppers in half, remove the seeds and ribs, and flatten them out. Cut the larger bell peppers into quarters. Cook the peppers, slim side down, until moderately blackened and soft. While cooking, add a few drops of olive oil and turn several times with tongs. Set aside. When cool, coarsely chop by hand or in a food processor.

4. When the garlic is done, remove it to a plate and raise the oven temperature to broil. Set a rack 5 to 6 inches [13 to 15cm] from the heat. Lay out the tomatoes on a baking sheet and broil, turning them with tongs until they are lightly blackened and softened, with skins split and peeling off, 7 to 10 minutes. As soon as they are cool enough to handle, peel off the skins, coarsely chop the tomatoes, and set them aside in a bowl along with their juices.

5. In the skillet, cook the onion in the remaining 1 tablespoon of the oil over medium heat until softened and lightly browned, about 5 minutes. Add the roasted garlic and cook for another minute, lightly mashing down a few of the garlic cloves. Add the mushrooms and cook until tender, about 5 minutes. Add the tomatoes with their juices. Cook over medium-low heat, stirring occasionally, until the tomatoes and garlic break down and the sauce begins to thicken.

6. Add 3 to 4 tablespoons of the roasted peppers and the cooked pasta to the tomato sauce. Toss until the pasta is heated through and completely coated with sauce. Season with salt and pepper to taste. Splash with vinegar and serve immediately. Toss with additional extra virgin olive oil, if desired.

SERVES 4 TO 6

note   The recipe calls for a relatively small amount of mixed peppers. However, I highly recommend that you roast a whole batch of them. Freeze some after roasting so you'll have them in the off-season.

A different kind of mac and cheese

Roasted vegetables, three cheeses—including my favorite, smoked mozzarella—and a hazelnut and macadamia topping make this version of mac and cheese a bit different—and more sophisticated. Gemelli, meaning "twins" in Italian, is a dense and chewy pasta shaped like two strands of spaghetti twisted together. If you can't find gemelli, look for radiatore, which is Italian for "little radiators," and that's exactly what they look like.

½ pound carrots, peeled and cut into thin sticks 2 inches [5cm] long [250g]

2 tablespoons olive oil

1 large red bell pepper, cut into strips 2 to 3 inches [5 to 8cm] long

1 small onion, thinly sliced

Salt and freshly ground pepper

4 ounces hazelnuts [125g]

4 ounces macadamia nuts [125g]

4 ounces sharp Cheddar cheese, shredded [125g]

4 ounces smoked mozzarella, shredded [125g]

4 ounces goat cheese, crumbled [125g]

1 pound gemelli [500g]

Salt and freshly ground pepper

6 scallions, thinly sliced on the diagonal, for garnish

1. Preheat the oven to 425°F [220°C]. In a medium bowl, toss the carrots with 1 tablespoon of the olive oil to coat lightly. Spread out on a baking sheet and roast for 15 minutes.

2. Toss the bell pepper strips and onion slices with the remaining olive oil in the same bowl to coat lightly. Add the peppers and onions to the carrots on the baking sheet and return to the oven for another 20 minutes. Ideally, the carrots should be golden brown, the onions soft and lightly browned, and the pepper soft, with a few lightly blackened edges. Season the roasted vegetables with salt and pepper and set aside.

3. In a large dry skillet, **toast** the hazelnuts and macadamias over medium heat, shaking the pan often to prevent burning, until fragrant and lightly browned, 3 to 5 minutes. Let cool slightly, then pulse the toasted nuts in a food processor until coarsely chopped.

4. **Toss** together all the cheeses and set aside.

5. Bring at least 4 quarts [4L] salted water to a vigorous boil. Add the pasta and stir immediately and often until the water returns to a boil. **Cook** until the pasta is al dente (slightly resistant to the bite), then drain it quickly in a ready colander. Shake out the water.

6. Pour the hot pasta into a large bowl and immediately add the cheeses and roasted vegetables. Toss to mix thoroughly. **Season** with salt and pepper to taste. Serve each portion hot, topped with the chopped nuts and sliced scallions.

SERVES 4 TO 6

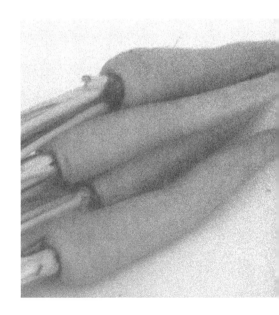

Whole wheat lasagna with caramelized onion, dinosaur kale, and basil

I'm from the cook-the-lasagna-noodles-in-the-sauce school. This may seem strange to some, but I like the convenience and the chewy texture of the pasta prepared this way. You will need more sauce than usual, as the dry noodles will suck up a lot of liquid. Special no-boil lasagna noodles are also available in some stores. Dinosaur kale is a dark-green, chewy, lemony leaf. It is very tasty and much more tender than regular kale, which can be substituted.

2 large onions, very thinly sliced

2 tablespoons olive oil

1 teaspoon salt

4 garlic cloves, minced

2 tablespoons unrefined cane sugar

1 tablespoon dried basil

1 tablespoon dried oregano

2 teaspoons fennel seeds

1 teaspoon crushed hot red pepper

½ cup port wine [125ml]

1 bunch (about 12 ounces) fresh dinosaur kale, coarsely chopped [350g]

3 cans (28 ounces each) organic tomato sauce [2.25L total]

Freshly ground black pepper

1 pound whole wheat lasagna noodles [500g]

1½ pounds regular or smoked mozzarella, sliced [750g]

½ pound ricotta cheese [250g]

12 ounces Parmesan cheese, shredded [375g]

Simple Béchamel Sauce (recipe follows)

½ cup coarsely chopped fresh basil

1. In a large heavy pot, sauté the onions in the olive oil over medium-low heat until soft and very brown, 25 to 35 minutes. Don't rush them; the key to their taste is that they have become tender and sweet, not burned or bitter. Stir the onions every few minutes. Season with ½ teaspoon salt.

2. While the onions are cooking, **mix** the following ingredients in a bowl: the garlic, sugar, basil, oregano, fennel, hot pepper, and remaining ½ teaspoon salt.

3. When the onions are nicely browned, **add** the port and bring to a simmer. With a wooden spoon, scrape off all the caramelized onion bits stuck to the bottom of the pot. Continue to cook, stirring often, until most of the liquid is evaporated.

4. Preheat the oven to 350°F [175°C]. Add the seasoning mixture to the caramelized onions and continue to cook for another 1 to 2 minutes, until the spices are fragrant. Add the kale and stir until the leaves wilt, 1 to 2 minutes. **Pour** in the tomato sauce and bring to a simmer. Season with a generous grinding of black pepper and continue to cook for 15 to 20 minutes.

5. Ladle a light layer of tomato sauce over the bottom of a lasagna pan measuring 9 by 13 inches [23 by 33cm]. **Layer** the noodles across lengthwise and top with more sauce, making sure the noodles are completely covered. Ladle an extra cup [250ml] or so of sauce, more than you normally might because the noodles are uncooked. Reserve ½ of the mozzarella. Add layers of the ricotta, Parmesan, and the remaining mozzarella. Top with more pasta, then cover with béchamel sauce. Add another layer of the cheeses and top with the last layer of pasta. Spoon all but 1½ cups [375ml] of the remaining tomato sauce over all.

6. Cover the pan with aluminum foil and bake for 30 minutes, or until the noodles are cooked all the way through. Test with a sharp paring knife. Raise the oven temperature to 400°F [200°C] and remove the foil. **Top** the lasagna with the remaining sauce and mozzarella and top with the fresh basil. Continue to bake for 10 to 15 minutes, until the top is browned and bubbly. Let rest for 15 to 20 minutes before serving. *Note:* When reheating, use any leftover sauce to moisten the lasagna.

SERVES 8 TO 10

Tip Make the lasagna several hours or a day ahead. Have as much as possible ready to go and prepped before you start cooking—cheese grated and cut, onions sliced, spices set aside in one bowl, tomato cans open, etc.—so you are not caught scrambling in the middle of your preparation. Prepare the béchamel sauce while the tomato sauce is simmering.

Simple Béchamel Sauce

1½ cups whole milk, preferably organic [375ml]

2½ tablespoons unbleached all-purpose flour

3 tablespoons butter, preferably organic

1. In a medium saucepan, **scald** the milk, but do not let it boil. Remove from the heat.

2. In another saucepan, **melt** the butter over medium-low heat. Add the flour and cook, stirring with wooden spoon, for 1 to 2 minutes, without allowing the mixture to color.

3. Remove the roux from the heat and slowly **whisk** in the milk, 2 to 3 tablespoons at a time, until about half has been added. Then slowly pour in the remaining milk and bring the sauce to a boil, whisking constantly, until it thickens. Reduce the heat to low and simmer for 5 minutes.

MAKES ABOUT 1 ½ CUPS [375ML]

Risotto

CREAMY AND SENSUOUS, risotto is a luxurious meal or a beautiful starter. Flavor bases for risotto are virtually unlimited. Here are some important points and tips to remember as you create the perfect risotto. Make fresh stock and keep it at a simmer right next to your risotto pot. Be creative with your stocks based on your final dish. For example, use a mushroom-based stock for a mushroom-flavored risotto or a light tomato base for a sun-dried tomato risotto. Retain any soaking liquid you may use and add that to your stock—from dried mushrooms, tomatoes, chiles, or the like.

The method of cooking classic risotto, while uncomplicated, is very specific. Classic risotto starts with onion sautéed in butter or oil. Then the rice is toasted for a minute or two. You must stir your rice continuously with a wooden spoon. Add hot stock by the ladleful only after any liquid in the pot has been absorbed. Repeat the ladling of hot liquid several times while stirring constantly. For 1 cup [200g] risotto you will use about 4 cups [750ml to 1L] hot stock. The amount will vary from recipe to recipe. I favor cooking risotto for 20 to 25 minutes, which creates a creamy texture while still leaving a hint of chewiness. The right texture and technique will come quickly after one or two goes at it.

The quantities given for liquid are always approximate. Be prepared to use a little more or a little less depending on the mood of your risotto. Use quality cookware for making risotto. Your saucepan must be heavy-bottomed, ideally coated with a stainless-steel alloy.

Important: No matter which risotto you choose, read the following recipe for Shiitake-Apple Risotto thoroughly and use it as your technique guide.

Shiitake-apple risotto

This risotto is tart, creamy, and luxurious. I have found that a sharp apple is always a pleasant surprise in a hot savory dish. This recipe serves two as a main course, four as a first course or side dish. Have everything prepped and ready to go on the counter before you begin cooking.

4 cups vegetable stock [1L]

1 small onion, finely chopped

1½ tablespoons olive oil or butter

½ pound fresh shiitake mushrooms, stemmed, caps thinly sliced [250g]

3 garlic cloves, minced

1 small Granny Smith apple, cored and cut into ½-inch [1-cm] dice

1 cup Arborio or other risotto rice [200g]

Salt and freshly ground pepper

2 tablespoons freshly grated Parmesan cheese

2 teaspoons fresh thyme, minced

1. **Bring** the vegetable stock to a simmer on the burner closest to your risotto pan. You will need a solid wooden spoon and a ½-cup [125-ml] ladle.

2. In heavy-bottomed saucepan, **cook** the onion in the olive oil over medium-low heat until softened and translucent, 3 to 5 minutes. While it's not the end of the world if you do so, try to avoid browning the onion. Add the mushrooms and garlic and cook until the mushrooms are soft, about 5 minutes.

3. Add the apple and stir once or twice. **Add** the rice and cook, stirring constantly, for 1 to 2 minutes, until the grains begin to turn opaque. Raise the heat to medium-high and ladle in 1 cup [250ml] simmering stock. The liquid should quickly boil and then simmer until you are finished. Find the right level on your stovetop so that the risotto is not at a rolling boil but at a constant light simmer.

4. Continue to stir without stopping, getting all sides and the bottom of the pan, so the rice does not stick or burn. You are now officially on your way. Keep stirring until the liquid is absorbed and evaporated. **Ladle** in ½ cup [125ml] more hot liquid and repeat the process until the pan is again void of much stock.

5. After 15 minutes or so of cooking, **season** with salt and pepper and get a quick taste. Is your rice too crunchy? It probably will be, but this is the time for you to make choices. Risotto should be tender but firm to the bite. You may add slightly less liquid now at each addition until you get your desired results in about 20 to 25 minutes total. I find I use from 3 to 3½ cups [750 to 875ml] total liquid, though once I used 4 cups [1L]. Be prepared to modify to the needs of the risotto.

6. When the risotto is done, remove it from the heat, **stir** in the cheese and thyme, and season again generously with salt and pepper. Serve immediately. Like a soufflé, properly made risotto waits for no one.

SERVES 2 TO 4

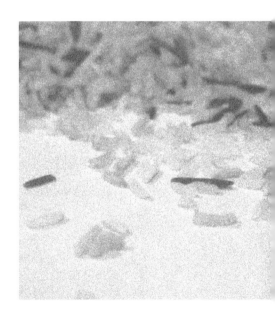

Asparagus and fennel risotto

This recipe has a slight bite and very **interesting** flavors and textures. Look for plump fresh fennel without blemishes. Cut from the softer white bulb rather than the woodier green stalks.

4 cups vegetable stock [1L]

1½ tablespoons organic butter or olive oil

1 small onion, finely chopped

½ cup finely chopped fresh fennel bulb, leaves reserved for garnish [60g]

½ pound tender fresh asparagus, tough ends removed, stalks cut into pieces 1 to 2 inches [2.5 to 5cm] **long** [250g]

1 fresh serrano or Thai pepper, seeds and ribs removed, minced

1 teaspoon unrefined cane sugar

1 cup Arborio or other risotto rice [200g]

Salt and freshly ground pepper

2 tablespoons freshly grated Parmesan cheese

1. **Bring** the vegetable stock to a simmer on the burner closest to your risotto pan. You will need a solid wooden spoon and a ½-cup [125-ml] ladle.

2. In a heavy-bottomed saucepan, **melt** the butter over medium-low heat. Add the onion and fennel and cook until the vegetables are softened, about 5 minutes. Add the asparagus and, stirring constantly, cook for about 1 minute, until it turns a brighter shade of green.

3. Add the serrano pepper and sugar and stir in the pan for 30 seconds or so. **Add** the rice and cook, stirring constantly, for 1 to 1½ minutes. Raise the heat to medium-high and ladle in 1 cup [250ml] simmering stock. The liquid should quickly boil and continue to simmer until you are finished.

4. Continue to **stir** without stopping, getting all sides and the bottom of the pan, so the rice does not stick or burn. Keep stirring until the liquid is absorbed and evaporated. Ladle in ½ cup [125ml] more hot liquid and repeat the process until the pan is again void of much stock.

5. After 15 minutes or so, **season** with salt and pepper and get a quick taste. Is your rice too crunchy? It probably will be, but this is the time for you to make choices. Risotto should be tender but firm to the bite. You may add slightly less liquid now at each addition until you get your desired results in about 20 to 25 minutes.

6. When the risotto is done, remove it from the heat, **stir** in the cheese, and season again generously with salt and pepper. Garnish with the reserved fennel leaves. Serve immediately.

SERVES 2 TO 4

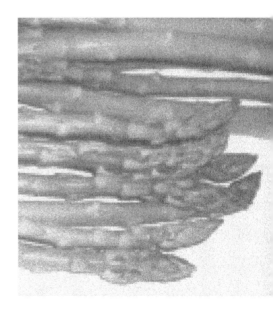

Kale-garlic risotto with fresh mango

Many risottos contain cheese, though I made this one without any for my vegan friends across the aisle. Of course, if you are not vegan, you can always stir in some Parmesan cheese at the end.

1½ tablespoons olive oil or butter

1 small onion, finely chopped

2 cups packed dinosaur or other green kale, tough stems removed, leaves coarsely chopped [500ml]

3 garlic cloves, minced

1 cup arborio or other risotto rice [200g]

4 cups vegetable stock [1L], simmering

Salt and freshly ground pepper

1 large fresh mango, sliced

1. In a heavy-bottomed saucepan, heat the olive oil over medium-low heat. **Add** the onion and cook until softened and translucent, about 5 minutes. Add the kale and, stirring constantly, cook for about 1 minute, until it begins to soften and turns a brighter shade of green.

2. Add the garlic and stir for 30 seconds. Add the rice and cook, stirring constantly, for 1 to 1½ minutes. Raise the heat to medium-high and **ladle** in 1 cup [250ml] simmering stock. The liquid should quickly boil and continue to simmer.

3. Continue to **stir,** without stopping, reaching all sides and the bottom of the pan so the rice does not stick or burn. Keep stirring until the liquid is absorbed and evaporated. Ladle in ½ cup [125ml] more hot liquid and repeat the process until the pan is again void of much stock.

4. After 15 minutes or so, **season** with salt and pepper and get a quick taste. Is your rice too crunchy? It probably will be, but this is the time for you to make choices. Risotto should be tender but firm to the bite. You may add slightly less liquid now at each addition until you get your desired results in about 20 to 25 minutes.

5. When the risotto is done, remove it from the heat and season again generously with salt and pepper. **Garnish** with fresh mango. Serve immediately.

SERVES 2 TO 4

Polenta

In Roman antiquity, those who prepared food would grind wheat, millet, spelt (farro), or barley to make various combinations of cereal porridges. Fast forward to the beginning of the sixteenth century, when corn arrived in northern Italy from the Americas, and polenta was born.

Polenta is a deeply satisfying and versatile culinary gem made from dried ground corn. Boiling water swells the starch in the corn, creating a delicious, comforting mush. It is an excellent accompaniment to an infinite variety of sauces and toppings. It can be served piping hot with your favorite tomato sauce, drizzled with warm rosemary-flavored olive oil, topped with freshly grated Parmesan cheese, or even as dessert, with brown sugar, cinnamon, nutmeg, honey, toasted nuts, and raisins. Served with cranberry sauce, polenta can also make an inspired addition to the holiday table.

Polenta is most often available in coarse, medium, and fine grinds. Coarsely ground corn retains some of its hull and germ, making it not only the most nutritious of the grinds but the most abundant in corn flavor. A very fine grind, available through major-brand companies, may lack a full corn taste. A medium grind, comparable to sugar granules (as opposed to salt), is the most versatile, yielding a smooth, creamy, yet hearty consistency, ideal for soft or firm polenta dishes.

Also available, but recommended only in an emergency, are the quick-cooking or instant brands of polenta. You can also buy tubes of precooked polenta, which reminds me of a funny story. My mother read one of my polenta recipes and decided she would try it. She called in a panic to say the recipe wasn't working. She couldn't get the polenta to stir in the pot like the directions indicated. It was just a mishmash of mush! After I explained to her that the tube kind was already cooked, we had good laugh.

Like all other grains, polenta must be seasoned while it cooks to avoid blandness. Salted water is always acceptable but for a truly rich and tasty polenta, substitute a light-colored stock or broth. The secret to smooth polenta is constant stirring, which means you'll want to avoid other kitchen tasks until it is finished. Cooking times will vary, but once the polenta pulls away from the side of the pot, it's done—theoretically, at least. In other words, you can eat the polenta as it is in just a matter of 10 minutes or so, but the longer you cook the polenta, the creamier and richer it will become.

Basic polenta recipe

You will follow this basic recipe for all the polenta recipes in this chapter (and one in chapter 3). It's straightforward and easy to follow. For the very best results, use light-colored homemade or prepared vegetable stock. The only alterations to this recipe will be if you are doubling the amount or if you need a softer or firmer consistency. Techniques follow for those two variations.

5 cups light-colored vegetable stock, such as Basic Vegetable Stock (page 45), or water [1.25L]

1½ teaspoons salt

1 cup polenta (coarse-ground cornmeal) [130g]

Freshly ground pepper

1. Bring the stock to a boil in a heavy medium pot. **Add** the salt and keep the water at a boil over medium-high heat.

2. Add the polenta in a very thin stream, either slowly from a measuring cup or letting a fistful of it run through nearly closed fingers, **stirring** all the while with a long-handled whisk to avoid lumps. Stirring constantly and keeping the water boiling, continue this procedure until all the cornmeal is added.

3. Reduce the heat to medium-low, enabling the cornmeal to simmer gently. You will realize the right temperature when the hot polenta no longer bubbles and pops back at you. (Remember, you want to enjoy the process of making polenta by not getting burned.) Continue stirring, switching to a long-handled wooden spoon. For an even, slow heat and to help avoid burning or sticking, use a flame-tamer or heat diffuser. **Stir** continuously and thoroughly, bringing the mixture up from the bottom and loosening it from the sides. Make sure to really scoop into the sides. Continue to stir for 15 to 25 minutes* or until the polenta is very creamy and pulls away from the sides of the pot. Season with additional salt and pepper to taste.

MAKES ABOUT 2 CUPS [500ML]

*For soft, loose polenta, cooking time is about 10 to 15 minutes. For firmer polenta, used for grilling or broiling, cook longer until it is thicker, about 20 to 25 minutes.

Variations

- For firm polenta, to broil or grill, pour the cooked mixture into a lightly oiled glass pie plate or baking dish. Smooth the top and let cool off completely. This will take about 2 to 3 hours in the refrigerator. When completely firm and cooled, cut the polenta into desired shapes. If you are eating dinner shortly and are feeling rushed for the polenta to cool and set, put it in the freezer for 15 minutes before returning to refrigerator.

- If you are serving polenta soft, it can be prepared up to 2 hours ahead. Remove from the cooking pot with a large rubber spatula and keep warm in a double boiler or a stainless-steel bowl placed over a pot of simmering water. Cover loosely with aluminum foil and stir every 10 or 15 minutes.

Polenta with white beans and sun-dried tomatoes

Simple luxury epitomizes what polenta is all about: the most basic of flavors, properly cooked—no more, no less. This recipe highlights that idea with a combination of soft white beans and the appeal of slightly chewy and tangy sun-dried tomatoes. For best results, serve this dish fresh from the pot, when the polenta is warm and soft. However, if you make it into firm cakes and reheat them the next day, you'll still have yourself a fine dish. Serve with a side of cooked or fresh greens.

1 recipe Basic Polenta (page 216)

1½ ounces sun-dried tomatoes [45g]

1 tablespoon olive oil

1 small onion, finely chopped

3 garlic cloves, minced

2 cups cooked white beans [330g]

Salt and freshly ground pepper

1. **Prepare** the Basic Polenta and keep warm in a double boiler.

2. Soak the sun-dried tomatoes in 1 cup [250ml] hot water until soft, 15 to 20 minutes. Drain, reserving ½ cup [125ml] of the soaking liquid. **Cut** the tomatoes into thin strips.

3. In a large skillet, **heat** the olive oil over medium-low heat. Add the onion and cook for 3 to 5 minutes, until soft and translucent. Add the garlic and sun-dried tomatoes and cook for an additional 30 seconds. Increase the heat slightly and add the reserved soaking liquid. Cook for 1 to 2 minutes, stirring frequently, until the liquid cooks reduces and the sauce thickens.

4. Add the beans and heat through for 2 minutes. **Season** with salt and pepper to taste and set aside on the stovetop.

5. **Pour** individual servings of hot polenta into bowls. Make a well in the center of each with a ladle and spoon in the white beans and sauce. Serve immediately.

SERVES 4

note This dish serves 6 as an appetizer.

Broiled polenta with chipotle-mushroom ragout

While the previous recipe relies mostly on the beauty of simplicity, this highlights a slightly more complex sauce that is **brash** in its savory heat and spice. Rather than featuring a mushlike polenta, this dish carries the day with polenta formed into a cake, then set under the broiler to slightly brown the top—offering an equally tasty result.

1 recipe Basic Polenta (page 216)

5 dried porcini or other dried mushrooms

1 to 2 chipotle chiles or 1 teaspoon chipotle chile powder

1 medium onion, finely chopped

3 tablespoons olive oil

2 garlic cloves, minced

5 ounces fresh shiitake mushrooms, stemmed, caps thinly sliced [150g]

½ pound white button or cremini mushrooms, thinly sliced [250g]

2 tablespoons tomato paste

1 tablespoon balsamic vinegar

Salt and freshly ground pepper

¼ cup coarsely chopped parsley [60ml]

1. Prepare the Basic Polenta and **pour** it into a lightly oiled 9-inch [23-cm] pie plate or a loaf pan. Refrigerate until cool and firm, at least 2 hours.

2. **Soak** the dried mushrooms in 1 cup [250g] hot water until soft, 15 to 20 minutes. Lift out the mushrooms and squeeze excess liquid from them back into the bowl. Finely chop the mushrooms. Strain the mushroom soaking liquid through a coffee filter or double thickness of cheesecloth and set aside.

3. Crack open the chipotle chile(s), remove the seeds, and soak in hot water until soft, 20 to 30 minutes. **Mince** the chile(s) and set aside.

4. In a large skillet, **cook** the onion in the oil over medium heat until soft and lightly browned, 5 to 7 minutes. Add the garlic, fresh and dried mushrooms, and chipotle chile. Cook an additional 4 to 5 minutes, or until the mushrooms are tender.

5. **Add** the reserved mushroom soaking liquid and bring to a boil. Cook until the liquid is reduced by about half. Reduce the heat slightly and blend in the tomato paste. Cook until thick, about 5 minutes longer, stirring frequently. Add the vinegar. Remove from the heat and season with salt and pepper to taste.

6. Preheat the broiler with the rack set 4 to 5 inches [10 to 13cm] from the heat. **Brush** the polenta with olive oil and broil for 1 to 2 minutes, or until slightly browned and just a touch crispy. Watch carefully so it doesn't burn. Cut into 4 to 6 triangles. Ladle the mushroom ragout over each piece of polenta. Garnish with parsley and serve.

SERVES 4 AS AN ENTREE, 6 AS AN APPETIZER

Polenta lasagna

What a culinary shocker—polenta substitutes for pasta noodles in this hearty, enlightened dish. And I find that, like traditional lasagna, this dish tastes better the next day, as the flavors pull together. As a matter of practicality, I recommend making the polenta the day or morning before preparing the rest of the dish. This will make the whole process much simpler as the polenta will be done and ready, freeing you to concentrate on the sauce and assembling the lasagna.

2 recipes Basic Polenta (page 216)

2 tablespoons olive oil

1 small onion, chopped

3 garlic cloves, minced

½ teaspoon dried oregano

1 bay leaf

⅛ to ¼ teaspoon crushed hot red pepper

1 small red bell pepper, diced

1 small zucchini, halved lengthwise and thinly sliced

1 carrot, peeled and thinly sliced

Salt and freshly ground black pepper

2 cans (28 ounces each) organic crushed tomatoes [875ml or 784g total]

2 tablespoons tomato paste

1 tablespoon balsamic or red wine vinegar

¼ cup plus 2 tablespoons freshly grated Parmesan cheese [40g]

8 ounces mozzarella cheese, thinly sliced [250g]

1. **Prepare** the polenta and pour into a lightly oiled 9 by 13 inch baking dish [23 by 33cm]. Let set until firm, at least 3 hours (or overnight) in the refrigerator.

2. In a large skillet, heat the oil over medium heat. **Add** the onion and cook until soft and translucent, 3 to 5 minutes. Add the garlic, oregano, bay leaf, and hot pepper. Cook for 1 minute longer. Add the bell pepper, zucchini, and carrot and cook another 2 minutes. Season lightly with salt and black pepper. Add the crushed tomatoes and tomato paste and simmer until the vegetables are soft but still slightly firm, 5 to 7 minutes. Remove from the heat. Stir in the vinegar and season with salt and black pepper to taste.

3. Preheat the oven to 350°F [175°C]. **Remove** the polenta to a clean cutting board by sliding a sharp paring knife around the edges to loosen it. Place the cutting board on top of the dish and, firmly holding both together, quickly flip them over. The polenta should pop right out onto cutting board. Depending on the size of the board, you may need someone to help you with this.

4. With a long, thin knife, **cut** the polenta in half vertically, then again in half horizontally. Gently return 2 of the halves to the baking dish.

5. Ladle about 2 cups [500ml] of the tomato sauce over the polenta in the baking dish. Sprinkle on half the Parmesan cheese and layer on half the mozzarella. **Top** with the remaining polenta pieces, another 2 cups [500ml] tomato sauce, and the rest of the cheese. Use any remaining sauce to pour over the finished lasagna.

6. **Bake** for 35 to 40 minutes, or until the cheese is browned on top and a knife inserted in the middle comes out hot.

IMPORTANT! Let the lasagna rest for at least at least 15 to 20 minutes before cutting and serving.

SERVES 8

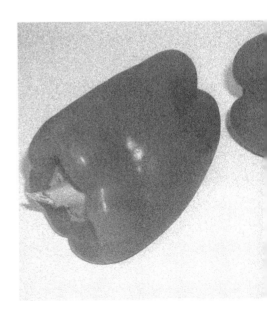

Italian fontina and roasted garlic polenta with creamy tomato sauce

Butter, Italian fontina cheese, and roasted garlic are superb additions to polenta. I stir the cornmeal above and beyond in this recipe to make sure it as creamy as possible. Freshly grated Parmesan broiled on top perfects the visual. Serve as suggested with the Creamy Tomato Sauce that follows or soft, simply topped with grated Parmesan cheese.

1 recipe Basic Polenta (page 216)

2 tablespoons butter

6 garlic cloves, roasted and mashed into a paste*

1 tablespoon maple syrup

3 ounces Italian fontina cheese, cut into small chunks [90g]

Salt and freshly ground pepper

3 tablespoons freshly grated Parmesan cheese

Creamy Tomato Sauce (recipe follows)

1. Prepare the Basic Polenta recipe and remove from the heat. Stir in the butter, roasted garlic, and maple syrup until well blended. Then stir in the fontina, mixing until the cheese is completely melted. Season generously with salt and pepper.

2. Pour into a medium-size oiled glass baking dish. This could be a 7 by 10 inch [18 by 25cm] rectangular dish, a 9-inch square [23-cm] or even a 10-inch [25-cm] pie dish. Sprinkle the Parmesan cheese over the polenta and let cool completely, at least 2 hours.

* To roast garlic: Preheat the oven to 300° to 325°F [150° to 160ºC]. Skin the garlic cloves and cut off the hard bits on the ends. (It's okay if the cloves get crushed while you peel the skin off them.) Coat the garlic with olive oil and cook in a covered baking dish for 30 to 40 minutes, or until lightly browned and very soft. You may toss them once or so while they are cooking.

3. Before serving, place under a hot broiler for 1 or 2 minutes, or until lightly browned on top. Watch carefully, as polenta can go from gorgeous golden to burned very quickly. **Cut** into squares or wedges and serve while hot. Drizzle a little Creamy Tomato Sauce over the polenta and pass the remainder in a bowl on the side.

SERVES 6

chef's note I use Italian fontina cheese here rather than Swiss fontina, which does not melt as smoothly.

Creamy tomato sauce

Frying sauce after it is prepared is a Mexican-inspired technique, which adds an extra mellowness and depth of flavor. This easy preparation is perfect over grilled polenta with a stuffed pepper. It is a simple, lively sauce. Alternatively, if you like a smoother sauce, press the mixture through a fine-mesh strainer before adding the crème fraîche.

2 pounds ripe tomatoes, cored and halved lengthwise [1kg]

1 medium onion, chopped

2 tablespoons olive oil

3 garlic cloves, minced

1½ teaspoons salt

1 cup vegetable stock [250ml]

¼ cup crème fraîche or heavy cream [60ml]

Salt

1. Preheat the broiler with the rack set 5 to 6 inches [13 to 15cm] from the heat. Place the tomatoes, cut side down, on a baking sheet. Broil until the tomatoes are lightly charred and the skins are wrinkled and peeling, 5 to 7 minutes.

2. Let the tomatoes cool, then peel and coarsely chop them, saving their juices. Place in a blender or food processor.

3. In a medium frying pan or cast-iron skillet, cook the onion in 1 tablespoon of the olive oil over medium-low heat until very soft and lightly browned, about 7 to 9 minutes. Add the garlic and cook for another minute.

4. Add the onion-garlic mixture to the tomatoes. Season with the salt and puree until smooth.

5. In the same pan, heat the remaining oil over high heat. Add the puree to the pan (it should sizzle and bubble), reduce the heat to medium-high, and cook for about 5 minutes, stirring constantly. *Warning:* The puree may splatter.

6. Stir in the vegetable stock and return to a boil, then reduce the heat to low and simmer uncovered for about 15 minutes, or until the sauce begins to thicken. Remove from the heat and stir in the crème fraîche. Season with additional salt to taste.

MAKES ABOUT 3 CUPS [750ML]

8

SEITAN:

The Power of Wheat Meat

A whole book could be written about seitan (pronounced *say-tahn*), a form of

wheat protein, also called *wheat meat* or *grain meat*. It is made from vital, or

high-gluten, flour. You will find vital gluten flour in the bulk section of most health

food stores or with other packaged flours in the baking aisle. When this protein is

combined with water and kneaded, it develops gluten, the same elastic element that gives bread its chewiness. This satisfying texture, combined with a generally neutral flavor, helps the seitan absorb the taste of its companion ingredients.

Depending upon how it is treated and what it is cooked in, seitan can mimic all kinds of meat dishes. Virtually anywhere animal meat is used, seitan can take its place. It's all in the texture of the dough, which becomes firm and chewy or crisp or soft and tender, depending on the cooking technique used. There are dozens of techniques and recipes and styles for seitan. What this chapter aims to do is give you a solid foundation in forming and cooking this amazingly versatile ingredient. Once you've made three or four recipes, you will be confident enough to explore further the finer points of seitan.

A well-seasoned braising liquid is a critical component of preparing wheat meat. Added flavor is what makes roasts, stir-fries, and other "meats" possible. Many of the recognizable tastes that we've associated with animal meat for so many years have less to do with the meat itself and more to do with the combination of spices, flavors, and cooking techniques. After seitan is fully prepared and sauced, it is not that different from animal meat, except that it contains no saturated fat.

Because seitan is relatively neutral in taste and does so well picking up the character of the ingredients it is cooked and marinated in, it's an ideal choice for many who like the different tastes and mouthfeel of meat dishes but prefer not to eat meat. Homemade seitan is easy to create. It does take a little time, though, so be prepared and be patient. The good news is that homemade seitan is substantially better than most store-bought seitan or packaged mixes. There are exceptions, of course (in some vegetarian Chinese restaurants, for example), but once you've made it yourself, you will gain a keen appreciation for the nuances and flavors of grain meat that you may not have had before. Although total preparation of seitan takes about 2 hours, 90 percent of that time is devoted to the actual cooking.

General tips

SEITAN COOKED IN a marinade takes on the flavors at hand, and these flavors continue to grow as it marinates overnight. While this also holds true for soy products, the good news is that unlike tofu or tempeh, which generally must marinate several hours or overnight for substantial flavor development, seitan absorbs a great deal of taste in just a couple hours of cooking.

There is a considerable amount of leeway involved in flavoring seitan. I have created some complex interesting flavors here. I am often disappointed with store-bought or restaurant dishes, which is why I go to the trouble of creating these more interesting recipes and flavors in the first place. If you prefer simpler dishes, you can certainly stick with the basics and use just basic flavorings like soy sauce, garlic, and fresh ginger.

Last resort

Remember, when all is said and done, if you simply are not feeling up to making your own seitan, you can use a store-bought brand in any of the recipes calling for prepared seitan. Just open the package and cut it up. One of the down sides to this is that packaged seitan is usually already marinated, with distinct flavors that may not go with the dish you are interested in making. Try different brands and experiment. Warning: Once you've made your own, you may never buy store-bought again.

Let's get started

1. Before you do anything, read through the recipes in this chapter and decide which one you want to make. This chapter is a tad tricky because the recipes are interconnected, so take it slow and easy.

2. If you decide you want to make one of the two roast recipes, proceed to the Basic Seitan Dough on page 230. Prepare the basic seitan dough as described, then continue with the roast recipe that you have chosen. Follow those directions to season the basic dough, then bake and baste for 2 hours.

3. If you are making *any other recipe* in this chapter, you will also make the Basic Seitan Dough first. You *will* then boil it in the flavoring liquid called for in either Light Meat Seitan on page 232 or Dark Meat Seitan on page 234, depending on the recipe you have chosen. After the seitan is cooked and cooled, you can cut it into appropriate-size pieces and add them to the dish you have chosen.

Basic seitan dough

This is the basic dough recipe that will lead you to all other seitan dishes. It is an indistinct "meat" that needs a flavoring, marinade, or sauce to make it stand out. If you haven't made wheat meat before, keep in mind it is simply one of those hands-on learning experiences best appreciated with practice. For example, depending on the humidity in the air and moisture content of your flour, the amount of water needed to create the basic dough may vary slightly from time to time. Extra water will create a softer meat; more flour, a firmer one. You will very quickly begin tweaking the recipes to your own liking, adjusting the texture and adding other flavors like minced garlic, onion powder, or soy sauce along with the water.

2 cups vital or high-gluten flour [250g]	2 teaspoons unrefined cane sugar
2 tablespoons nutritional yeast	2 teaspoons salt
1 tablespoon toasted wheat germ	1⅔ cups water [400ml]

1. In a large bowl, **combine** the flour, nutritional yeast, wheat germ, sugar, and salt. Toss to mix.

2. Add the water and knead the dough with your hands until the liquid is completely absorbed and the dough is firm and springy, about 5 minutes. Continue to **knead** for 2 to 3 minutes longer to get the dough tight and the flavors firmly incorporated.

3. If you plan on making one of the two roast seitan recipes, proceed *to* Savory Seitan Roast, page 236, or Free-Range Roasted Seitan, page 240. If not, **divide** the seitan into 3 equal oblong loaves. Lay down 3 pieces of cheesecloth, 8 to 10 inches [20 to 25cm] long. At this point, there are three ways to wrap the seitan:

     ❧ Place a loaf in the middle of a piece of cheesecloth and fold the cloth over on all four sides to secure your package, not unlike a gift-wrapped present. Tie the string around the package firmly but allow some give, as the "meat" will expand as it cooks.

- If you are using cheesecloth and no string, roll the seitan up in the cloth and bring the two ends together in a light knot.

- Finally, you can skip the cheesecloth altogether and just plunk the uncooked seitan in the boiling braising liquid as is. The advantage is a little less hassle. The disadvantage is that you will end up with odd-shaped pieces without a consistent shape, nor will they be quite as firm as if they were wrapped. Experiment, if you like, by wrapping two pieces of seitan dough and dropping the third in unwrapped. See which you like better.

4. Prepare either the Light or the Dark Meat Seitan, depending on which your selected recipe calls for. Cook the seitan in the liquid as instructed.

MAKES ABOUT 1 ½ POUNDS [750G] (4 SERVINGS)

note You will need cheesecloth and white kitchen string for this recipe if you plan on boiling. (Alternatively, if you don't have string or don't want to bother, you can tie the ends of the cheesecloth together, like a bundle of laundry.) If you are making either of the roast recipes, you will *not* need cloth or string.

Light meat seitan

If you are making Ken Pow Seitan with Asparagus, you will prepare your Basic Dough, wrap it, and cook it in this highly seasoned braising liquid that will flavor the dough as it cooks.

The liquid is a combination of flavors that you are probably familiar with—many that might be associated with a chicken broth or soup. There is enough liquid to cook one batch of Basic Seitan Dough.

5 cups prepared or homemade vegetable stock [1.25L]

5 cups water [1.25L]

1 cup dry white wine [250ml]

3 tablespoons olive oil

1 tablespoon soy sauce

1 tablespoon white wine vinegar

6 garlic cloves, minced

1 bay leaf

1½ tablespoons nutritional yeast

2 teaspoons unrefined cane sugar

2½ teaspoons onion powder

1 teaspoon powdered mustard

1 teaspoon fennel seeds

1 teaspoon dried thyme

½ teaspoon crushed hot red pepper

½ teaspoon celery seed

1 teaspoon salt

½ teaspoon freshly ground black pepper

Uncooked prepared dough from Basic Seitan Recipe (page 230), wrapped according to recipe directions

1. In a large pot, bring all the ingredients except the seitan to a boil. Place the wrapped seitan packages in the pot and reduce the heat to a simmer. Partially cover the pot with a lid and cook for 1 hour.

2. Use tongs to turn the seitan over so all sides get adequately exposed to the braising liquid. Continue to cook for another 1 to 1½ hours. (The longer you cook the seitan, the firmer it will become; at any point after 1½ hours total you may remove the seitan from the liquid and unwrap it to check out the taste and firmness and decide whether you want to continue cooking.) If you see that the liquid has evaporated and more than half of the seitan is exposed, add an additional 1 to 2 cups [250 to 500ml] stock. The seitan will be firm after braising, but it will continue to firm up overnight.

3. Let cool, remove the string (if using) and cheesecloth, and slice the seitan into rounds ½ inch [1cm] thick, or cut the loaves into other desired shapes (such as dice, fingers, or thin strips) and proceed with the recipe of your choice.

4. Store light meat seitan in the refrigerator, completely immersed in the braising liquid and well sealed, for up to 3 days.

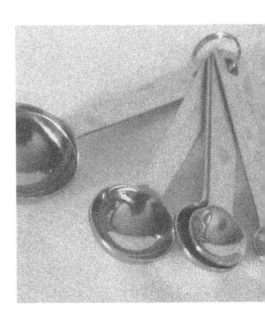

Dark meat seitan

If you are making Udon Noodles with Seitan, Crispy Sweet and Hot Orange Seitan, Savory Seitan Strips, or Seitan à la Bourguignonne, prepare your Basic Dough, wrap it, and cook it in this highly seasoned braising liquid that will flavor the dough as it cooks.

The flavors in this braising liquid are rich, savory, and a touch smoky. There is enough liquid to cook one batch of Basic Seitan Dough.

2 tablespoons olive oil

2 tablespoons red miso

2 tablespoons molasses

2 tablespoons tomato paste

1 tablespoon soy sauce

1 tablespoon balsamic vinegar

4 garlic cloves, minced

1 tablespoon dried basil

1 tablespoon dried oregano

2 teaspoons paprika

2 teaspoons salt

1 teaspoon whole peppercorns

1 heaping teaspoon onion powder

¼ teaspoon cayenne powder

1 cup port or Madeira [250ml]

5 cups vegetable stock [1.25L]

5 cups water [1.25L]

Uncooked prepared dough from Basic Seitan Recipe (page 230), wrapped according to recipe directions

1. In a medium bowl, **mix** together the olive oil, miso, molasses, tomato paste, soy sauce, balsamic vinegar, and garlic into a paste. Add the basil, oregano, paprika, salt, peppercorns, and onion powder. Stir to blend. Set the paste aside.

2. In a large nonreactive pot, **combine** the wine, vegetable stock, and water. Bring to a boil. Ladle about 1 cup [250ml] of the hot liquid into the seasoning paste. Stir until well incorporated. Stir everything back into the pot and return to a boil.

3. Place the wrapped seitan packages in the pot and **reduce** the heat to a simmer. Partially cover the pot with a lid and cook for 1 hour.

4. Use tongs to **turn** the seitan over so all sides get adequately exposed to the braising liquid. Continue to cook for another 1 to 1½ hours. (The longer you cook the

meat, the firmer it will become; at any point after 1½ hours total you may remove the seitan from the liquid and unwrap it to check out the taste and firmness and decide whether you want to continue cooking.) If you see that the liquid has evaporated and more than half of the seitan is exposed, add an additional 1 to 2 cups [250 to 500ml] stock. The seitan will be firm after braising, but it will continue to firm up in the refrigerator overnight.

5. Let cool, remove the string (if using) and cheesecloth, and slice the seitan into rounds ½ inch [1cm] thick or cut into other desired shapes (such as dice, fingers, or thin strips) and proceed with the recipe of your choice.

6. Store dark meat seitan in the refrigerator, completely immersed in the braising liquid and well sealed, for up to 3 days.

Savory seitan roast with burgundy garlic sauce

In this recipe, the uncooked seitan dough is mixed with a highly seasoned marinade and then baked rather than boiled for 2 hours. The result is a delicious vegetarian meat that is sausage-like and tender on the inside, crisp on the outside. It's a very comforting dish and makes an excellent presentation. Top with Burgundy Garlic Sauce, or serve the sauce on the side along with mashed potatoes, gravy, and a side of vegetables.

Vegetable oil

Uncooked prepared dough from Basic Seitan Dough (page 230)

BRAISING LIQUID

2 tablespoons maple syrup

2 tablespoons port or red wine

2 tablespoons balsamic vinegar

1 tablespoon molasses

2 teaspoons soy sauce

4 garlic cloves, minced

4 whole cloves

1 tablespoon fennel seeds

2 teaspoons paprika

1 teaspoon onion powder

1 teaspoon caraway seeds

1 teaspoon dried basil

1 teaspoon dried oregano

1 teaspoon freshly ground black pepper

½ teaspoon crushed hot red pepper

GLAZE

2 tablespoons port or red wine

2 tablespoons maple syrup

2 tablespoons balsamic vinegar

2 tablespoons olive oil

1 tablespoon soy sauce

Burgundy Garlic Sauce (recipe follows)

1. **Preheat** the oven to 375°F [190ºC]. Liberally oil a 9 by 5 by 3 inches [23 by 13 by 8cm] loaf pan and set aside. Prepare the Basic Seitan Recipe dough through Step 1.

2.   Combine all the braising liquid ingredients in a large bowl and **mix** well. Do the same for the glaze in a small bowl or measuring cup and set aside.

3.   Add the prepared dough to the braising liquid. **Knead** together for about 2 minutes, until the ingredients are very well incorporated. Put the seasoned dough in the oiled loaf pan and pack down as much as possible to press out any air bubbles. The dough will expand during cooking, so don't worry about any extra space. (The loaf can be made ahead to this point up to 24 hours in advance. Cover tightly with plastic wrap and refrigerate.)

4.   Cover the pan with aluminum foil and **bake** for approximately 2 hours. During the first hour, baste twice with the pan juices. After that time, use the glaze to baste a couple more times during roasting. Remove the foil for the last 5 minutes of cooking. The finished roast should be firm but still springy to the touch, and the glaze on top should crisp slightly and be lightly browned. Remove from the oven and let rest for a few minutes. Remove to a cutting board and cut into ½-inch [1-cm] slices with a sharp serrated knife. Serve topped with the Burgundy Garlic Sauce.

SERVES 4 TO 6

Burgundy garlic sauce

A simple, classically inspired sauce restructured slightly by adding soy sauce and miso for a deeper flavor.

1 bottle burgundy or other red wine [750ml]

2 teaspoons soy sauce

6 garlic cloves, crushed through a press

2 cups vegetable stock [500ml]

2 tablespoons whole wheat flour

2 tablespoons butter or olive oil [30g]

1 tablespoon unrefined cane sugar

½ teaspoon red miso

½ teaspoon salt

1. In a large nonreactive saucepan, **combine** the wine, soy sauce, and garlic. Bring to a boil over medium-high heat. Cook until the wine is reduced by half. Add the stock and return to a boil. Again cook until the liquid is again reduced by about half. Set aside.

2. In a large dry skillet, **toast** the flour over medium-low heat, shaking the pan constantly, until the flour is fragrant and beige, 1 to 2 minutes. Watch carefully, because flour can burn quickly.

3. Immediately add the butter and **whisk** until melted and smooth. Gradually whisk in the wine reduction. Bring to a boil, whisking, until the sauce is smooth and thickened. Reduce the heat to low and continue to whisk for 30 to 60 seconds longer.

4. Stir in the sugar, miso, and salt. **Simmer** for 1 to 2 minutes longer.

MAKES ABOUT 2 CUPS [500 ML]

Savory seitan strips with sweet and sour sauce

This makes great use of the Dark Meat Seitan Braising Liquid. After cooking the seitan, the leftover marinade is reduced to concentrate the flavors. The sweet and sour sauce is added for an unusual combination. Almost by accident, I found that when the two liquids are combined, a very enjoyable taste develops that unites yet continues to highlight each flavor in just the right blend. Serve hot over rice or noodles.

TIP: You will need to make the Sweet and Sour Sauce first, I suggest doing this while the Dark Meat Seitan is cooking.

1 recipe Dark Meat Seitan (page 234)

1 medium onion, chopped

2 tablespoons olive oil

½ pound cremini mushrooms, thinly sliced [250g]

½ teaspoon salt

⅛ teaspoon freshly ground pepper

1¼ cups Sweet and Sour Sauce (page 243) [325ml]

1 tablespoon arrowroot

1. Remove the cooked seitan from its braising liquid and cut it into sticks measuring about 2 inches by ½ inch [5 by 1cm]. Strain the braising liquid into a measuring cup, pouring enough to equal 1½ cups [375ml]. Reserve separately.

2. In a large skillet, sauté the onion in the olive oil over medium-high heat oil until slightly browned, 3 to 5 minutes. Add the mushrooms and cook for another 5 minutes, or until they have softened. Season with the salt and pepper. Add the reserved liquid, reduce the heat to medium-low, and simmer for 10 minutes, stirring occasionally. Add the Sweet and Sour Sauce and simmer 10 minutes longer.

3. Stir the arrowroot into the remaining ½ cup [125ml] liquid and mix until smooth. Stir into the mushroom sauce in the pan and bring to a boil, stirring for another minute or so, until thickened and smooth.

SERVES 4

Free-range roasted seitan with mushroom ragout

This is essentially the same recipe as the Light Meat Seitan (page 232), with slight modifications for a roasted dish. While good any time, this dish, topped with a savory mushroom ragout, may be especially appropriate around the holidays if you are looking for a vegetarian substitute for turkey or chicken. Serve with rice or mashed potatoes.

Vegetable oil

Uncooked prepared dough from Basic Seitan Recipe (page 230)

BRAISING LIQUID

1 tablespoon nutritional yeast

2 teaspoons unrefined cane sugar

1 teaspoon mustard powder

1 teaspoon dried thyme

1 teaspoon onion powder

½ teaspoon crushed hot red pepper

½ teaspoon celery seed

½ teaspoon fennel seeds

½ teaspoon dried rosemary

½ teaspoon dried sage

3 garlic cloves, minced

½ teaspoon salt

½ teaspoon freshly ground black pepper

¼ cup dry white wine [60ml]

2 tablespoons olive oil

2 teaspoons soy sauce

2 teaspoons white wine vinegar or lemon juice

GLAZE

¼ cup dry white wine [60ml]

2 tablespoons olive oil

2 teaspoons soy sauce

2 teaspoons lemon juice

1 teaspoon unrefined cane sugar

Mushroom Ragout (recipe follows)

1. Preheat the oven to 375°F [190ºC]. Liberally oil a 4½ by 8½ inches [11 by 22cm] loaf pan and set aside. **Prepare** the Basic Seitan Recipe dough through Step 1.

2. Combine all the braising liquid ingredients in a large bowl and **mix** well. Do the same for the glaze in smaller bowl or measuring cup and set aside.

3. Add the prepared dough to the liquid. **Knead** together for about 2 minutes, until the ingredients are very well incorporated. Put the seasoned seitan and any remaining liquid in the loaf pan and press the dough down as much as possible. If the dough separates from itself after kneading, fold the edges under. At this point, the dough will not fill the pan; it will expand during cooking. (The loaf can be made ahead to this point up to 24 hours in advance. Cover tightly with plastic wrap and refrigerate.)

4. Cover the pan with aluminum foil and **bake** for about 2 hours. During the first hour, baste twice with the pan juices. After that time, use the glaze to baste a couple more times. Uncover for the last 5 minutes of cooking. The finished roast should be firm but still springy to the touch. Remove to a cutting board, let rest 5 minutes, then cut into ½-inch [1-cm] slices with a sharp serrated knife. Add the seitan slices to the hot Mushroom Ragout and simmer for 2 minutes before serving.

SERVES 4 TO 6

Mushroom Ragout

2 tablespoons olive oil

1 medium onion, thinly sliced

½ pound combination of various fresh mushrooms (chanterelle, cremini, portobello), thinly sliced [250g]

6 dried shiitake or porcini mushrooms, soaked in 1 cup [250ml] hot water, drained, water reserved

2 garlic cloves, crushed through a press

1 tablespoon unbleached all-purpose flour

2 teaspoons minced fresh thyme

1 tablespoon tomato paste

1 teaspoon red miso

1 teaspoon salt

¼ teaspoon freshly ground pepper

1 tablespoon balsamic vinegar

1. In a large skillet, **heat** the olive oil over medium-high heat. Add the onion and cook, stirring occasionally, until golden, about 5 minutes. Add the fresh and dried mushrooms and the garlic and cook, stirring often, until the mushrooms soften and give up their juices, 5 to 7 minutes longer.

2. **Sprinkle** the flour and thyme over the mushrooms. Cook, stirring, about 1 minute. Pour in the reserved mushroom soaking liquid and bring to a boil, stirring until the liquid is smooth and thickened. Stir in the tomato paste, miso, salt, and pepper. Reduce the heat to low and simmer for 3 minutes. Stir in the vinegar.

Crispy sweet and hot orange Seitan

A crispy beef recipe I used to eat a lifetime ago in a Chinese restaurant far, far away **inspired** this dish. I use my sweet and sour sauce recipe with two slight changes: orange juice for the mango and a bit more sugar. For this recipe, you'll need both a large cast-iron skillet and a wok. Serve with rice and a salad.

Sweet and Sour Sauce (recipe follows)

2 tablespoons peanut or safflower oil

10 dried Thai or other hot red chiles (1 to 3 broken open)

3 garlic cloves, minced

½ recipe Dark Meat Seitan (page 234), cut into thin strips

2 carrots, cut into thin strips

3 stalks celery, cut into thin strips

1. Make the Sweet and Sour Sauce and set aside.

2. Preheat the oven to 375°F [190ºC]. **Heat** 1 tablespoon of the peanut oil in a cast-iron skillet over medium-high heat. Add the chiles and garlic and cook for 30 seconds, stirring often. Add the seitan strips and stir a few times. Add the sweet and sour sauce and bring to a simmer. Cook, stirring constantly, for 10 minutes, or until most of the sauce has been absorbed by the seitan and the rest coats the strips.

3. Transfer the seitan in the skillet to the oven and **bake** for about 20 minutes, stirring once or twice. Remove and let cool; the seitan will become crisp.

4. In a wok or a large skillet, **heat** the remaining 1 tablespoon oil over high heat. Add the carrots and celery and cook, stirring often, until barely softened, about 1 minute. Add the seitan and continue to cook, stirring, until heated through, about 1 minute.

SERVES 2

Sweet and sour sauce

½ cup finely chopped onion [70g]

1 tablespoon peanut or safflower oil

1 cup frozen or fresh pitted cherries, coarsely chopped [150g]

1¼ cups orange juice [325ml]

⅔ cup sherry vinegar or red wine vinegar [150ml]

⅓ cup unrefined cane sugar [70g]

1½ teaspoons tamarind paste

1. In a nonreactive medium saucepan with a heavy bottom, **cook** the onion in the peanut oil over medium-low heat until very soft but not brown, 5 to 7 minutes.

2. **Add** the cherries, orange juice, vinegar, and sugar. Bring to a boil, cover, and reduce the heat to a bare simmer. Cook for 10 minutes. Uncover and cook 10 minutes longer, stirring occasionally so the sauce does not stick to the bottom or sides of the pan.

3. Pass the sauce through a food mill or fine mesh strainer and **press** through until the solids are practically dry. Return the sauce to the pan, stir in the tamarind paste, and simmer uncovered for 5 minutes, or until the sauce is reduced enough to coat a spoon heavily.

MAKES ABOUT 1 ½ CUPS [375G]

Ken pow seitan with asparagus

You may have heard of *kung pao* chicken in Chinese restaurants. Well, here's my vegetarian version. It's worth digging out the wok for this dish, but a large skillet will work. The more chiles you break open, the **hotter** Ken Pow will get.

IMPORTANT: You will use the Light Meat Seitan for this recipe. Make sure to eliminate the thyme, rosemary, and sage from the marinade.

½ recipe Light Meat Seitan (page 232; thyme, rosemary, and sage omitted from the seasoning paste), or Free-Range Roasted Seitan (page 240), cooked and cooled

2 tablespoons soy sauce

2 teaspoons mirin

2 teaspoons unrefined cane sugar

1 teaspoon toasted sesame oil

1 teaspoon vegetarian Worcestershire sauce

1 teaspoon black bean sauce

¼ teaspoon freshly ground pepper

1 tablespoon arrowroot

1 tablespoon peanut oil

1 carrot, thinly sliced into diagonal half-moons

12 asparagus spears, cut into 1-inch [2.5-cm] slices

3 garlic cloves, minced

10 dried small red chiles (1 to 3 broken open)

½ red bell pepper, cut into ¾-inch [2-cm] squares

¼ cup unsalted roasted peanuts [35g]

6 scallions, thinly sliced

1 can (8 ounces) water chestnuts [250g]

1. **Cut** the seitan into ½-inch [1-cm] dice. Set aside.

2. In a small bowl, **combine** the soy sauce, sugar, sesame oil, Worcestershire sauce, black bean sauce, pepper, arrowroot, and ¼ cup [60ml] water. Mix well. Set the sauce aside.

3. In a hot wok or large heavy frying pan, **heat** the peanut oil over high heat. Add

the carrot and asparagus and cook, tossing with a spatula frequently, for about 1 minute. Pour in ¼ cup [60ml] water and let steam for another minute.

4. Add the seitan, garlic, and chiles and cook, tossing, for another 30 seconds or so. Add the bell pepper and peanuts and **stir-fry** for another 30 to 60 seconds, until the bell pepper has softened slightly. Give the sauce a stir and pour it into the wok. Toss with the spatula until the sauce thickens. Stir in the scallions and water chestnuts and toss once or twice. Serve at once.

SERVES 4

tip   As with all stir-fry recipes, you must have everything prepped and ready to go before starting. I recommend serving a big bowl of sticky white rice alongside.

Udon noodles with seitan, broccoli, and napa cabbage

Thick udon noodles nearly melt in your mouth. When they are matched with a salty, savory sauce, I find them **addictive.** Look for fresh refrigerated noodles in your local Asian specialty shop. Boiling them just before adding them to the wok or frying pan will break them up and make them easier to handle. This dish makes a beautiful presentation and is a full meal on its own.

¼ ounce dried shiitake mushrooms [7g]

2 tablespoons peanut oil

10 dried small red chiles (1 to 3 broken open)

3 garlic cloves, minced

1 piece of ginger, 1 inch [2.5cm], thinly sliced into matchsticks

1 medium onion, thinly sliced

½ recipe cooked Dark Meat Seitan (page 234) or Savory Seitan Roast (page 236; omit sauce), thinly sliced

1½ cups napa cabbage, shredded [375ml]

1 medium carrot, shredded

1 pound fresh udon noodles [500g]

1½ cups cooked broccoli florets [80g]

1½ tablespoons toasted sesame oil

1 tablespoon black bean sauce

1 tablespoon unrefined cane sugar

1 teaspoon soy sauce

¾ to 1 cup bamboo shoots, thinly sliced

1 tablespoon rice wine vinegar

2 teaspoons fresh lime juice

Salt

1 handful of fresh bean sprouts

1 to 2 tablespoons shredded nori*

2 tablespoons black and white sesame seeds

Lime wedges, for garnish

*You can buy sheets of nori sea vegetable and toast and cut them yourself, or you can save yourself a lot of time and buy them already toasted and shredded. You will likely find this product in your Asian or Chinese specialty store.

1. Bring a large pot of water to a boil. You will **drop** your noodles in just before adding them to your wok or pan in Step 5.

2. In a medium heatproof bowl, **soak** the mushrooms in hot water to cover until soft, about 15 minutes. Lift out the mushrooms and squeeze excess liquid back into the bowl. Strain the soaking liquid through a coffee filter or double thickness of dampened cheesecloth and reserve.

3. Heat the peanut oil in a wok or large frying pan over high heat. Add the chiles, garlic, and ginger. **Cook,** stirring constantly, for 30 seconds, or until the garlic is fragrant but not brown. Add the onion and cook until softened and lightly browned, 2 to 3 minutes.

4. **Add** the seitan and cook for a minute or so. If the ingredients begin to stick at this point, add a couple of tablespoons of the reserved mushroom soaking liquid.

5. Reduce the heat slightly. Add the cabbage and carrot and cook until the cabbage wilts, about 1 minute. At the same time, add the udon noodles to the boiling water and cook for 30 seconds, or until heated through and separated. **Drain** and add to the wok. Add the broccoli and stir well. Stir in the sesame oil, black bean sauce, sugar, soy sauce, and bamboo shoots.

6. Remove from the heat. **Stir** in the vinegar and lime juice and season with salt to taste. Serve the noodles hot, topping each portion with bean sprouts, nori, and sesame seeds. Garnish the plates with a lime wedge.

SERVES 6

tip   Blanch your broccoli for about 1 minute in the same boiling water you are using to cook the udon noodles. Cool under cold water and set aside until ready to add to the wok.

Seitan à la bourguignonne

With no apologies to boeuf à la bourguignonne, here is my version of the French stew cooked in red wine. This vegetarian version is incredibly rich, **slightly sweet, and very satisfying. Serve over rice or noodles.**

¼ cup unbleached all-purpose flour [30g]

About ¾ portion cooked Dark Meat Seitan (page 234), cut into bite-size chunks*

3 tablespoons olive oil

1 onion, thinly sliced

1 leek (white and tender green parts), sliced into half-moons

¾ pound cremini or portobello mushrooms (or a combination), thinly sliced [375g]

1 tablespoon fresh thyme, minced

2 teaspoons fresh rosemary, minced

2 carrots, cut into bite-size chunks

3 garlic cloves, thinly sliced

1 teaspoon salt

¼ teaspoon freshly ground pepper

2 cups burgundy or other dry red wine [500ml]

3 tablespoons tomato paste

1 bay leaf

1 cup vegetable stock [250ml]

2 tablespoons balsamic vinegar

2 to 3 tablespoons parsley, coarsely chopped

1 tablespoon fresh lemon juice

1. Place the flour in a sealable plastic bag. **Add** the seitan and shake until all the pieces are well coated. Put the coated seitan on a plate and set aside.

2. In a Dutch oven or large soup pot, **heat** 2 tablespoons of the olive oil over medium-high heat. Fry the seitan in batches without crowding until browned on all sides. Use tongs to turn the pieces. You may have to add more oil as you go along. Remove the seitan and set aside.

3. **Heat** another 1½ tablespoons oil in the same pot. Add the onion and leek and cook over medium heat until very soft and lightly browned, 5 to 7 minutes. Add the

*You may substitute 8 ounces [250g] of store-bought seitan.

mushrooms, thyme, and rosemary and cook, stirring often, until the mushrooms are tender, about 3 minutes. Add the carrots and garlic and cook for another minute. Season with the salt and pepper.

4. Add the wine and bring to a boil. Cook for 10 minutes, stirring frequently. Stir in the tomato paste and add the bay leaf. Reduce the heat to a simmer, cover with the lid ajar, and cook for 45 minutes.

5. Stir in the stock and vinegar. Continue to simmer uncovered for about 15 minutes longer, stirring often, until the stew is thickened to your liking. Stir in the parsley and lemon juice and season with additional salt and pepper to taste.

SERVES 4 TO 6

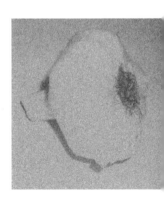

9 VEGETABLES

and GRAINS

on the Side:

All the Best

Accompaniments

I offer these sides to complement more complex vegetarian main dishes or for combining with other sides to make a composed meal. The timeless classic of a main thing (meat) plus a starch thing plus a vegetable thing may live on forever. But vegetarians want a balanced meal, too, and I have no quarrel with mimicking traditional plates that feature a main course, starch, and vegetable.

Who wouldn't want a crunchy char-grilled piece of marinated tofu with a side of savory mashed potatoes and an ear of buttered corn, for example? But I'm looking further when I examine a plate of food. While I do keep in mind nutritional balance, I look at the symmetry of textures, colors, and mouthfeel. So no, I wouldn't serve lentil soup with a side of baked beans, red bean salad, and a black bean burger just because they are all vegetarian dishes. Too many beans, too many soft things, and not enough dissemination of salty, savory, sweet, and sour tastes, and so on. And, of course, a plate of sides has the same rule. But that's the beauty of exquisite vegetarian cuisine.

Experienced vegetarians know that there are really no "sides" on a round plate, meaning a menu featuring Roasted Potatoes with Arugula and Aged Vinegar plus Quinoa Pilaf and Gold and Red Beets would make an interesting and tasty meal. You've got distinctions of flavor: the tang of the vinegar. You've got differences in mouthfeel: the crunch of sugar snap peas versus the softness of eggplant. You've got the variety of colors: red beets, green spinach, orange carrots. And without much thought, it's a nutritious meal, as well.

This chapter, as most throughout the book, introduces you to recipes that include flavors, foods, and cooking techniques you may not be familiar with or may never have even heard of.

If you've never tasted quinoa (pronounced KEEN-wah), you must try this high-protein staple of the ancient Incas, who referred to it as the "mother grain." It is cooked like rice but takes a much shorter time. It is light and spices up extremely well, picking up the flavors of garlic, soy sauce, or herbs, for example, with ease.

And if you've never roasted vegetables (it always surprises me how many people have not), then you're in for one of life's simply sophisticated pleasures. Done properly—crisp on the outside, tender on the inside—roasted vegetables are both beautiful and enticing, the perfect accompaniment to any number of other dishes.

So join me in this chapter with eyes wide open and palates at attention. Be ready to savor the effortless wonders of simple foods cooked just so and the refined techniques of more intricate recipes prepared professionally. In both cases, or anywhere in between, "Vegetables and Grains on the Side" will help you see how just the right touch, just the right flavor, and just the right color will make your vegetarian plate perfect.

Caramelized sweet potato with toasted pumpkin seeds

This colorful side dish makes a beautiful presentation. It's especially appropriate in the fall and winter months, and, of course, is perfect for the holiday table. I find a well-seasoned cast-iron skillet works best here, but a nonstick skillet will do.

2 medium beets, scrubbed and cut into ⅜-inch [1-cm] dice

1 medium sweet potato, scrubbed and cut into ⅜-inch [1-cm] dice

3 tablespoons fresh pumpkin seeds

½ pound green beans, stem ends and strings removed [250g]

1 tablespoon plus 2 teaspoons olive oil

2 tablespoons fresh lemon juice

Salt and freshly ground pepper

1. Set the beets on one half of a steamer rack and steam for about 10 minutes, until they begin to soften slightly. **Arrange** the sweet potato on the other half of the rack. A few overlaps are okay, but the key is try to keep the vegetables as separate as possible so the beets don't bleed all over the sweet potato. Continue to steam until both vegetables are tender.

2. While the sweet potato and beets are cooking, place the pumpkin seeds in a large dry skillet, preferably cast-iron, over medium-high heat. **Shake** the pan or stir frequently until most of the seeds have popped, about 30 seconds. Immediately remove from the pan and set aside.

3. In the same skillet, **sauté** the green beans in 2 teaspoons of the olive oil for 2 to 3 minutes, stirring and tossing frequently, until softened but still slightly crunchy. You may choose to brown them slightly for extra flavor. Set the beans aside in the middle of a round platter.

4. **Spoon** the cooked beets around the beans. In the same skillet, sauté the steamed

sweet potato in the remaining 1 tablespoon oil over high heat, tossing, until lightly browned, about 2 minutes.

5. Spoon the sweet potatoes on top of the beets. Drizzle the lemon juice over the vegetables and season with salt and pepper to taste. Sprinkle the toasted pumpkin seeds over all.

SERVES 4

Asian-inspired sugar snap peas and red peppers

Bright-green sugar snap peas, so tender they are eaten pod and all, along with scarlet bell peppers make a striking pair. The combination is versatile enough to accompany a wide range of other dishes. Serve with Citrus-Marinated Tofu Cutlets (page 122) and Cauliflower Puree (page 261).

1 large red bell pepper, cut into 1-inch [2.5-cm] strips

2 teaspoons olive oil

8 ounces fresh sugar snap peas, stemmed, strings removed [250g]*

2 teaspoons toasted sesame oil

2 teaspoons soy sauce

½ teaspoon sugar

Salt and freshly ground pepper

1. In a large nonstick skillet, sauté the bell pepper strips in the olive oil over medium-high heat until bright red and just slightly softened, about 2 minutes.

2. Add the sugar snap peas and cook, tossing, until they are crisp-tender and bright green, 1 to 2 minutes longer.

3. Add the sesame oil, soy sauce, and sugar and remove from the heat. Season with salt and pepper to taste. Toss and serve at once.

SERVES 4

*Substitute snow peas if sugar snaps are not available.

Green beans and garlic baby spinach

I like the soft mellowness of baby spinach combined with the sharpness of the garlic. Cooked for just a minute or two, the spinach is done when it turns bright green. If cooked longer, the leaves will throw off too much liquid and shrivel up. For additional color and flavor, sauté finely diced red bell peppers with the spinach. Serve with Shiitake-Apple Risotto (page 210) and Blackened Fruit Jerk Tempeh (page 150).

⅓ cup finely chopped onion [50g]

1 tablespoon olive oil

4 garlic cloves, minced

½ teaspoon crushed hot red pepper

12 ounces baby spinach leaves [375g]

¼ cup vegetable stock or water [60 ml]

Salt and freshly ground pepper

1. In a large skillet, cook the onion in the olive oil over medium heat until very soft and lightly browned, about 5 minutes. Add the garlic and hot pepper and continue to cook for 1 minute longer.

2. Raise the heat to medium-high and add the spinach and vegetable stock. Season with salt and pepper. Use tongs or 2 wooden spoons to mix and turn the leaves several times. The spinach will wilt and turn a vivid green quickly. Remove with a slotted spoon and serve.

SERVES 2

Moroccan carrots with cumin and lemon

Tangy, **tasty**, and pretty to look at, this dish can be served warm, cold, or at room temperature. Baby carrots—the real ones with their green tops still intact, not bagged—prepared the same way as the whole ones called for here also make an outstanding presentation.

8 medium carrots, roughly the same length, peeled, ends trimmed, left whole

3 tablespoons fresh lemon juice

2 teaspoons olive oil

1 garlic clove, crushed through a press

½ teaspoon ground cumin

½ teaspoon sweet paprika

½ teaspoon unrefined cane sugar

¼ teaspoon salt

2 tablespoons coarsely chopped parsley

1. **Steam** the carrots until tender, 7 to 10 minutes.

2. While the carrots are steaming, **mix** together the lemon juice, olive oil, garlic, cumin, paprika, sugar, and salt in a small bowl to make a dressing.

3. When the carrots are done, transfer them to a shallow serving dish. **Drizzle** the dressing over the carrots and roll them with your fingers to make sure they are well coated. Garnish with the parsley.

SERVES 4

Glazed carrots with fresh nutmeg

The history of nutmeg goes back many centuries. As with many herbs and spices, long before nutmeg was used in the kitchen, it was valued for other perceived valuable properties. It was used medicinally, as an aphrodisiac, and as a fumigant. Culinarily speaking, freshly grated is the ideal way to use this spice. Ground nutmeg loses its flavor very quickly. If you don't have a nutmeg grater, I recommend this inexpensive purchase; you will really appreciate the results.

5 medium carrots, peeled and cut into diagonal slices about ¼ inch [.5 cm] thick

1½ tablespoons butter [25g] or olive oil

1½ tablespoons unrefined cane sugar

¼ teaspoon freshly grated nutmeg

Salt

1. Steam the carrot slices until just barely tender, 5 to 7 minutes.

2. In a large cast-iron skillet or sauté pan, melt the butter or heat the olive oil over medium-high heat.

3. Add the carrots and sauté until lightly browned on both sides, tossing and stirring frequently, 2 to 3 minutes.

4. Add the sugar to the skillet and toss until it melts and the carrots are glazed, about 1 minute. Remove from the heat, dust with the nutmeg, and season with salt to taste.

SERVES 4

Roasted root vegetables

Roasting **caramelizes** the sugar in vegetables, highlighting their natural sweetness and enhancing their flavor. If they are organic, simply scrub and cut as directed. Done correctly, roasted vegetables are really beautiful—simple but delicious. I recommend topping the vegetables with Cranberry Balsamic Vinaigrette (page 282) and serving Almond Coconut Dal (page 177) on the side.

3 or 4 Jerusalem artichokes, scrubbed and sliced

½ celery root, peeled and sliced

2 large carrots, scrubbed and sliced

1 head of garlic, cloves separated, peeled, and left whole

3 shallots, thinly sliced

3 cippolini or 1 medium onion, sliced

2 parsnips, peeled and sliced

1 medium sweet potato, scrubbed and sliced

1 medium baking potato, scrubbed and sliced

1½ tablespoons extra virgin olive oil

Salt and freshly ground pepper

Splash of cider vinegar or balsamic vinegar

1. **Preheat** the oven to 375°F [190°C]. Place all the cut vegetables in a large bowl. Add the olive oil and toss to coat.

2. Spread out the vegetables on a large baking sheet or shallow baking dish. **Season** with salt and pepper to taste.

3. Roast for 45 minutes to 1 hour, turning with a wide spatula several times, until lightly browned and soft. You want a slightly crisp, brown outside while maintaining a soft center. **Transfer** to a serving bowl and toss with a splash of vinegar.

SERVES 4

chef's tip

For a professional-looking presentation, stack roasted vegetables in an imaginative way, like kindling for a fire, making sure they are evenly distributed among servings.

Stuffed japanese eggplant

Believe it or not, eggplant is actually a fruit, specifically a berry. There are several interesting varieties besides the fat oblong, round, or pear-shaped types we are accustomed to. One of them, the Japanese eggplant, which I prefer in this recipe, is a beautiful, slender, light purple specimen with tender, slightly sweet flesh. It has a lovely creamy texture and attractive purple skin.

1 medium red potato, scrubbed and cut into small dice

½ pound tomatoes [250g]

2 Japanese eggplants

2 tablespoons pine nuts

1 small red onion, finely chopped

2 tablespoons olive oil

3 garlic cloves, minced

1 teaspoon dried oregano

1 teaspoon dried basil

1½ teaspoons red miso

1 to 2 tablespoons fresh lemon juice

Salt and freshly ground pepper

4 ounces Monterey Jack cheese, shredded [125g]

Shredded fresh basil, for garnish

1. Steam or boil the diced potatoes until tender, about 5 minutes. Drain and rinse under cold running water; drain well. Put the potatoes in a medium bowl.

2. Preheat the broiler with the rack set 5 to 6 inches [13 to 15cm] from the heat. Place the tomatoes on a baking sheet and broil, turning with tongs, until the skin is blistered and slightly charred all over, 3 to 5 minutes. Peel off the skins and coarsely chop the tomatoes. Add to the potatoes.

3. Preheat the oven temperature to 350°F [175°C]. Slice the eggplants in half lengthwise; brush lightly with oil and place cut side down on the baking sheet. Bake for 20 minutes, or until just tender. Remove from the baking sheet and let cool. Slice each piece lengthwise in half again so you have 8 long wedges.

4. With a spoon, gently **scoop** out the cooked eggplant, being careful not to tear the skin. Coarsely chop the eggplant and add to the potatoes and tomatoes. Set the skins aside separately.

5. **Toast** the pine nuts in a large dry skillet over medium heat, stirring often, until lightly browned, 2 to 3 minutes. Set aside in a small dish.

6. In same pan, **cook** the red onion in the olive oil over medium heat until very soft and lightly browned, 5 to 7 minutes. Add the garlic, oregano, and basil and stir for about 30 seconds, until fragrant.

7. Increase the heat to medium-high. **Add** the potatoes, tomatoes, chopped eggplant, miso, and 1 tablespoon of the lemon juice. Cook, stirring often, until the excess liquid evaporates and the mixture begins to thicken, 3 to 5 minutes. Remove from the heat and stir in the pine nuts. Season with salt and pepper to taste. Add more lemon juice, if desired.

8. Let the vegetable mixture cool a bit, then spoon into the eggplant skins. **Top** with shredded cheese and place on a lightly oiled baking sheet. Ideally, cover and refrigerate the dish at this point, giving everything a chance to set nicely. When ready to eat, place the eggplant boats under a preheated broiler until the stuffing is reheated and the cheese melts, about 2 minutes. Garnish with basil before serving.

SERVES 2 TO 4

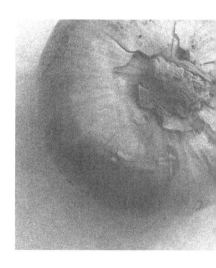

Golden and red beets with toasted garlic

Beets are very **nutritious** and one of nature's best internal bodily cleansers and detoxifiers. Overlap the beets in a circle; toss the garlic on top or in the center. Alternately, if the beets are super-large, cut them in half before slicing.

1 large round red beet, peeled and sliced into ¼-inch [.5-cm] rounds

1 large round golden beet, peeled and sliced into ¼-inch [.5-cm] rounds

2 tablespoons extra virgin olive oil

1 head of garlic, cloves separated and peeled, hard bits cut off, sliced in half

Salt and freshly ground pepper

1 teaspoon red wine vinegar

1. **Steam** the beets, either separately in 2 batches or in a double-decker steamer, until just tender, 7 to 10 minutes. Remove to separate plates and let cool.

2. In a large cast-iron or nonstick skillet, **heat** the olive oil over medium heat. Add the garlic and cook, stirring often, until lightly browned, about 2 minutes. With a slotted spoon, remove the garlic to a small bowl.

3. Add the beets to the garlic oil left in the pan. **Cook** over medium heat until heated through and well coated with the oil, about 2 minutes. Toss in the garlic for one last twirl around the pan. Season with salt and pepper and a spritz of vinegar.

SERVES 4

Cauliflower millet puree

Millet, which in North America is grown primarily for birdseed, has been around since ancient times. It was a mainstay of the Chinese diet even before rice. It is a nutritious grain, with a profusion of minerals and vitamins. Its somewhat bland flavor makes it appealing as a base on which to build other flavors.

This is a very comforting side dish, much like mashed potatoes but with a slightly nutty flavor. It also happens to be extremely nutritious. It makes an excellent accompaniment to three dishes: Roasted Vegetables (page 257), Crisp Tempeh with Honey-Mustard Sauce (page 152), and Citrus Tofu Cutlets (page 122).

1 pound cauliflower, cut into florets [500g]	½ cup millet [100g]
2 large shallots or 1 small onion, minced	1¼ cups vegetable stock or water [325ml]
3 garlic cloves, minced	¼ cup plain yogurt, preferably organic [60ml]
3 tablespoons olive oil	Salt and freshly ground pepper

1. Boil or steam the cauliflower florets until tender, about 10 minutes. Drain and run under cold water until cool. Set aside.

2. In a medium, heavy-bottomed saucepan, cook the shallots and garlic in 1 tablespoon of the oil over medium heat until softened but not browned, about 2 minutes.

3. Add the millet and toast for another minute, stirring frequently with a wooden spoon. Add the stock and bring to a boil. Reduce to a simmer and cook until tender. If the liquid evaporates before the millet is done, add a small amount of water and continue cooking until tender.

4. In a food processor, puree the cauliflower until smooth. With the machine on, add the remaining 2 tablespoons oil, the yogurt, and a generous amount of salt and pepper. Add the millet and blend again until well incorporated. If not serving right away, keep warm in the oven or on the stovetop over very low heat.

SERVES 4

Curried cauliflower, carrots, and potatoes

Packed with lively taste, this vegetable ragout can serve as a substantial side dish or as a satisfying entree, depending on the rest of the meal. The rich brown sauce tastes complex, but it's your secret that the ingredients are simple: curry, white wine, a little miso, tomato paste, and sugar. If serving as a main dish, add a cup of chickpeas or some cubes of tofu for additional protein.

2 carrots, cut into bite-size chunks

3 medium-size red potatoes, cut into ¾-inch [2-cm] chunks

¼ pound cauliflower, divided into florets [125g]

½ onion, minced

1 tablespoon olive oil

2 tablespoons curry powder

1 cup dry white wine [250ml]

1 tablespoon tomato paste

2 teaspoons unrefined cane sugar

1½ teaspoons chickpea miso

Salt and freshly ground pepper

1 cup frozen peas

½ tart apple, coarsely chopped

1. Steam the carrots and potatoes until tender, about 10 minutes. Add the cauliflower and cook for an additional 2 minutes, or until tender but not mushy. Set aside.

2. In a large skillet, cook the onion in the olive oil over medium heat until lightly browned, about 5 minutes. Add the curry powder and cook, stirring, 30 to 60 seconds longer.

3. Increase the heat slightly and add ½ cup [125ml] of the wine. Bring to a boil and stir in the tomato paste, sugar, and miso. Add the remaining wine. Cook, stirring, until a nice thick sauce forms. Season with salt and pepper to taste.

4. Add the steamed vegetables and stir to coat well with the curry sauce. Add the peas and apple, reduce the heat to low, and simmer for 2 minutes.

SERVES 4 TO 6

Twice-baked potatoes with roasted garlic and crispy shallots

This is so tasty and so easy, it's just plain remarkable. **Serve with a side of sautéed Sugar Snap Peas and Red Pepper (page 253) or a salad.**

2 baking potatoes, 10 to 12 ounces [300 to 350g] **each**

4 garlic cloves, roasted

2 tablespoons grated sharp Cheddar cheese

1 teaspoon fresh thyme, minced, or ½ teaspoon dried thyme

¼ cup plain soy milk [60ml]

Salt and freshly ground pepper

Extra virgin olive oil

⅓ cup canola or safflower oil [75ml]

4 medium shallots, thinly sliced

1. Preheat the oven to 375°F [190°C]. Bake the potatoes until soft, 45 minutes to 1 hour. Remove the potatoes, but leave the oven on.

2. Roast the garlic cloves in a dry cast-iron skillet over medium heat, turning often, until softened and browned in spots, 10 to 15 minutes. Peel and coarsely chop.

3. As soon as the potatoes are cool enough to handle, slice a piece off the top 3 to 4 inches long [8 to 10cm] and about ½ inch deep [1cm]. Gently scoop out the potatoes into a bowl, being careful not to tear the shell. Add the roasted garlic, cheese, and thyme and mash all together until the potato is smooth. Blend in the soy milk. Season with salt and pepper to taste. Scoop the mashed potato back into the shells.

4. Place the stuffed potatoes in a small baking dish. Drizzle the olive oil over the tops and return to the oven. Bake for 10 to 15 minutes, until lightly browned on top.

5. While the potatoes are baking the second time, heat the canola oil in a small saucepan over medium-high heat. Fry the shallots in small batches until golden brown, 2 to 3 minutes per batch. With a slotted spoon, scoop out the shallots and drain on paper towels. Sprinkle with salt. Cascade the crispy shallots over the top of the twice-baked potatoes and onto the plate.

SERVES 2

Roasted potatoes with arugula and aged vinegar

Roasted potatoes, much like roasted vegetables, are a quintessentially **elegant** food. They are uncomplicated but exceedingly rich in flavor. They even taste good cold. To complement their smoky taste, use your best aged vinegar. I recommend serving this dish with Light Meat Seitan (page 232) and a salad.

1 pound red potatoes, cut into quarters or eighths, depending on size [500g]

2 tablespoons olive oil

Salt

½ red onion, thinly sliced

1 small bunch of arugula, tough stems removed

1 tablespoon aged sherry vinegar or balsamic vinegar

1. Preheat the oven to 375°F [190°C]. **Toss** the potatoes with 1 tablespoon of the olive oil to coat. Season liberally with salt. Spread out on a baking sheet and roast, turning with a spatula once or twice, for 40 to 50 minutes, or until browned and crispy on the outside and tender inside. Set aside in a medium bowl.

2. In a medium-size cast-iron or other heavy skillet, **heat** the remaining tablespoon oil over medium-high heat. Add the red onion and sauté until lightly browned, about 5 minutes. Add the arugula and toss for 15 to 30 seconds, until just wilted and still bright green.

3. Add the onions and arugula to the roasted potatoes and mix well. **Sprinkle** on the vinegar, toss, and serve warm.

SERVES 4

Roasted cauliflower and mushroom bhutanese red rice

Cooked Bhutanese red rice has a beautiful red russet color. Its slightly nutty taste blends perfectly with browned butter and pine nuts, giving it a real sassy flavor. Roasting cauliflower is an excellent technique, which enhances a vegetable that admittedly can be a tad on the boring side.

4 ounces cremini mushrooms, sliced [125g]

12 ounces cauliflower, trimmed and cut into slices ½-inch [1-cm] thick

1½ tablespoons olive oil

1⅛ teaspoon salt

1 cup Bhutanese red rice [200g]

2½ cups vegetable stock or water [625ml]

4 tablespoons unsalted butter, preferably organic

½ cup pine nuts [100g]

Chopped parsley, for garnish

1. Preheat the oven to 400°. On a large baking sheet, arrange the mushrooms and cauliflower separately. Toss both with the olive oil to coat lightly. Sprinkle with ⅛ teaspoon of the salt.

2. Roast for 15 to 20 minutes, until the mushrooms are soft and slightly shriveled. Remove the mushrooms to a plate and set aside. Turn over the cauliflower and continue to roast until it is tender and lightly browned around the edges, 5 to 10 minutes longer.

3. Meanwhile, cook the rice in the stock with the remaining 1 teaspoon salt, covered, until tender, about 15 minutes. Set aside in the covered pot.

4. In a small pan, melt the butter over medium-low heat. After the foam has settled, add the pine nuts. Continue to cook for another 1 to 2 minutes, stirring often, until the nuts begin to brown. Remove from the heat.

5. In a large bowl, toss the rice, cauliflower, and mushrooms. Pour the butter and pine nuts over the rice mixture. Garnish with parsley and serve.

SERVES 4 TO 6

Wild rice and barley with olives and almonds

What I find interesting about this **full-bodied** dish is that two disparate grains cook well together and at the same time. They hold their individual colors and complement each other: one with a slight crunch, the other with a familiar creaminess.

This dish is an exceptional "bring along" for a potluck. It matches beautifully alongside Frittata with Oven-Dried Tomatoes (page 76).

¾ cup wild rice [150g]

½ cup pearled barley [100g]

4 cups vegetable stock or water [950ml]

1½ teaspoons salt

¼ cup kalamata olives, pitted and sliced [50g]

¼ cup toasted almonds, slivered [50g]

½ fresh tart apple, diced

½ small red onion, thinly sliced, rinsed under cold water

2 tablespoons fresh lemon juice

3 scallions, thinly sliced

1. In a medium saucepan, **bring** the wild rice, barley, stock, and 1 teaspoon salt to a boil. Reduce the heat, cover, and simmer for 45 to 50 minutes, or until the rice and barley are tender. Remove from heat and set aside, covered to keep warm.

2. Meanwhile, in a large bowl, **toss** together the olives, almonds, apple, red onion, olive oil, and lemon juice. Add the wild rice and barley to the bowl and mix thoroughly. Serve warm or at room temperature.

SERVES 4 TO 6

Jasmine rice with toasted garlic

Because jasmine rice cooks so quickly, it's **excellent** for a fast side dish. Feel free to toast the garlic in advance so you don't have to rush and risk burning it while you're busy making the rest of the meal.

2 tablespoons olive oil

6 garlic cloves, thinly sliced

Salt

1 cup jasmine rice [200g]

2½ cups vegetable stock or water [625ml]

1. In a small saucepan, **heat** the olive oil over low heat. Add the garlic and cook very slowly, stirring frequently, until lightly browned and toasted, 3 to 5 minutes. The key is to cook at a snail's pace so the garlic doesn't burn and turn bitter. Immediately scoop out the garlic with a slotted spoon and set aside on a small plate. Season lightly with salt.

2. Raise the heat to medium-high, **add** the rice, and stir for about 1 minute, until most of the grains turn from opaque white to translucent. Add in the stock and 1 teaspoon salt and bring to a boil. Cover and reduce to a simmer; cook until tender, about 15 minutes.

3. Keeping the pan covered, remove from the heat and let stand for 5 minutes before serving. **Top** each serving with some of the toasted garlic slices.

SERVES 4

chef's note

Rice is often the perfect accompaniment for so many dishes. Some are surprisingly simple, and that's just the way you want them. Others are complex, both in flavor and preparation—and that's okay, too, for the right occasion. But no matter how easy or hard, rice can be a tricky proposition. Prepare it the exact same way on different days, and it comes out differently each time. Maybe the lid wasn't tight enough or the heat was slightly higher or the rice was older or the saucepan was not heavy enough. I guess it's like cooking in general—influenced by a variety of nuances. So take your rice cooking with a grain of salt, so to speak, and just enjoy.

Mexican brown rice with jalapeños and tomatillos

Fragrant jasmine rice also comes in a less-processed brown form, which has a great chewy texture. Here it becomes a beautiful green thanks to tart tomatillos and mildly hot jalapeño peppers.

4 tomatillos, husked and rinsed

¼ cup pine nuts [30g]

2 fresh jalapeño peppers

3 garlic cloves, unpeeled

¼ cup coarsely chopped cilantro [60ml]

2 teaspoons unrefined cane sugar

1 teaspoon salt

2½ cups plus 3 tablespoons vegetable stock [625ml plus 3 tablespoons]

½ white onion, chopped

1 tablespoon olive oil

1 cup brown jasmine or other long-grain brown rice [200g]

1. **Preheat** the broiler with a rack set 4 to 5 inches [10 to 13 cm] from the heat. Lay out the tomatillos on a baking pan and broil, turning until they are slightly blackened and softened, about 7 to 10 minutes. Coarsely chop the tomatillos and set them aside in a bowl along with their juices.

2. While the tomatillos are broiling, **toast** the pine nuts in a dry skillet over medium heat until they brown lightly. Toss and turn constantly so they don't burn. Set aside on a plate.

3. For your next step, make sure your kitchen is well ventilated. In the same skillet, **dry-roast** the jalapeño peppers and garlic cloves, turning every so often, until lightly blackened all over. Remove the stems from the hot peppers and coarsely chop.

4. In a blender or food processor, **combine** the tomatillos, roasted peppers and garlic, cilantro, sugar, salt, and 3 tablespoons stock. Puree until smooth.

5. In a medium saucepan, **sauté** the onion in the olive oil until very soft, 3 to 4 minutes. Add the rice and stir continuously for about 1 minute. Raise the heat to high and add the tomatillo sauce (it should sizzle); stir for about 30 seconds.

6. **Add** the remaining stock and bring to a boil. Cover, reduce to a simmer, and cook for 20 to 25 minutes, or until the rice is tender. Remove from the heat and let stand, covered, for 10 minutes before serving, garnished with the pine nuts.

SERVES 4

note If the rice is not done but the liquid has evaporated, add ¼ cup [60ml] boiling water (from a kettle) and continue to cook. Repeat if necessary.

Red chile roasted tomato rice

This rich red rice is **perfect** with Mexican Marinated Tofu (page 134). The two chiles I recommend here are mild to medium on the heat scale. Top with avocado slices or chopped scallions.

2 guajillo or red New Mexico chiles, seeded and stemmed*

½ pound plum tomatoes [250g]

3 garlic cloves, unpeeled

1 teaspoon unrefined cane sugar

1 teaspoon salt

½ white onion, cut into small dice

1 tablespoon olive oil

1 cup brown jasmine or other long-grain brown rice [200g]

2½ cups stock or water [625g]

½ cup frozen peas [60g]

1. In a small covered bowl or large covered glass, **soak** the chiles in very hot water until soft.

2. Preheat the broiler with a rack set 4 to 6 inches [10 to 15cm] from the heat. Lay out the tomatoes on a baking pan and broil until they are lightly blackened and softened and the skins are popping off, 5 to 7 minutes per side. **Turn** with tongs. Let cool, remove the skins, and set the tomatoes aside in a bowl with their juices.

3. While the tomatoes are broiling, in a cast-iron skillet over medium heat, **roast** the unpeeled garlic. Turn over with tongs occasionally but allow to get slightly blackened, 10 to 15 minutes. When cooled, peel and chop the garlic and add to the bowl with the tomatoes.

4. In a blender, puree the softened chiles, tomatoes, garlic, sugar, and salt. **Pour** the sauce back into the bowl.

*When the chiles have softened, taste the soaking water. If it is not bitter, substitute ½ cup [125ml] for ½ cup [125ml] stock.

5. In a saucepan, **cook** the onion in the olive oil over medium heat until very soft, 3 to 4 minutes. Add the rice and stir continuously for about 1 minute. Turn up the heat to high and add the tomato-chile sauce (it should sizzle); stir for about 30 seconds. Add the stock and bring to a boil. Cover, reduce to a simmer, and cook for 45 minutes, or until tender.

6. **Stir** in the peas. Remove from heat and let stand, covered, for 10 minutes before serving.

SERVES 4

note If the rice is not done but the liquid has evaporated, add ¼ cup [60ml] more boiling water and continue to cook. Repeat if necessary.

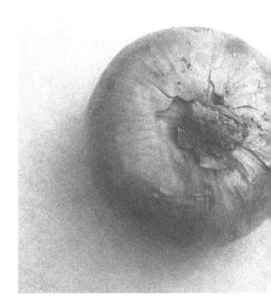

Roasted corn and mushroom salad

Your options are endless as to what you might put in this salad. Some of the ingredients are cooked and some are raw to take advantage of a **variety** of flavors and textures.

4 ears of corn

½ onion, chopped

2 tablespoons plus 2 teaspoons extra virgin olive oil

2 garlic cloves, minced

10 fresh shiitake mushrooms, stemmed, caps sliced

2 teaspoons ground cumin

1 teaspoon chickpea miso or white miso

Salt and freshly ground pepper

Juice of 1 lime

½ red bell pepper, finely diced

½ cucumber, peeled, seeded, and finely diced

2 teaspoons apple cider vinegar

1 avocado, sliced

Chopped watercress or other greens, for serving

1. **Shuck** the corn and set the kernels aside. Scrape any excess milk from the cobs with the back of a knife and set it aside in a large bowl. In a very hot cast-iron skillet, roast the corn kernels until lightly browned, stirring often with a wooden spoon. If the corn sticks excessively, add a few drops of oil. Add the roasted corn to the bowl with the corn milk.

2. Cook the onion in the same skillet in 2 tablespoons of the olive oil over medium-high heat, until lightly browned, 3 to 5 minutes. **Add** the garlic and mushrooms. Cook until the mushrooms are soft, about 5 minutes. Stir in the cumin and miso. Season with salt and pepper to taste.

3. Add the contents of the pan to the corn and mix well. Let cool slightly. Add the lime juice, bell pepper, and cucumber. **Toss** with the vinegar and remaining oil and season again with salt and pepper. Top with the avocado slices. Serve on a bed of chopped watercress or other greens.

SERVES 4 TO 6

Marinated grilled portobello mushrooms

Grilled portobellos with a good marinade are like heaven. They have a smoky, succulent, meaty flavor and make an excellent sandwich with almost any savory spread. You can fry portobellos in a sauté pan, but don't expect the same results. The fire and smoke from the grill create a flavor and texture that the kitchen stove cannot replicate.

4 portobello mushrooms, 3 to 4 inches [8 to 10cm] in diameter

¼ cup toasted sesame seed oil [60ml]

3 tablespoons dry red wine

1 tablespoon soy sauce

1 tablespoon balsamic or red wine vinegar

Juice of ½ lemon

2 garlic cloves, crushed through a press

Salt and freshly ground pepper

1. Remove the mushroom stems; save them for stock, if you like. Wipe the caps clean with damp paper towels. Mix all the remaining ingredients except the salt and pepper together in a small shallow bowl to make the marinade.

2. One at a time, submerge each mushroom in the marinade for just a few seconds. Lift out and twist gently to squeeze any excess liquid back into the bowl.

3. Light a medium-hot fire in a barbecue grill. Place the mushrooms gill side down on the oiled grill rack. Cook for 3 to 5 minutes, brushing the tops once with some of the marinade left in the bowl, until the bottoms have begun to soften but the mushrooms have not yet given up their juices. Turn over, brush again with marinade, and grill for another 4 to 6 minutes, until the mushroom caps are tender and lightly browned and the juices have welled up in the hollows.

4. Transfer the mushrooms to a cutting board, being careful not to spill the juices. Let them rest for a few minutes to allow the juices to penetrate. With a sharp knife, slice each cap into thin strips. Fan out the slices on a place, splash with vinegar, and season lightly with salt and pepper.

SERVES 4

Caramelized pearl onions with toasted almonds

Looking for a fun holiday dish—maybe something a little different—guaranteed to solicit raves and cravings for more? Caramelized pearl onions are uncomplicated yet rather clever. This is a side dish with the sweet qualities of a dessert, not unlike other popular Thanksgiving standards, like candied sweet potatoes. Most of this recipe can be prepared ahead of time, making it ideal when you're asked to bring a side dish. The finishing touches can be done in just a few minutes.

½ cup slivered almonds [40g]

2 tablespoons canola or safflower oil

24 to 35 small pearl or white onions, peeled

½ teaspoon salt

3 to 4 tablespoons maple syrup

1. Preheat the oven to 325°F [160°C]. Spread out the almonds in a small baking dish and toast in the oven for 7 to 10 minutes, stirring several times, until lightly browned. Watch them carefully, as nuts can burn quickly and often unexpectedly.

2. Heat the canola oil in a large skillet over medium heat. Add the onions and salt and cook, rolling the onions about from time to time to prevent burning, for 20 to 25 minutes, or until they are golden to dark brown.

3. Reduce the heat to low. Drizzle the maple syrup over the onions. Cook, stirring, for 1 to 2 minutes, until the onions are glazed.

4. Remove from the heat. Add the toasted almonds and stir to mix.

SERVES 4 TO 6

note If not serving right away, prepare the onions through Step 2; cover and set aside at room temperature for up to 2 hours, or refrigerate. When ready, reheat the onions, then add the maple syrup and almonds.

Spicy mustard potato salad

I like two kinds of potato salad—traditional, with mayo and celery, and crazy, mixed-up, and wild, as in this recipe. Okay, so it's not that wild. But I did add a few ingredients not always found in potato salad, like caraway, jalapeño, lemon juice, and roasted red bell peppers. I'll leave it up to you whether to keep it vegan or not by choosing mayonnaise or my tofu-based sour "cream."

1 pound medium red potatoes, scrubbed, cut into quarters or eighths, depending on size

1 small fresh jalapeño pepper, seeds and ribs removed, minced

1 tablespoon stone-ground or Dijon mustard

1 tablespoon caraway seeds

1 tablespoon finely diced roasted red bell pepper

1 tablespoon fresh lemon juice

1 tablespoon extra virgin olive oil

½ cup frozen peas

1 teaspoon salt

¼ teaspoon freshly ground pepper

3 to 4 tablespoons Simple Sour Cream (page 48) or mayonnaise

2 scallions, thinly sliced on the diagonal

½ to 1 teaspoon paprika

1. **Steam** the potatoes just until tender. While they are cooking, put the jalapeño, mustard, caraway seeds, roasted peppers, lemon juice, and olive oil in a large bowl. Add the warm potatoes and mix very well.

2. Keep the water in the steamer boiling and add the peas. Steam until just tender, 3 to 5 minutes; drain. While the peas are cooking, season the salad with the salt and pepper. **Stir** in the Simple Sour Cream or mayonnaise and gently mix well. Add the peas, scallions, and paprika and mix again.

SERVES 4

Curried chickpeas

If you have fresh chickpeas, use them, of course, but if you're in the mood for curry in a hurry, toss in a couple of cans for a presto-chango deluxe side dish in minutes.

1 onion, chopped

2 tablespoons olive oil

4 cups cooked chickpeas

2 garlic cloves, minced

1½ tablespoons curry powder

⅔ cup vegetable stock or dry white wine

1 tablespoon tomato paste

2 teaspoons chickpea miso or white miso

Salt and freshly ground pepper

Fresh lemon juice

1. In a large skillet, cook the onion in the olive oil over medium heat until very soft and lightly browned, 7 to 9 minutes.

2. Add the chickpeas and garlic, then stir in the curry powder. Cook for about 1 minute, stirring often. Turn up the heat to medium-high and add the stock. Bring to a simmer.

3. Stir in the tomato paste and miso and season with salt and pepper. Cook, stirring, until the liquid has reduced and thickened, about 2 minutes. Remove from the heat and splash with lemon juice. Season again with salt and pepper to taste.

SERVES 4

Cranberry
hazelnut relish

Highly refreshing, raw cranberries are a $great$ palate pleaser, especially next to a spicy or savory dish. Try a spoonful in your mashed potatoes
and then ask who's the bold vegetarian chef.

2 juicy tangerines

3 cups fresh cranberries [300g]

2 ripe Anjou pears, peeled, cored, and cut
into chunks

½ cup chopped toasted hazelnuts [45g]

⅓ to ½ cup maple syrup [75 to 125ml]

2 teaspoons grated fresh ginger

2 tablespoons fresh lime juice

Pinch of salt

1. Peel off the skin and as much of the white pith as possible from the tangerines.
Peel the membrane from each segment and remove all seeds. Work over a bowl to
catch as much of the juice as possible.

2. Place the tangerines and their juice, the cranberries, pears, hazelnuts, ⅓ cup [75 ml]
of the maple syrup, the ginger, lime juice, and salt into a food processor. Pulse a
few times until chopped but still chunky. Taste and add the remaining maple syrup if
you feel it's needed. Cover and refrigerate for at least 1 hour, or until serving time.

SERVES 6 TO 8

Crazy pecan cranberry sauce

During the holidays, I love tradition as much as the next guy, but some-times I just get bored with the same old thing. If Mexico had Thanksgiving, I think they might serve this spicy, sassy cranberry dish and its knockout topping. I like to decorate the top of the sauce with tangerines angled around in a circle.

1½ pounds fresh cranberries [750g]

¼ cup unrefined cane sugar [50g]

½ to 1 fresh jalapeño pepper, minced

½ cup coarsely chopped cilantro [125ml]

½ cup coarsely chopped pecans [50g]

1 tablespoon minced fresh ginger

Peeled sections from 2 seeded tangerines or oranges, for garnish*

1. In a large nonreactive saucepan, cook the cranberries with the sugar over medium heat until the berries soften and begin to pop, about 5 minutes.

2. Transfer to a bowl and stir in all the remaining ingredients except the tangerines. Mix well. Cover and refrigerate until cool.

3. Before serving, decorate with the tangerine sections.

SERVES 6

*In a pinch, mandarin orange sections will do.

GREEN 10

SALADS: Crisp and Well Dressed

When I go into a restaurant, I often find the quality of the starter salad a telltale sign of the restaurant's character and thus, the rest of the meal. Whether you prefer your greens before, with, or after the main course, a great salad is commonly paired with a meal of equal stature. Of course there are exceptions, but I've found that, more often than not, chefs who take care in the quality of their salad take equal care with the rest of the meal.

I look for intensely fresh produce that is appropriately dressed and heaped or stacked on the plate in an appealing way. I also look for something extra, a bonus that brings it all home, like a smattering of just the right cheese, or a grilled vegetable, fresh fruit, herbs, or croutons. And speaking of croutons, don't take them for granted. They should be made from good bread and, of course, be properly crunchy, with no hint of rancidity from old oil.

The dressing or vinaigrette should be appropriately divided among tart, sweet, and savory tastes. This area is very personal. I know many people who like more vinegar, while others prefer more oil. Some like dressings bold, others light. Some can't get enough garlic; others abstain. In this section of the book, the recipes are especially adaptable to your own tastes.

Washing and storing greens

WASHING YOUR GREENS is simple, yet what may seem an obvious procedure is often done improperly by the home cook. Here's my way. Fill a large bowl or a clean sink with cold water. Completely submerge your greens in the water. Dunk them a few times, swishing them around with your hands. Lift out the greens, leaving the water behind. What you'll probably find on the bottom of the sink or bowl is sand or dirt and a bug or two. You will be transformed; after you have washed greens this way once or twice, there is a very good chance you will never again hold your lettuce leaves under the tap, trying to rinse them one or two at a time.

Next, spin your greens completely dry in a salad spinner. (If you don't have one—get one.) If not using the greens right away, place them in a bowl and cover with lightly dampened paper towels or a clean kitchen towel, or place them in an aerated plastic bag with a lightly dampened paper towel inside. Keep in a cool place or refrigerate until ready to make your salad.

Each green salad in this chapter has two dressings to choose from. They are my favorites, but if you have your own or, for convenience, prefer to use a bottled brand, feel free to improvise.

Bibb lettuce salad with tempeh croutons

This is a simple salad with **bold** taste. The buttery, smooth leaves are a perfect match with the crisp, savory tempeh croutons. Choose a dressing that features the sharpness of garlic or the tartness of cranberries; either will liven up the greens and cause guests to sit up and notice.

¼ cup canola or safflower oil [60ml]

8 ounces tempeh, cut in half [250g]

Salt

1 large head of Bibb* or butter lettuce, thoroughly washed and dried, torn into bite-size pieces

Freshly ground pepper

¼ cup [30g] fresh raspberries or ¼ cup [40g] dried cranberries (optional)

CHOOSE YOUR DRESSING

Raspberry Garlic Dressing (recipe follows)

Cranberry Balsamic Vinaigrette (recipe follows)

1. In a medium skillet, **heat** the oil over medium-high heat. When just shimmering, add the tempeh squares and fry on one side until nicely browned and crisp but not burned, 2 to 3 minutes. Turn the tempeh over and brown the other side. Drain on paper towels. Sprinkle with salt while still warm.

2. When cooled, **cut** the tempeh into small cubes. Use a very sharp regular knife or a serrated knife for best results.

3. **Toss** the lettuce with 2 to 3 tablespoons of the dressing. Add the tempeh croutons and toss lightly again. Divide among 4 salad plates or bowls. Add a generous grinding of pepper and serve. Pass the remaining dressing on the side. If using raspberry dressing, top with a few fresh raspberries; if using cranberry, garnish the salads with dried cranberries.

* Sometimes Bibb is available in small heads only, so buy 2 or 3 depending on how many servings you need.

SERVES 4

Raspberry garlic dressing

This is an outstanding summer taste sensation. Raspberries and fresh garlic make an excellent combination and a naturally thick and creamy dressing. Be sure to reserve additional berries to toss in your salad.

2 tablespoons fresh raspberries

2 garlic cloves, minced

1 tablespoon unrefined cane sugar

1 tablespoon raspberry vinegar

2 tablespoons extra virgin olive oil

½ teaspoon salt

Puree all the ingredients in a blender until very well mixed. If you are a perfectionist, strain to remove the raspberry seeds.

MAKES ABOUT ⅓ CUP [75ML]

Cranberry balsamic vinaigrette

This is a rich, distinctively flavored dressing, perfect for a Bibb lettuce salad, mesclun greens, a warm wilted greens salad, or over grilled fruit or vegetables. Some stores have dozens of bags of cranberries frozen from the fall holiday season. If you haven't saved any yourself and are making this out of season, see if you can find a store that carries them.

2 tablespoons fresh or frozen cranberries

2 tablespoons your best balsamic vinegar

2 tablespoons plus 1 teaspoon extra virgin olive oil

2 to 3 tablespoons maple syrup

Salt and freshly ground pepper

Combine the cranberries, vinegar, olive oil, and 2 tablespoons maple syrup in a blender or mini food processor. Puree until very smooth. Season with salt and pepper to taste. If too tart, add more maple syrup.

MAKES ABOUT ½ CUP [125ML]

Roasted radicchio with arugula, endive, and fresh mozzarella

If you have never cooked radicchio, you are in for a **visual** and taste sensation. Its slightly charred burgundy-red leaves and mellowed nutty flavor are a sophisticated change of pace. I think cooking improves the traditional bitter-tart salad (radicchio and endive) with a savory, sweetened edge.

Roasted Garlic Dressing goes very well with this salad. If you prefer something with a sweet tang, try the Chipotle-Date Dressing with Lime, which has a modest bite.

2 tablespoons olive oil

1 head of radicchio, sliced into quarters, root ends removed

1 bunch of arugula, cleaned, tough stems removed

1 head of Belgian endive, cored and cut lengthwise into thin strips

6 ounces fresh mozzarella, diced [180g]

3 medium-size ripe tomatoes, seeded and cut into chunks

Salt and freshly ground pepper

CHOOSE YOUR DRESSING

Creamy Roasted Garlic Dressing (recipe follows)

Chipotle-Date Dressing with Lime (recipe on page 285)

1. In a large cast-iron skillet, **heat** the olive oil over medium-high heat until very hot. Add the radicchio and grill, turning, until browned and lightly blackened on at least 2 or 3 sides. Use tongs to turn the radicchio about so all sides are exposed to the skillet. Remove and let cool.

2. In a large salad bowl, **toss** the grilled radicchio with the arugula. Add 2 to 3 tablespoons of the dressing and toss again. Gently fold in the endive. Top with the mozzarella and tomatoes. Season with salt and pepper to taste. Serve immediately. Pass the remaining dressing on the side.

SERVES 4 TO 6

Creamy toasted garlic dressing

This savory, slightly tangy dressing is creamy, with a beautiful pale yellow color.

6 garlic cloves, skins on

1 teaspoon mellow white miso

2½ tablespoons extra virgin olive oil

1 tablespoon apple cider vinegar

1 tablespoon lemon juice

1½ teaspoons honey

½ teaspoon salt

1. Heat a dry cast-iron skillet or heavy frying pan over medium heat. **Toast** the unpeeled garlic, turning over with tongs occasionally. Allow the garlic to brown in spots, about 15 minutes. Let cool, then peel and coarsely chop.

2. **Puree** the garlic along with the rest of the ingredients in a blender or mini food processor until smooth. Let the dressing stand for 1 hour before serving.

MAKES ABOUT ⅓ CUP [75ML]

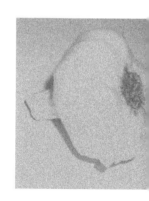

Chipotle-date dressing with lime

The date in this recipe sweetens and thickens the dressing. It also dampens the heat of the chile while allowing the flavor and smokiness to shine through. As chiles vary widely in heat, start with half a chipotle. After blending, taste to see if the heat and flavor are where you want it. The key to this dressing is to achieve just a hint of heat and smoke.

I also like to use this dressing to top roasted veggies. With the addition of ¾ cup [200ml] apple juice or a combination of citrus juices, it makes a nice tofu marinade.

½ to 1 small chipotle chile, cracked open, stem and seeds removed

2 fresh dates, pits removed, quartered

3 tablespoons fresh lime juice

2 tablespoons juice from honey tangerine, tangelo, or other orange

3 tablespoons extra virgin olive oil

1 tablespoon sherry vinegar or good-quality balsamic vinegar

1 teaspoon unrefined cane sugar

¼ teaspoon salt

Freshly ground pepper

1. **Soak** the chipotle chile in 1 cup [250ml] hot water until soft, about 30 minutes. Remove from the water and coarsely chop.

2. In a blender or mini food processor, **combine** the chipotle with the dates, lime juice, citrus juice, olive oil, vinegar, sugar, salt, and a generous grinding of pepper. Puree until very smooth, scraping down the sides 2 or 3 times with a rubber spatula. For a smoother texture, press though a fine mesh strainer with a whisk.

MAKES ABOUT ½ CUP [125ML]

Chard, fresh fennel, and red onion salad with feta and mint

Modesty aside, this is an **outstanding** salad with all the characteristics of a classic. The Creamy Italian Dressing is a perfect accompaniment with its dried herb base. Roasted Tomato Vinaigrette goes beautifully, too, as a sweet-savory-tangy addition to the feta and herbs.

2 tablespoons olive oil

½ large red onion, very thinly sliced

1 fresh fennel bulb (about 6 ounces), stems removed, very thinly sliced, leaves reserved and coarsely chopped [180g]

Salt and freshly ground pepper

1 bunch of Swiss, red, or rainbow chard, tough stems removed, leaves thoroughly washed and dried, torn into bite-size pieces

4 sorrel leaves, shredded (optional)

6 mint leaves, shredded

4 ounces feta cheese, crumbled or cubed [125g]

CHOOSE YOUR DRESSING

Creamy Italian Dressing (recipe follows)

Roasted Tomato Vinaigrette (recipe on page 288)

1. In a large cast-iron skillet, **heat** the oil until very hot. Add the red onion to one side of the pan, the fennel to the other. Slowly cook over medium heat, turning and stirring with tongs, until soft and lightly browned. The onion and fennel may finish cooking at different times, so remove them as they are done. Season lightly with salt and pepper and set aside to cool while preparing your salad.

2. In a large bowl, **toss** the chard, sorrel, and mint. Toss again with 3 to 4 tablespoons of the dressing. Fold in the red onion and fennel. Top with the feta cheese.

SERVES 4

Creamy italian dressing

This is somewhat like the Creamy Fresh Herb Dressing, but it has a distinctively Italian cast to it. So while it is also wide open to interpretation, given the blank slate of the tofu and herbs, it is geared to Mediterranean flavors.

¼ teaspoon dried thyme

¼ teaspoon dried basil

¼ teaspoon dried oregano

3 ounces silken tofu [90g]

1 teaspoon minced shallot

1 garlic clove, minced

1 tablespoon plus 1 teaspoon extra virgin olive oil

1 tablespoon red wine vinegar

1 teaspoon unrefined cane sugar

¼ teaspoon salt

1 tablespoon vegetable stock or water

1. **Combine** the thyme, basil, and oregano in a mortar and crush them with a pestle until well blended. If a mortar and pestle are not available, crumble the herbs between your fingers to release their flavors.

2. In a blender or food processor, **combine** the herbs with all the remaining ingredients and puree until very smooth and creamy. Add more liquid if you like a thinner dressing.

MAKES ABOUT ½ CUP [125ML]

Roasted tomato vinaigrette

A hint of cheese flavor comes in this bright and very savory dressing from the nutritional yeast. Besides being a bold vinaigrette for salads, this makes an excellent dip for fresh bread, in place of plain olive oil.

4 plum tomatoes, cored and halved lengthwise

1 tablespoon red wine vinegar

2 tablespoons extra virgin olive oil

1 teaspoon nutritional yeast

1 teaspoon unrefined cane sugar

1 garlic clove, minced

Salt and freshly ground pepper

1. **Preheat** the broiler with a rack set about 4 to 6 inches [10 to 15cm] from the heat.

2. Set out the tomatoes on a baking sheet, cut sides down. **Broil** until they are soft and the skins are cracked and lightly charred, 5 to 7 minutes. Let the tomatoes cool, then place them in a fine strainer set over a bowl.

3. With a whisk, **press** the tomato juice through the strainer. Continue to turn the sieve and whisk until all that is left is dry pulp. Discard the pulp or freeze it in your vegetable stock bag. Don't forget to scrape off the liquid that clings to the bottom of the strainer.

4. Whisk the vinegar, olive oil, nutritional yeast, sugar, and garlic into the roasted tomato juice. **Season** with salt and pepper to taste. If there is time, let the dressing stand for 1 hour at room temperature before serving, then mix well again.

MAKES ABOUT ¼ CUP [60ML]

Spinach, tomato, and cucumber salad with garlic croutons

Trying to get the kids to eat salad? They might like this one. I've included Russian dressing as one choice; because it has ketchup in it, they very well might go for it. You might too if you have a craving for the good old days of mayonnaise and ketchup. By the way, the croutons are extra special, so don't leave them out.

½ loaf of slightly stale French or Italian bread

6 tablespoons olive oil

5 large garlic cloves, thinly sliced

Salt and freshly ground pepper

1 large cucumber

1 bunch of fresh spinach (⅔ to 1 pound), tough stems removed, thoroughly washed, torn into bite-size pieces [300 to 500g]

2 large ripe tomatoes, seeded and cut into chunks

CHOOSE YOUR DRESSING

Creamy Fresh Herb Dressing (recipe follows)

Russian Dressing with Sun-Dried Tomatoes (recipe on page 291)

1. Preheat the oven to 375°F [190°C]. Cut the bread into thick slices, then into fat cubes. If not stale, leave in a bowl overnight or lightly toast in the oven.

2. In a large cast-iron or other ovenproof skillet, heat the olive oil over medium-low heat. Add the garlic and cook until it just begins to brown. Immediately remove with a slotted spoon and set the toasted garlic aside.

3. Add the bread cubes to the oil in the skillet and quickly stir with a spoon so as many cubes are coated with oil as possible. Continue to cook, stirring, for 1 or 2 minutes. Season lightly with salt and pepper.

4. Transfer the skillet to the preheated oven and bake for 10 to 15 minutes, until the croutons are crisp and nicely browned. **Toss** the toasted garlic with the croutons. Let cool and set aside. If you not using all of the croutons, seal the remainder in a plastic bag and store in a cool place.

5. **Peel** the cucumber, cut it lengthwise in half, and scoop out the seeds. Cut the cucumber into slices—thick or thin, as you prefer.

6. In a large bowl, toss the cucumber slices, spinach, and tomatoes. Add 3 or 4 tablespoons of the dressing and toss again. **Season** with salt and pepper to taste. Top with the croutons and garlic and serve. Pass the remaining dressing on the side.

SERVES 4 TO 6

Creamy fresh herb dressing

In this luscious dressing, tofu is used for the base, citrus as a conduit for flavor, and the herbs for an accent. Really, there is no wrong way to make this recipe. The options are wide open. Use whatever fruit and fresh herbs you have on hand.

4 ounces silken tofu [125g]

¼ cup fresh citrus juice (any combination of orange, lime, tangerine, and lemon) [60ml]

1 tablespoon chopped mixed fresh herbs (lemon thyme, mint, basil, tarragon)

2 tablespoons extra virgin olive oil

1½ tablespoons red wine vinegar or cider vinegar

Vegetable stock or water (optional)

Salt and freshly ground pepper

Puree the tofu, citrus juice, herbs, olive oil, and vinegar in a blender or food processor until very smooth. Add a little vegetable stock or water if you like a thinner consistency. Season with salt and pepper to taste. If you have time, let the dressing stand for at least 1 hour before serving to let the flavors develop.

MAKES ABOUT 1 CUP [250ML]

Russian dressing with sun-dried tomatoes

This popular bold dressing is especially thick. It works well with a hearty salad of greens and tomatoes or a spread for sandwiches. Add more tomato soaking liquid if you prefer a thinner dressing.

5 sun-dried tomatoes

4 ounces silken tofu [125g]

2 teaspoons bottled plain (not creamed) red or white horseradish

1 tablespoon ketchup

1 small shallot, minced

1 teaspoon vegetarian Worcestershire sauce

1 tablespoon extra virgin olive oil

½ teaspoon salt

Freshly ground pepper

1. **Soak** the tomatoes in 1 cup [250ml] hot water until soft, 15 to 20 minutes. Drain, reserving the soaking liquid. Coarsely chop the tomatoes.

2. Puree all the ingredients except the reserved soaking liquid in a blender or food processor, scraping down the sides 2 or 3 times until very smooth. With the machine on, **drizzle** in ⅓ to ½ cup [75 to 125ml] of the soaking liquid to achieve the desired consistency. Use more if necessary.

MAKES ABOUT 1 CUP [250ML]

Rainbow ribbon salad

Presentation is a very important part of this salad, so take your time and do it just right. The salad is bright, beautiful, and full of color. The shredded beet is essential to bringing it all together. Tofu adds a nice warm touch and a firm mouthfeel to accent the softer vegetables.

3 tablespoons vegetable oil

½ pound firm tofu, pressed of water, cut lengthwise in half [250g]

Salt

½ red bell pepper, cut into thin strips

½ yellow bell pepper, cut into thin strips

½ cucumber, seeded and cut into thin strips

1 medium carrot, peeled and cut into thin strips

½ green apple, cut into thin strips

½ cup shredded peeled fresh beet

CHOOSE YOUR DRESSING

Chipotle-Date Dressing with Lime (page 285)

Chinese Mustard Dressing (page 32)

1. In a cast-iron skillet, heat the vegetable oil over medium-high heat. Add the tofu cutlets and sauté until lightly browned and crispy on both sides, 2 to 3 minutes per side. Drain on paper towels. Sprinkle with salt while still warm. Cut into ½-inch [1-cm] cubes and set aside.

2. In a large bowl, toss the bell peppers, cucumber, carrot, and apple with 2 or 3 tablespoons of the dressing.

3. With tongs, portion out servings of the vegetable and apple mixture in the center of 4 salad plates, leaving the outer portion of the plate free for the tofu. Top each pile of rainbow salad with shredded beet. Place 4 or 5 tofu cubes around the outside of each plate. Serve immediately. Pass any remaining dressing on the side.

SERVES 4

Wilted greens with miso-tamarind sauce and caramelized pears

This is the kind of salad that often surprises people. It's unusual and interesting in flavor, and it looks beautiful in a large bowl or on individual plates. The browned pears are a special treat. This is a very nice salad for the fall season.

1 head of hearty leafy greens (for example: mustard, romaine, radicchio, endive, oak leaf, chard), cleaned and very coarsely chopped

1 firm but not hard Bosc pear

2 tablespoons vegetable oil

2 teaspoons maple syrup

1 teaspoon red miso or barley miso

1 teaspoon tamarind paste

1 teaspoon tomato paste

1 garlic clove, crushed through a press

1 tablespoon minced fresh ginger

½ cup vegetable stock or water [125ml]

1. **Prepare** the greens and set aside in a large bowl.

2. Quarter the pear and cut out the stem and core. **Cut** each quarter into 2 or 3 thin slices.

3. In a large skillet, **heat** the oil over medium-high heat. Add the pear slices and sauté until browned on both sides, 7 to 9 minutes. Drain on paper towels and set aside. Pour off any oil or juices in the skillet.

4. In a medium bowl, combine the maple syrup, miso, tamarind, tomato paste, garlic, ginger, and vegetable stock. **Whisk** until smooth. Pour into the pan and bring to a boil over medium-low heat. Cook, stirring, until the dressing begins to thicken, 1 to 2 minutes.

5. Immediately **pour** the hot dressing over the greens and toss until they are well coated and wilt slightly. Divide among salad plates (tongs work well) and top with pear slices. Serve immediately.

SERVES 2 TO 4

Herbed feta cheese with tomatoes and cucumbers

Man . . . if you'll pardon the expression—this is good stuff. Very simple to make and a wonderful presentation. This salad is especially suited to a summer meal or party. Serve the marinated cheese over tomatoes and cucumbers, as suggested here, or over your favorite mix of greens. Add a splash with balsamic or red wine vinegar if you prefer a bit of acid.

10 ounces feta cheese, cut into bite-size cubes [300g]

¼ cup extra virgin olive oil [60ml]

2 tablespoons fresh rosemary, coarsely chopped

2 tablespoons fresh oregano, coarsely chopped

Freshly ground pepper

3 large tomatoes, preferably beefsteaks or heirlooms, seeded and cut into bite-size cubes

1 large cucumber, sliced

1. Place the feta cheese, olive oil, rosemary, oregano, and a generous grinding of pepper in a heavy-duty sealable plastic bag. Refrigerate overnight, turning the bag 2 or 3 times.

2. Serve the cheese with its marinade over the tomatoes and cucumbers.

SERVES 6

Vegan caesar salad

Here is a classic that has a bold, zesty flavor yet a fraction of the fat and calories of the original. No anchovies, no eggs, and no cheese, but all the bright taste.

1 large head of romaine lettuce

1 garlic clove, cut in half

1 cup bread or tempeh croutons [250ml]

½ recipe Hail Caesar Dressing (recipe follows)

Freshly ground pepper

1. **Separate** the lettuce leaves and tear them into large bite-size pieces. Rinse well and whirl dry in a salad spinner.

2. Rub a large salad bowl with the cut sides of the garlic. **Add** the lettuce, three-quarters of the croutons, ¼ cup [60ml] of the dressing, and a generous grinding of black pepper. Toss to mix well.

3. **Garnish** the salad with the remaining croutons and serve at once. Pass the remaining dressing on the side.

SERVES 4 TO 6

Hail Caesar Dressing

2 tablespoons slivered blanched almonds

2 garlic cloves, chopped

3 tablespoons Dijon mustard

3 tablespoons nutritional yeast

½ sheet toasted nori, crumbled

½ teaspoon salt

⅛ teaspoon freshly ground pepper

3 tablespoons fresh lemon juice

2 tablespoons soy sauce

1 tablespoon extra virgin olive oil

About ¼ cup water [60ml]

Mix all the ingredients in blender, adding the water in increments until you achieve the thickness you desire. Scrape down the sides 2 or 3 times until very well mixed. Let the dressing rest for 1 hour before serving. Store any extra in a covered jar in the refrigerator for up to 3 days.

MAKES ABOUT 1 CUP [250ML]

11 JUST DESSERTS: Sweetness and Light

You won't find any rich, extravagant chocolate cakes in this chapter. Yes, I'm disappointed, too. But I know there are already so many places you can find super-deluxe, extra-rich desserts that there is no need for more in this book. Let's just say the desserts in this chapter balance sweetness with good sense. Yet they don't taste fake or processed as those you might find in the natural or health foods section of your grocery store.

What you will find are several desserts featuring silken tofu—from puddings to cakes to crèmes. You'll also find a few fruit desserts that I think you'll find very refreshing at the end of a meal.

I firmly believe in desserts that taste good, whether they're vegan or not. Not all, by any means, but I think some desserts in the natural foods world are lackluster in taste. No wheat, no sugar, no dairy, no butter can mean dry texture and flavor that leaves you wanting. On the other hand, traditionally made pastry-shop desserts can sometimes be sickly sweet or rich. I have humbly tried to create a collection of desserts somewhere in the middle of these two roads.

There seems to be a distinct line drawn in the sand between those who have acquired a taste for soy desserts or have a positive attitude about trying them and those who simply, for whatever reason, will not accept any substitute for traditional dessert fare. As hard as I try, I can do very little for the latter individuals. Serve my desserts, and maybe you can be the one to spread the good word when these people taste your version of crème caramel, chocolate vanilla cashew cake, and so on.

Some ideas to keep in mind: When a dessert calls for silken tofu, don't substitute any other kind. Most of the time, extra-firm style is the best bet, as it has the least amount of water, which leaves more room for flavor and a texture firm enough to hold its body. Silken tofu has a specific creamy texture and clean taste that generally cannot be found in regular tofu. If you use regular tofu for a pudding, pie, or crème, it's likely you'll experience a subtle grainy texture and an aftertaste that is not apparent in most savory dishes but may be unpleasant in a dessert.

Four important tips to remember with tofu in desserts:

1. Blend, blend, and blend some more. Make your tofu as creamy as possible.

2. Let your completed dessert rest. Flavors in tofu must have time to build.

3. Taste. It may sound obvious, but tasting is a significant factor in getting the flavors right. If a dessert tastes good now, it will taste great later. If the taste is mediocre now, don't expect it to improve notably after a few hours.

4. Expect the unexpected. Tofu varies from brand to brand in taste and in water content. There is no industry standard when it comes to soft, firm, extra-firm, etc. One brand's firm may be another's extra-firm. You will have to do some work on your own to see which works best.

No-bake chocolate cashew cake

Who would have thought of couscous for dessert? The bland grain presents an interesting texture and a perfect vehicle for picking up flavorings. The cake itself is composed of two rich layers in which all my favorite dessert flavors—at least the flavors I like: chocolate, vanilla, and coconut—are merged.

¼ cup shredded unsweetened coconut [15g]

1 cup raw, unsalted cashews [120g]

1½ cups coconut-pineapple juice* [375ml]

1¼ cup unrefined cane sugar [225g]

1 cup couscous [150g]

1½ tablespoons vanilla extract

10 ounces vegan or regular semisweet chocolate chips [300g]

2 packages (12.3 ounces each) firm or extra-firm silken tofu [700g total]

¼ cup maple syrup [60ml]

Pinch of salt

1. **Preheat** the oven to 350°F [175°C]. Place the coconut on a baking sheet and toast it in the oven until golden, about 5 minutes. Watch carefully, as it will burn quickly. Transfer to a plate and let cool.

2. In a blender, **puree** the cashews with 1 cup water [250 ml] until very smooth. In a medium saucepan, **combine** this cashew milk, the coconut-pineapple juice, sugar, and couscous. Mix well. Bring to a simmer and cook, stirring often, until thickened, 5 to 10 minutes. Remove from the heat and stir in the vanilla. Spread into an ungreased 9-inch [23-cm] springform pan. Let cool.

3. In a double boiler, **melt** the chocolate chips over low heat, stirring until smooth. Scrape into a food processor. Add the tofu, maple syrup, and salt. Process until very smooth.

4. Pour the chocolate tofu over the couscous layer. **Sprinkle** the toasted coconut evenly over the top. Refrigerate until the cake is set, at least 2 hours or, ideally, overnight.

SERVES 10 TO 12

*Knudsen brand makes a coconut-pineapple juice. It blends and unifies beautifully with the other flavors. If you cannot find it, substitute apple juice.

Vanilla maple pudding

This pudding goes beyond just mixing tofu with a particular flavoring. I felt compelled to challenge the status quo with a dairy-free pudding that had a proper mouthfeel and a taste you might expect from a more traditional pudding. The key seems to be the oil (don't substitute or leave out!) and the combination of a thickener, like arrowroot, and the vegetarian gelatin, agar.

1 package (12.3 ounces) firm or extra-firm silken tofu [350g]

¼ cup flavorless vegetable oil [60ml]

½ cup maple syrup [125ml]

1 tablespoon fresh lemon juice

Pinch of salt

2 tablespoons arrowroot

1 cup vanilla rice milk or soy milk [250ml]

1 cup apple, peach, or pear juice [250ml]

1 tablespoon agar flakes

2 tablespoons vanilla extract

Fresh strawberries or blueberries, for garnish

1. In a food processor, **combine** the tofu, oil, maple syrup, lemon juice, and salt. Blend until very smooth, at least 1 minute, scraping down the sides once or twice. Set aside.

2. In a measuring cup, **whisk** the arrowroot into the milk until blended.

3. In a medium saucepan, **heat** the apple juice over low heat. Add the agar and bring to a bare simmer, whisking constantly, until the flakes are completely dissolved. This may take several minutes, so be patient.

4. Reduce the heat to low. **Whisk** the milk-arrowroot mixture into the juice and continue to cook, stirring, until the mixture thickens, 1 to 2 minutes.

5. **Pour** the juice mixture into the tofu in the food processor. Add the vanilla and pulse just enough to blend. Do not overmix here, or the arrowroot may break down. Pour the mixture into individual dessert dishes or a single bowl. Decorate with berries while still warm. Cover and refrigerate until firmly set, about 2 hours.

SERVES 4

Crème caramel

I'm not against traditionally made desserts (actually, I'm usually all for them), but for some crazy reason I wanted to challenge myself to see if I could make a crème caramel as creamy and luscious as the original but made without eggs and white sugar. I got a lot of enjoyment out of creating and re-creating this dish, trying to get it just right. As I've said, many vegan desserts are a disappointment to me, but I think this one is a winner.

Vegetable cooking spray

¾ cup light-colored unrefined cane sugar [150g]

Pinch of salt

4 teaspoons egg replacer powder (look for Ener-G brand)

1 tablespoon arrowroot

1½ cups vanilla soy milk [375g]

1 pound extra-firm silken tofu [500g]

½ cup maple syrup [125g]

1½ tablespoons Kahlúa*

1. **Preheat** the oven to 350°F [175°C]. Prepare eight 6-ounce [180-g] custard cups or ovenproof ramekins by coating them lightly with cooking spray.

2. Put the sugar in a small heavy saucepan, then add ¼ cup [60ml] water. Bring to a boil over medium heat without stirring, gently swirling the pan by the handle until a syrup begins to form. **Cover** and cook for 2 minutes. Uncover and continue to boil until the sugar is thick and dark amber, another 2 or 3 minutes.

3. Quickly and carefully, **pour** the caramel into the custard cups, tilting to make sure the bottoms are completely covered.

4. In a medium bowl, combine the egg replacer, arrowroot, and ¼ cup [60ml] of the milk. **Whisk** until very smooth. Add the remaining milk and blend well.

*Look for the mini bottles in the liquor store if you don't want to buy a whole bottle.

5. In a blender or food processor, **puree** the tofu until very smooth, at least 1 minute. Add the soy milk mixture, maple syrup, and Kahlúa. Blend until very smooth.

6. **Pour** the tofu mixture into the prepared cups and place them in a larger baking dish or roasting pan. Fill the larger pan with enough warm water to reach one third up the sides of the cups.

7. Bake for 40 minutes, or until the crème caramel is firm to the touch but still slightly jiggly in the center. Let cool, then **refrigerate** for at least 2 hours or overnight. Before serving, loosen the sides of the crème caramels with a sharp paring knife. Place a plate, serving side down, over each cup and invert quickly to unmold. Serve immediately.

MAKES 8 PORTIONS, ½ CUP [125ML] EACH

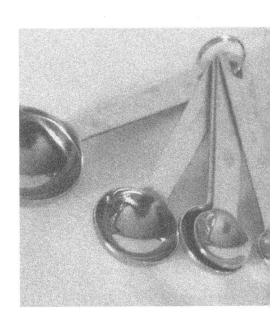

Mango-glazed lemon pie

You might call this dessert a hybrid. It looks like a cheesecake but contains no eggs or cream. It does, however, include a small amount of sour cream, which complements the flavor and texture, making it **smoother** and lighter. The cream also smooths out the tofu. Unless you're a vegan, why not? You want soy in your diet and you may eat dairy. I'm a rule breaker—what can I say?

If you *are* a vegan, try *soy* sour cream, yogurt, or cream cheese. I purposely left those out because personally I don't care for the ingredients, and I won't make a substitute for substitute's sake when I feel quality is sacrificed. I do, however, recommend that everyone use organic sour cream, as it won't contain fillers, stabilizers, and other unwanted additives. Ener-G brand makes a good powdered egg replacer.

For this recipe, you will need a 9-inch [23-cm] springform pan, a larger pan (roasting or baking pan) for your water bath, and some aluminum foil. This pie really is not hard to make. Just prep and organize your ingredients, and you'll be done in no time.

CRUST

10 double graham crackers

2 tablespoons maple syrup

3 tablespoons canola or safflower oil

FILLING

¾ cup coarsely chopped fresh mango (about 1 mango) [120g]

¾ cup light-colored unrefined cane sugar [150g]

1½ pounds extra-firm silken tofu (two 12.3-ounce packages) [750g total]

4 ounces sour cream, preferably organic [125g]

3 tablespoons egg replacer

¼ cup plus 2 tablespoons fresh lemon juice

2 teaspoons vanilla extract

Pinch of salt

2 cups coarsely chopped fresh mango or whole blueberries [300g mango or 250g blueberries]

¼ cup plus 1 tablespoon water [75ml]

1 tablespoon arrowroot

1. **Preheat** the oven to 350°F [175°C]. Place a 9-inch [23-cm] springform pan on a large piece of aluminum foil. Fold up and wrap the foil around the entire outside of the pan. The purpose is to keep water from leaking from the water bath into the pie. Set the wrapped springform in a larger pan at least a couple of inches wider.

2. Prepare the crust by grinding the graham crackers to fine crumbs in a food processor. Add the maple syrup and oil. **Process** until the crumbs are evenly moistened. Turn into the springform pan. Using a small glass, start pressing down the crumbs. Take your time, slowly going round and round until the crumbs are evenly distributed on the bottom and partway up the sides.

3. To prepare the filling, rinse out the crumbs from the processor and puree the mango until very smooth. **Add** all the remaining filling ingredients and blend and blend and blend until the mixture is as creamy as possible, 2 to 3 minutes.

4. Pour the filling into the prepared springform pan and smooth the top with a rubber spatula. **Pour** enough hot water into the larger pan to reach about halfway up the sides of the springform. The water helps ensure a slower, more even cooking process.

5. **Bake** for 45 minutes. Turn off the heat and leave the pie in the warm oven for another 30 minutes without opening the door. Remove from the oven and let cool.

6. While the pie is cooling, make the glaze. In a nonreactive medium saucepan, combine the mango or blueberries, sugar, and ¼ cup [60ml] water. **Simmer** for 10 minutes, stirring frequently. Mix the arrowroot with 1 tablespoon water to form a paste and stir the paste into the glaze. Cook and stir for another minute or so until thickened. Remove from the heat and let cool.

7. **Spread** the cooled glaze over the pie. Cover and refrigerate for several hours or, ideally, overnight. When ready to serve, gently remove the rim of the springform pan. Use a sharp knife to cut the pie into slices.

SERVES 10 TO 12

Sweet yogurt with raspberries

If you've never made yogurt cheese, you must try it. It's a very simple technique that does two things: It removes excess water from the yogurt, making it thicker and creamier, and it yields a sharper, tangier flavor. This particular combination makes an outstanding summer dessert when raspberries are at their plump finest.

32 ounces (2 quarts) plain yogurt, preferably organic [2L]

8 ounces crème fraîche [250ml]

1 teaspoon vanilla extract

9 tablespoons unrefined cane sugar [115g]

1½ pints fresh raspberries [375g]

Fresh mint leaves, for garnish

1. **Line** a fine mesh strainer with 2 layers of cheesecloth. Use enough cloth so that it hangs over the sides. Set the strainer over a bowl so there is 1 to 2 inches [2.5 to 5cm] of space between the bottom of the strainer and the bottom of the bowl. Pour the yogurt into the strainer and cover with plastic wrap or a plate. Refrigerate overnight.

2. Pour the crème fraîche into a medium bowl and stir until softened. Add the vanilla and 3 tablespoons of the sugar. **Stir** until the sugar dissolves.

3. Fold in the yogurt cheese and mix well. **Distribute** evenly among six 8-ounce [240g] custard cups or ramekins. Ideally, you'll want to leave ½ inch [1cm] or so of room for your topping. Refrigerate for at least 15 to 30 minutes.

4. In the meantime, place the raspberries into a bowl and set aside. **Add** the remaining sugar and ¼ cup [60ml] water to a saucepan over medium heat and bring to a light boil. Cook for 2 to 3 minutes, stirring frequently, until the sugar thickens slightly and turns golden.

5. Immediately **pour** the syrup over the raspberries and mix gently so they are well coated. Let cool for a few minutes. Spoon the raspberries and syrup over the yogurt cups and return to the refrigerator. Chill for 1 hour. Garnish with mint before serving.

SERVES 6

Orange and dried cherry salad

A mix of fresh and dried fruit makes for a perfectly light, slightly sweet, and fragrant dessert. Orange blossom water is available in Middle Eastern and Indian specialty shops.

5 large navel oranges

2 ounces dried tart cherries [60g]

2 teaspoons orange blossom water

2 teaspoons unrefined cane sugar

½ teaspoon ground cinnamon

¼ cup toasted, coarsely chopped almonds [25g]

Fresh mint leaves, for garnish

1. Using a sharp knife, cut off the entire skin and white pith from the oranges. Place a strainer over a bowl to catch the juices and section the oranges between the white membranes so that you are left with nothing but orange—no skin or seeds.

2. Place the orange sections and dried cherries in a clean bowl. Add the orange blossom water, sugar, cinnamon, and almonds. Toss lightly to mix. Serve chilled, garnished with mint.

SERVES 4

Rum rice pudding

I've liked rice pudding since I was a kid. I like it mostly traditional, with white rice, milk, and sugar. Rum adds a respectful touch.

Vegetable cooking spray

½ cup raw long-grain white rice [100g]

2 ¼ cups whole milk [550ml]

½ cup light-colored unrefined cane sugar [100g]

¼ teaspoon salt

3 tablespoons dark rum

½ teaspoon vanilla extract

⅓ cup toasted slivered almonds [30g]

Freshly grated nutmeg

1. Preheat the oven to 350°F [175°C]. Coat a covered baking dish with vegetable oil spray. In a medium bowl, mix together the rice, 2 cups [500ml] of the milk, the sugar, and the salt. Scrape into the baking dish. Cover with foil.

2. Bake for 45 minutes. Remove from the oven and give the pudding a good stir. It will still be quite loose. Don't worry; it is still in its infancy at this point.

3. Reduce the oven temperature to 325°F [160°C]. Return the dish to the oven and bake, covered, for another 20 to 30 minutes, or until most of the milk is absorbed.

4. Remove from the oven and, while still hot, stir in the rum, vanilla, and almonds. Stir in the remaining ¼ cup [60ml] milk. Dust with nutmeg. Serve warm.

SERVES 4

Berry-ginger merlot sauce over ice cream

This recipe is **perfect** for cranberries you froze in the fall. Or use your favorite seasonal berries. Blueberry, strawberry, blackberry—the combination is your choice.

1 cup berries [250ml]

1 teaspoon safflower or canola oil

2 teaspoons finely minced fresh ginger

1 cup Merlot [250ml]

2 to 3 tablespoons unrefined cane sugar

Vanilla ice cream

1. In a nonreactive medium skillet, **cook** the berries in the oil over medium heat for a minute or so, stirring often.

2. Add the ginger and continue to cook and stir for another minute. **Add** the wine and bring to a boil. Cook until the berries are softened, about 2 minutes.

3. Mash the berries with the back of a large spoon. **Stir** in the sugar—the amount you add will depend on the sweetness of the berries—and continue to cook until the wine is substantially reduced and the sauce is thickened.

4. **Spoon** over vanilla ice cream and serve at once.

SERVES 4

Summer compote with cashew vanilla crème

For best results, make this comforting but luxurious dessert the night before and serve it chilled. The Cashew Crème is also best when made ahead; give it at least 2 to 3 hours to chill. In preparing the fruit, you may choose to leave on the skin. I prefer to peel most fruits except those with soft skins, like peaches.

1 tart apple, peeled and cut into large dice

1 cup diced peeled mango [150g]

1 cup diced peach [150g]

½ cup sliced strawberries, cut in half or quarters, depending on size [70g]

1 cup apple juice [250ml]

½ cup unrefined cane sugar [100g]

1 tablespoon lemon juice

Cashew Vanilla Crème (recipe follows)

1. Put the apple, mango, peach, and strawberries into a medium saucepan. **Add** the apple juice, sugar and 1 cup [250ml] water; bring to a boil, stirring to dissolve the sugar. Reduce the heat and simmer, stirring occasionally, until the fruit is tender but still holds its shape, 5 to 7 minutes. With a slotted spoon, transfer the fruit to a bowl.

2. Bring the liquid in the saucepan to a boil. **Cook** for 10 to 15 minutes, or until reduced and syrupy. Stir in the lemon juice and pour over the fruit. Cover and refrigerate until chilled, several hours or, preferably, overnight.

3. To serve, **spoon** the compote into individual dessert bowls and top with a dollop of Cashew Vanilla Crème.

SERVES 4

Cashew vanilla crème

¾ cup raw unsalted cashews [90g]

½ cup apple juice [125ml]

2 tablespoons light-colored unrefined cane sugar

2 tablespoons fresh lemon juice

½ teaspoon vanilla extract

1. **Puree** all the ingredients in a blender or food processor until creamy and smooth. The key here is the blending. Just keep blending and scraping down the sides and blending some more for 2 or 3 minutes.

2. Transfer to a small bowl. **Cover** and refrigerate until chilled.

SERVES 4

chef's tip

Add a bit more lemon juice or a little water if the cream is too thick.

Index